Communal Riots After Independence

Communal Riots After Independence

A Comprehensive Account

ASGHAR ALI ENGINEER

Centre for Study of Society and Securalism, Mumbai

SHIPRA

(First HB Ed. Published in 2004)

Rs. 995

ISBN: 978-93-88691-93-2

2027
(First Soft Cover PoD in 2022)

Communal Riots After Independence

Published by:
SHIPRA PUBLICATIONS
LG 18-19, Pankaj Central Market
I.P. Ext., Patparganj, Delhi 110092, India
91 11 47322068; 96500 28065, 9810522367
info@shiprapublication.com
www.shiprapublication.com

Preface

Centre for Study of Society and Secularism is an organisation which lays emphasis on research along with activism. It, therefore, undertook the project for documenting the communal riots which took place in post-independent India since 1950. The data was not easy to come by. Though India is a secular country, large number of communal riots took place even after the Britishers left. And the Centre thought it is important to document these riots.

It required real hard work and immense patience to find the data and still there remains gaps which is not easy to fill. The press has reported generally only major riots in which large number of people were killed. However, our researchers did their best to collect the data. I also prepare annual survey reports for communal violence which came handy. I had also investigated most of the major riots, especially during the decade of eighties which was very critical decade from the viewpoint of communal violence. All this data was used for this research.

Our research is continuing and any further data which is unearthed will be included in the subsequent editions. This book covers the period from 1950 to 2002.

Contents

List of Tables

List of Figures

Introduction

The study of communalism and communal violence in post-independence India is of great significance. Our leaders like Jawaharlal Nehru and others were of the opinion that with the creation of Pakistan the communal problem has been solved and it would not raise its ugly head in independent India. Also, they thought that with the spread of modern scientific education people's mindset would change, communalism become a thing of the past, people's outlook would become more scientific and they would not be motivated in their social and political behaviour by their religious affiliations. But, as we see, these assumptions were not entirely true, and the availability of education has remained limited to a small section of urban and rural population. The nature of education imparted is also quite problematic. It is far from secular and scientific as was assumed by Nehru. He was too optimistic in this regard. Education is a state subject and the Central Government could hardly influence the educational policy. Those who have communal outlook, control most of the educational institutions. The textbooks could not be changed even after fifty years of independence. The history textbooks are still quite distorted and are written with communal outlook. Thus, education has become a powerful instrument of spreading communal outlook.

Also, the functioning of democracy in a country like India creates its own problems. Caste and communal affiliations are very strong in the traditional society. The motivating cause of Pakistan, distribution of power along communal lines, has hardly been mitigated. It has been further strengthened not only along communal but also caste line. Communal and casteist parties have multiplied and these parties campaign for votes on these lines. Jan Sangh, the Hindu communal party, has always targeted the minority communities and accused the Congress of appeasing them for their votes. And the Congress, the minorities felt, has been making false promises, which are never fulfilled. The minorities feel that most of the Congressmen are basically communal in outlook. Some even accuse that while the Jan Sangh is the A party of Hindus, the Congress is their B party. There is some truth in it.

In such social and political atmosphere it was not surprising if communalism as a social, political and even as an ideology was strengthened. Communalism and communal violence are two stages of the same phenomenon. If communal tendencies become stronger in the society, it is much easier for communal forces to organise communal violence. Spread of communalism is a necessary condition for communal violence. To organise communal violence, communal atmosphere needs to be generated. Communal issues always formed an important part of political campaigning in the last fifty years. This tendency became much stronger during the eighties. And it was precisely during the eighties and early nineties that maximum communal violence erupted in India.

It is thus very important to understand the socio-political dynamics of the country to understand the nature of communal violence, be it in pre-or-post independent India. India is essentially a pluralist society. There is tremendous plurality and diversity in this country. It is regional, linguistic, cultural and religious in nature. This diversity could be both strength as well as a problem for the democratic society. It all depends on how political parties and political forces treat it. One can build a strong and healthy democracy on the basis of diversity and plurality and one can also create violent conflicts taking advantage of this diversity and plurality.

When power is sought on communal and caste lines, diversity becomes a source of conflict rather than a source of strength. The communal forces in this country exploited diversity—specially the religious diversity—for creating conflict and have thus tried to monopolise the votes of one particular community.

The communal forces, especially of the majority community, have always attacked religious diversity whereas the minority communities emphasise that communal forces from the majority community have always treated diversity as a source of weakness for the country. While the communal forces in the Muslim community in pre-partition period raised the slogan of nationalism based on religion and talked of Islamic nationalism (though strictly speaking a term in contradiction) the Hindu communalists raised the slogan of Hindu Rashtra, i.e., Hindu nationalism. Thus it will be seen that communal forces are hostile to diversity and they try to emphasise homogeneity. Thus while for democratic and secular forces diversity is a source of strength, for communal forces it is a source of weakness and should be wiped out. It is precisely for this reason that minorities find themselves at the receiving end in authoritarian societies. Minorities can find justice only in a democratic society.

Thus the Hindutva agenda has been one language, one law and one country. Also the Hindutva forces adopted an agenda, which included doing away with Article 370 (according special status to Jammu and Kashmir), Ram Mandir and Common Civil Code. Demolition of Babri Masjid and constructing Ram Mandir became symbols of a homogenised Hindu society wherein Muslims and other minorities are treated as second-class citizens. Ramjanambhoomi-Babri Masjid controversy became a very major communal controversy in the history of post-independent India. A controversy, which historians should have debated, was politicised by the communal forces resulting in several major communal riots. In fact, politicians who do not specialise in the discipline of history had no business to indulge in such controversies and beg for votes on that basis. It is very dangerous for composite nation building. Before this controversy another major religious controversy, which also was sought to be politicised, was the Shah Bano controversy. A Muslim divorcee sued her husband for maintenance beyond the *iddah* period, which was granted to her by the Supreme Court. The religious and political leaders of Muslims exploited this as being against Muslim personal law and interference in it endangering Muslim identity. It also became a major controversy and was partly responsible for giving rise to the Ramjanambhoomi-Babri Masjid controversy.

This raises an important question about the politics of identity in a modern nation state, which is composite in nature. The Indian society is highly diverse and pluralistic. There is linguistic, cultural, religious and caste diversity. Each group emphasises its own identity not only to mark itself out from other groups but also for political mobilisation. In a society where distribution of political power and economic resources is highly uneven and monopolised by a few upper caste groups, group identity plays very significant mobilisatory role. It is a well-known phenomenon that voting also takes place along these group lines and hence group identity (which includes religious, cultural, linguistic and caste and sub-caste identities) acquires great significance and group clashes between Hindus and Muslims taking place on that basis have acquired phenomenal proportions. Now the Sangh Parivar has been inciting Hindu-Christian clashes also. The caste conflicts have also greatly increased. It is important to note that the dynamics of modern nation building in a pluralistic society like that of India results in complex processes. Certain processes bring about consolidation of nationhood and others promote intense conflicts as power equations between different groups change. Deepening of democratic processes results in breaking down of hierarchical relationship among certain groups and builds up more equalising and democratic relationship. This shift in power relations is not smooth and democratic and often tends to be very violent in nature.

Thus, the dynamics of this group clashes between Hindus and Muslims should not be sought in religion or caste but in other material factors like distribution of economic and political power resources. Creation of Pakistan also was basically motivated not by Islam or Islamic teachings but by the political dynamics of the time. The Muslim elite found their situation in the then prevailing power equation *vis-à-vis* the Hindu elite rather unfavourable and hence they began to demand a separate political domain for themselves wherein they would wield power unchallenged. Had the Hindu and Muslim elite worked out a satisfactory equation between themselves—as for example, number of parliamentary seats to be shared between them, partition could have been avoided. However, Islam and Islamic nationalism were invoked both for legitimisation as well as for mobilisation.

Having thrown some light on the nature of communalism and communal violence it would be interesting to study the occurrence of communal violence and its different phases in the post independent India. Each phase was characterised by some major political controversy. The occurrence of communal violence in post-independence period can be divided into five phases: 1951 to 1960; 1961 to 1970; 1971 to 1980; 1981 to 1993; and 1993 to 1999 to 2002. The period immediately after partition saw eruption of communal violence between Hindus and Muslims on an unprecedented scale resulting in massacre of more than half a million people. This was direct result of partition and displacement of population on a massive scale. This partition violence continued right up to 1950.

The period between 1950 and 1960 was relatively calm. One finds very few instances of communal violence during this period. Muslims in India were terrified by the partition riots and were keeping a low-key existence. This non-assertiveness on the part of Muslims was an important factor in maintaining communal peace. One finds more linguistic violence during this decade, especially after constituting the linguistic states. There were major clashes between the Marathi speaking and Gujarati speaking people of Bombay. Not that there were no communal clashes during this decade, but they were minor and few and far between.

The next decade 1961 to 1970 proved to be more convulsive. There was a major riot in Jabalpur in which several hundred people were killed. By now the Muslims had regained their confidence in Indian democracy and were asserting themselves for their rights. The process of democratisation made them more assertive for their rights. It was the beginning of communal violence on a major scale in post-independence India. This was followed by a series of riots in eastern parts of India like Jamshedpur, Rourkela, Ranchi and several other places. Most of these riots were instigated by the tales of woes of Hindu refugees from East Pakistan (now called Bangladesh). Some riots also took place due to Indo-Pak war in 1965.

But towards the end of sixties some major riots in western India took place due to basic changes in Indian politics. Mrs. Indira Gandhi succeeded in sidelining the big political bosses in the Congress Party and consolidated her position as the supreme Congress leader besides being Prime Minister. This brought about split in the Congress Party and those opposed to her regrouped along with other opposition parties and tried to weaken her position by instigating communal violence. Thus, Gujarat witnessed major communal riots in 1969 where Morarji Desai's faction, who was opposed to Mrs. Gandhi, was in power. Again, Bhivandi-Jalgaon in Maharashtra saw eruption of communal violence in 1970 mainly instigated by the Shiv Sena, which had emerged on the political scene and was trying to consolidate its position in Maharashtra politics.

The period from 1971 to 1977 was again relatively peaceful firstly due to India's involvement in liberation of Bangladesh and then Nation's attention was focussed on Jay Prakash Narayan's movement against corruption. As a result of this movement Mrs. Gandhi imposed emergency in 1975, which lasted up to 1977. Because of these developments communal clashes subsided during this period. Also, during emergency those responsible for instigating communal violence were in jail.

But a fresh bout of communal violence broke out in 1978 to 1980, which ended with cataclysmic Moradabad riot in which more than 1000 persons perished. Most of these riots, for example the ones in Jamshedpur, Aligarh and Benaras (1978-79) were instigated by the RSS to assert its existence which was then threatened because of merger of the Jan Sangh in the newly formed Janata Party. The dual membership controversy (membership both of Janata Party and the Rashtriya Swayam Sevak Sangh on the part of the Jan Sangh members was severely objected to by the socialist members of the Janata Party) led to these riots. However, the Moradabad riot had its own dynamics and was a result of competition between the Punjabi businessmen and the emergent Muslim traders in that town.

The decade beginning with 1981 witnessed maximum number of communal riots. They are due to either political controversy or economic competition. The first riot of this decade took place in 1981 in Biharshariff due to land dispute between Muslims and Hindus. It was followed by a series of riots, which ended with 1992-93 riots of Bombay and Surat after demolition of Babri Masjid on 6th December 1992. Most of these riots during this decade were the result of either the Shah Bano or Babri Masjid–Ramjanambhoomi controversy. There have been very few riots on major scale in the post–Babri demolition period with some exceptions (for example the Coimbatore riot of November 1997).

It is very important to document these riots, which took place in post-independence India. Thus the Centre for Study of Society and Secularism undertook this documentation and used news papers like *The Statesman, The Times of India, The Indian Express* and *The Hindu* as primary sources. We have tried to document number of persons killed (Hindus as well as Muslims), properties destroyed and places where these riots took place. This documentation can be of great importance for many future scholars working in this field. As the main sources of this documentation are various newspapers, errors and biases of reporters are unavoidable. The Home Ministry, Government of India, treats its records as secret and had declined our request to provide us with information. We had no other recourse but to rely on the newspaper reports.

We hope this study will enhance understanding of the underlying causes of communal violence and this understanding will enable us to find solution for the communal frenzy, which claims lives of hundreds of innocent people every year. There has been some decline in communal violence in the post-Babri demolition period. It was in 1992-93 that communal violence peaked and people began to understand the real designs of those responsible for instigating violence. The communal forces at least for the time being, find it difficult to evoke response from the people. Let us hope this phase lasts for longer, even forever.

A Commentary on Communal Violence

With the partition of the country, it was hoped that ill feeling between the diverse religious communities would give way to amity and friendship. However, unfortunately the majority communal forces still question the loyalty of the Indian Muslims to the country. In many religio-political processions, slogans like "Mussalman Jao Pakistan Ya Qabrastan" (O Muslims go to Pakistan or to cemetery) are still being raised to arouse the passions of the majority community. As India is celebrating the 53rd year of Independence, it is fitting to take stock of the communal riots that erupted time and again in different parts of the country. Though India had declared herself secular, she continued to witness communal tensions and riots year after year in the post-partition era. How can this be explained?

Communal violence can never be explained in terms of religion alone. The religious factor is only apparent; but not real. Religion is being exploited by vested interests to suit their own ends. Religion is emotionally appealing and thus acts as a powerful instrument of mobilisation of potential and latent elements. When religious sentiments and cultural ethos are manipulated for selfish gains the result is communal tension. Religious and cultural differences indeed exist. But these differences assume antagonistic proportions due to conflicting political vested interests, which in turn are linked with economic motives.

Scholars agree that modern democratic politics and capitalist society play an important role in instigating communal problems. Both democratic politics and modern capitalism being essentially competitive in nature, often lead to trouble. Communal forces take advantage of "vote bank politics" in a competitive and ballot box oriented democracy.

This study, based on data collected on communal violence in India during the period 1950-2002, provides a narrative of communal riots. Certain conclusions have been drawn on the basis of the collected data.

A. National Level Trends

The data collected indicates that in the period between 1950 and 1960, the communal disturbances were fewer. In fact, the decade between 1950-60 can be described as a decade of communal peace. Probably, the general political and economic stability contributed in reducing communal tension. It must also be recalled here that other issues like the reorganisation of States or the land reforms overshadowed this period. Also after partition, Muslims were maintaining a low profile.

Supporting the general perception, the collected data shows a rising curve of communal violence from mid-1960s peaking in 1969-70. Moreover, whereas the communal riots during the 1950s appear to be more the result of sudden and spontaneous outbursts of group violence, communal violence during the 1960s seem to be systematically contrived and engineered. The loss of life in communal riots, during 1950s was much less. During 1960s it increased considerably. An analysis of the trends of communal riots shows that in 1964 alone 346 people were killed at Rourkela, Jamshedpur, and Raigarh.

Most importantly, the data shows that more riots occurred during 1967-70 and also during 1978-80 when the Union or Central government authority was weak. It is interesting to note that the Congress Party, which had provided stability to the political system, was split into two factions, i.e., Congress (Indira) and Congress (Others) in 1969.

The strong wave of communal violence that swept across the country in 1967 and continued till 1970 was followed by a substantial decline during 1971-77. The collected figures show that the 1971-77 period as one with low level of communal violence.

The country was under Emergency rule for eighteen months during 1975-77. The low trend of reports on communal incidents and the total absence of major communal riots in 1976 can be to a certain extent, attributed to Emergency. Apart from restrictions on media coverage, probably the emphasis on class unity rather than communal solidarity also had an impact.

During the Emergency period, all the Rashtriaya SwayamSevak Sangh, Jamat-e-Islami, and Jan Sangh leaders were arrested. There was no one to incite communal passions and therefore during this period the communal situation remained by and large under control.

The Janata Period (1977-80) witnessed a number of major communal riots in Jamshedpur, Varanasi, Aligarh, and other places in which several hundred innocent lives were lost. This was reported to be due to the strong Rashtriya Swayam Sevak Sangh (RSS) influence on the Jan Sangh. The Rashtriya Swayam Sevak Sangh had been alleged to have a direct hand in most of the communal riots that rocked the country during this period.

The demolition of the Babri Masjid in December 1992 was followed by great bouts of communal violence in different parts of the country, particularly in Bombay and Surat. The year 1993 also began with great communal tension and rioting in Mumbai, Ahmedabad, and Surat besides other places. Compared with the preceding years, 1992 and 1993, the data shows the year 1994 as a year with less serious communal incidents. Unfortunately, the Idgah flag hoisting issue in Hubli, Karnataka on 15th August 1994 resulted in the loss of six lives.

The year 1995 was also not entirely free from communal violence. Both Aligarh and Moradabad, the two most communally sensitive towns of Uttar Pradesh, once again came under the spell of communal violence. Significantly, since both the riots were spontaneous and unplanned, they were easily and speedily brought under control.

In 1996, the data does not show any political party provoking riots. The riots during this year were results of some local incidents, not of planned provocation, with low intensity. Police and administration were able to put them speedily under control.

In 1997, the data shows that most of riots were spontaneous outbursts and controlled easily with minimum loss of life and property. Coaimbatore of Tamil Nadu, which until then was a peaceful place, turned violent and got a respectable place in the list of riot prone cities of India.

In 1998, the data show that most of the riots were minor and spontaneous. Another trend we observed is that the states where Bhartiya Janata Party was in power (Gujarat and Uttar Pradesh) the Vishwa Hindu Parishad and Bajrang Dal acted as if it was an unbridled Hindu Raj. During this year Christians also came under systematic attack.

The year 1999 was just like 1998 with no major communal riot. The year started with the Mangalore riots and a yearlong continuous attack on Christians. There was a series of attacks on Christian prayer halls in hilly areas of Dangs and other parts of Gujarat. The government functionaries insisted it was wrong to say that churches had been targeted as only small hutment's serving as prayer halls had been attacked.

B. State Level Trends

The data shows Bihar, one of the most communal states, remained riot free during the most surcharged situation following the demolition of the Babri Masjid. Administrative alertness probably helped in averting communal flare up.

The data makes it clear that not only the northern states (Uttar Pradesh and Bihar specially), but also western states (Gujarat and Maharashtra mainly) are greatly affected by communal violence. Many western Uttar Pradesh towns (Aligarh, Meerut, Moradabad) appear as "riot-prone" towns. Rajasthan, a state in the Western region, which had a low history of communal violence, joined the list of communally sensitive states with the events of 1989 and 1990. Udaipur emerged as a communally sensitive town of Rajasthan. There is an element of business competition between the Sindhis (who came to Udaipur after the partition) and the Bohra Muslims. Noticeably Orissa, a state on the eastern region which had not witnessed major communal violence since the Rourkela riots in 1964, got caught in the communal violence and rioting in the wake of the Mandir-Masjid dispute. The data also shows the presence of a substantial number of communal disturbances in Madhya Pradesh. Hence, one can say that communal conflict was confined mostly to north, central and western India.

In South India, Hyderabad registered a significant number of communal incidents. In fact, the data shows Hyderabad as one of the major centres of communal conflicts in the South. During the Ramjanambhoomi agitation, Karnataka, another southern State appeared as a highly communally sensitive state. Violence that erupted in the capital city of Bangalore in October 1995, on the question of telecast of Urdu program on Doordarshan clearly indicated the communal atmosphere in the state of Karnataka.

Tamil Nadu otherwise a state of communal peace finds a place in the list of riot prone states with Coimbatore riots and bomb blast which killed many persons. Hindu and Muslim fundamentalists worked hard to create the situation conducive to communal violence.

In Gujarat when Bhartiya Janata Party came to power, Vishwa Hindu Parishad and Bajrang Dal started acting as if they were a part of Hindu Raj. They systematically attacked Christians; their Prayer halls were destroyed in Dang and other areas in Gujarat.

The marked disparity in the rates of occurrence of communal violence between the North and the South can be attributed to socio-historical factors. People in the south are generally more religious and orthodox but less fanatical. The North mainly had experienced the burden of invasion and the rule by various Islamic dynasties. The Muslims entered into North India as invaders but into the South they entered as traders. Further, only the North had borne the actual brunt of the partition of the country. The high degree of cultural assimilation of the people of South, cutting across religious barriers, also contributed in creating a communal free atmosphere. If language and culture are same and only religion is different, hostility somewhat becomes muted; though it does not disappear altogether. If religious minorities have different culture and speak different languages, hostility definitely increases.

It has already been noted that Gujarat was not free from communal problem. But the holocaust was not so regular there. But whenever it occurred, the violence reached very high magnitude. Long periods of peace had been very often followed by long periods of violence. In contrast, the occurrences of violence in other communally sensitive states had been more frequent.

Karnataka had also become communally sensitive during the last few years. The Bangalore riots and Mangalore riots are testimony to this

C. Town Level Trends

Surat, a fast growing city of southern Gujarat, which was never on the communal map of Gujarat, got caught in the communal fervor after the demolition of the Babri Masjid. Surat, noticeably, had remained peaceful even during 1969 and 1985-86 communal riots elsewhere. Here, the relationship between Hindu and Muslim traders had been more cooperative than competitive thus ruling out the business rivalry. However, soon Surat acquired all the features of a fast growing urban conglomeration. Surat is a centre for diamond cutting, silk weaving and textiles. A high level of construction activity is being accompanied by a great deal of immigration. The growth and expansion of the area are both the cause and the effect of immigration. The immigration from outside disturbs the historical balance of homogeneity of population, leading to its new plurality or heterogeneity.

It is generally believed that communal violence is usually an urban phenomenon. The data provides ample evidence that communal riots erupt more often in medium-sized towns than in large urban conglomerates and cosmopolitan centres. Social conservatism or religious orthodoxy generates more often and more quickly a communal atmosphere in medium and small-sized towns. The outbreak of communal riots in Bombay in 1992-93 may be treated as an exceptional one, not negating the general perception of communal free cosmopolitan centres. Of course over the years large urban conglomerates too like Ahmedabad and Baroda have become permanent bastions of communalism. Ahmedabad appears now as one of the most communally sensitive cities in the country despite the fact that Ahmedabad has only 13% Muslim population. Surprisingly, Boroda known to be a hot bed of communal violence remained comparatively unaffected during the disturbances in the rest of the country after the demolition of the Babri Masjid in Ayodhya. In large urban conglomerates wherever and whenever the minorities find solace in clinging to their respective caste and communal fold due to their rootlessness and insecurity leading to psychological barriers, they tend to get exploited by the vile politicians for their selfish gains.

The rural areas too got caught in the communal frenzy after the Ramjanambhoomi controversy. Certain minor communal riots had taken place in some pockets of rural India even before that incident, but have now gathered momentum. In order to know more we need to take up a special study on the subject, *"The Communal Riots in Rural India."*

Medium sized towns like Aligarh, Jamshedpur, Moradabad, Bhiwandi, Malegaon, Varanasi, Godhra, etc., have been communally very sensitive.

The people from Tamil Nadu and Kerala are said to be spiritually religious. The people of one religion sometimes even worshipped gods of another religion. But the cities in these states also showed intense communal trouble. During February 1998 to April 1999, Tamil Nadu witnessed communal trouble in Coimbatore and Chennai and there was a bomb blast; and the Muslim and Hindu fundamentalists could vitiate the social and religious fabric of the State at a very high level.

D. Economic Trends

Our data supports the perception that either electoral politics or economic competition were behind some of the major riots during 1980s. Certain districts of western Uttar Pradesh which have more than 20 per cent Muslim population and which also have a newly emerging Muslim entrepreneur class saw much more communal violence than other districts. For example, the relative success and prosperity of Muslim businessmen in the **brassware trade** could be the cause of much business jealousy and antagonism of Hindu businessmen in Moradabad, which witnessed communal rioting in 1980. The Muslims in Moradabad were traditionally artisans making brassware vessels but of late some of them started their own manufacturing units and were exporting their product to the West Asian countries. The Hindu Punjabis who so far had the monopoly in brassware trade were greatly disturbed by the Muslims entering into this field, even on a small scale. The West Asian connection, due to commonality of religion, perhaps magnified their adverse perception of the problem. Aligarh is another medium sized town where the perceived threat to trade interest ultimately resulted in fanning the fires of communalism. Here unauthorised power tapping by the owners of lock manufacturing units often gives rise to rivalry between the members of the two communities.

Godhra, a district town in the Panch Mahal district of Gujarat, experienced communal carnage continuously for almost one year during 1980-81. The fight was between the Ghanchi Muslims of Godhra and the Sindhis who came to this town after the partition and are a community of petty traders. In addition to their traditional activity of cultivation, the Ghanchi Muslims, who are a very old Muslim community of Godhra, have taken to transport business. There has been intense hostility between the Sindhis and Ghanchis since the days of partition. Very often arguments, over positioning of stall-boards or vendorcarts boil over into communal violence.

Land disputes sparked off the Biharshariff riots (1981) and the Meerut riots (1982). The ghastly Biharshariff riot of April/May 1981 was mainly due to economic factors. Here the main dispute centred on a cemetery land between the Yadavas and the Muslims. This town in the Nalanda district of Bihar has a large proportion of Muslim population around 35 per cent. There are quite a few Muslim cemetery lands and many of them have fallen into disuse.

Biharshariff, it is to be noted is a fast expanding town with land prices skyrocketing. The Yadavas, a backward cultivating caste, naturally, therefore had their eyes on the unused cemetery lands belonging to the Muslim community. This intensified communal tension, which ultimately led to communal violence.

In most of riot prone towns the Muslim artisans and businessmen have achieved a relative degree of economic prosperity. From the data collected it appears that communal violence occurred mostly in towns where there is a particular Hindu-Muslim population balance, the presence of large number of partition refugees or a large and prosperous Muslim artisan population. Economic competition obviously results in social tension, which is often given a communal colour by exploiting certain situations on the occasion of religious festivals etc. This actually happened in the case of Moradabad (1980), and Bhiwandi (1970).

Further, comparative economic prosperity among the Muslims leads to greater political aspirations among them. This too results in a communally dangerous situation. Bhiwandi, a thriving centre of powerloom industry, witnessed communal riots in 1970. Apart from a large number of Muslim artisans working as weavers, there are a few Muslims owning powerlooms. A section of Muslims with their rising prosperity due to the power loom industry developed greater political aspirations challenging the traditional leadership. Not surprisingly Municipal politics had its visible impact on communal violence that took place in Bhiwandi in 1970.

E. Communal Riots: Hidden Economic Issues

Our data contains instances of several communal disturbances, which were sparked off by business rivalries. The "Tazia Procession", was only a pretext, but the real cause of the communal riots in Baroda, in October 1982, was the changing economic fortunes of the two communities.

Economic factor was the underlying element in communal violence that took place in the industrial belt of Bhiwandi-Thane-Bombay in May 1984. The causative factor, here, was political. In the case of Aurangabad riots (May 1988) the existing economic discrepancy between Muslims and Hindus was also exploited by petty-minded politicians to realise their own ends.

Business rivalry naturally causes heartburn. Our data provides certain cases of communal discords resulting from stiff economic competitions. The two communal riots that had occurred at Udaipur in 1965 and 1966 can be categorised as rioting resulting from purely economic factor, especially, when the economically prosperous Bohra Muslims were targeted, notwithstanding the fact that trouble started due to a *quarrel* between a Hindu and a Sunni Muslim. At Godhra (1980-81) the communal fury was caused by economic factor. The question of residential accommodation and the competition to capture the prevailing petty trades of the town resulted in violence.

The Moradabad riots in 1980 were essentially caused by the economic competition between the Punjabi Hindu traders and upcoming Muslim artisans, challenging the Punjabi monopoly of brass-ware business.

Significantly, our data also show, that Aligarh, a University town in Uttar Pradesh and famous as a Centre of lock manufacturing, is a communally sensitive town.

The collected data also show Benaras or Varanasi, which is famous for the silk fabrics industry, as a riot-prone area. The city witnessed frequent communal riots, especially after the Ayodhya controversy. Traditionally, the Muslims constitute the weaver's class; the wholesale business of silk fabrics was in the hands of Marwaris, Khatris, and Aggarwals. But now the master-weaver themselves, are becoming wholesale dealers. There were reports of delayed payments as well as under-pricing of product in the aftermath of the Ayodhya controversy.

Land dispute resulted in communal riots in Biharshariff, a small town in Bihar in 1981. This was mainly because of the fact that the parties involved in the dispute belonged to two different religious communities. Power hungry politicians used the resentment of one community against the other to suit their own ends.

F. Political Trends

After the split in the Congress, Mrs. Indira Gandhi sought legitimacy for her factional leadership by wooing the scheduled castes and scheduled tribes and the minorities. Hence, she played what was then called "the minority card" or policy of "appeasement of Muslims". This was seen as a danger signal by the upper caste Hindus and they reacted by exacerbating communal feelings. Many did not take the "populist image" which Mrs. Indira Gandhi was trying to project by nationalising banks and abolishing privy purses nicely. "Bank nationalisation" for instance, was done without taking the then Finance Minister, Mr. Morarji Desai into confidence. Not surprisingly, Gujarat (1969) witnessed communal riots on a very high scale. Gujarat then was the strong hold of Congress (Others) and Mr. Hitendra Desai, the then Chief Minister of Gujarat, was a close confidant of Mr. Morarji Desai. At the same time the Jan Sangh was becoming strong in Gujarat. Being a Rightist Party, the Jan Sangh was definitely against socialism. So naturally they joined or came close to Congress (Others). Thirdly, the Swatantra Party, representing the feudal and capitalist class, was also opposed to Mrs. Gandhi's bank nationalisation. They were already upset with Mrs.Gandhi for abolition of privy purses. To counter the populist image of Mrs.Gandhi, all these forces took recourse to emotive "communal card".

The respite on the communal front in the country during the early seventies can also be attributed to the Bangladesh liberation war. In 1971, the Indian defense forces entered Dhaka and defeated the Pakistan army; and Bangladesh was born. Mrs. Indira Gandhi was at the height of her popularity for her role in liberating Bangladesh and hence she commanded great respect even from the opposition.

The decade of eighties saw the highest degree of communalisation of Indian polity. It can be said that the decade of eighties was communally the worst for India. Mrs. Indira Gandhi came back to power in 1980 with a reduced majority. Being unsure of the minority votes, particularly of Muslim votes, Mrs. Gandhi tried to cultivate the support of the middle caste Hindus, who had acquired economic clout due to the land reforms, the Green Revolution, and so forth, and had also become politically far more assertive. Hence, her emphasis on secularism was not as strong as during the late sixties. The controversy about the conversion of a few Dalits to Islam in the Meenakshipuram district of Tamil Nadu, was alleged to have been exploited by Mrs. Gandhi to mobilise the upper and middle caste Hindu support for retaining political power. She was alleged to have even lent support to the Vishwa Hindu Parishad (VHP). During this period a wave of communal violence had begun with riots in Moradabad in 1980, Biharshariff in 1981, Meerut, Baroda, Pune, and Solapur in 1982 and Bombay, Bhiwandi in 1984. Interestingly, these were all Congress ruled states.

The Bombay-Bhiwandi riots that took place in 1984 owed there genesis to political factor. This was due to the campaign on the part of the Shiv Sena to revive the party that was then going through a bad phase. Trouble started after Shiv Sena Chief Bal Thackaray delivered a controversial speech about the Prophet Mohammed. Serious communal disturbances that took place in the late eighties, like the Meerut riot of 1987 and the Bhagalpur riot of 1989 which were directly the result of the Ramjanambhoomi-Babri Masjid controversy. Undoubtedly, the controversy is essentially political in nature. The—election frenzy had sparked off the riots in Aurangabad in 1988. Aurangabad riots are a clear indication of the dangerous implications of political parties fighting election-shouting slogans like "Garva se Kaho Hum Hindu Hai!" ("Say with pride we are Hindus".)

G. Causes of Communal Riots

It has been already observed how repeatedly social and religious factors coupled with political and economic rivalries activate vulnerable communal situations. It is difficult to single out only one factor as the sole cause for eruption of communal violence even at any point of time in any single area. However the instrumental and accidental role of a given factor in a particular riot cannot be easily ignored. On the basis of the available data an attempt has been made to classify communal riots that had caused havoc to innocent lives. The objective is to show why and how an insignificant or minor issue can unexpectedly cause communal turmoil resulting in untold miseries to common man for no fault of his. The criterion followed here is the classification of communal riots by incidents. The various causes for the outbreakof riots are:

a) Rumour: An Instigating Variable

According to the data, the instigating role of rumours has been apparent. Rumours always came in handy for the communalists. Communal riots occurred in a number of districts of West Bengal in January 1950. The situation had become tense after rumours were spread about alleged ill treatment of Hindus in certain districts of East Bengal. Reports of alleged forcible mass conversion to Islam, desecration of images of Hindu Gods, invoked communal violence.

The distinct role of rumours was again experienced in the case of Jabalpur riots in February 1961. The rioting was provoked by rumours about a Hindu girl being assaulted by two young Muslims. In the case of Bhagalpur riots (1989) too, the role of rumours was evident.

b) Trivial Issues Taking a Communal Turn

The collected data have also thrown light on the fact that very often-personal conflicts, petty clashes, or quarrels over trivial matters triggered communal clashes. For instance, communal rioting occurred in Srinagar in August 1967, following the conversion of a Pandit (Brahmin) girl to Islam and her marriage to a Muslim.

Communal riots that took place in Ahmedabad from September 18-24, 1969 were one of the worst outbreaks of communal rioting in India since Independence. Trouble started when a herd of cows belonging to a Hindu temple accidentally knocked down a number of Muslims hurting some children.

Later, this incident sparked off major riots in Ahmedabad and other places in Gujarat. In Ahmedabad alone more than 1,000 people were killed, a large majority of them were Muslims. So intensified were the riots that trains were attacked on a number of occasions by mobs searching for Muslims. Being an industrial city, the communal rioting that took place in Ahmedabad naturally had left an adverse impact on the Indian economy. Property worth crores of rupees was destroyed; there was a loss of income of at least Rs.33 thousand and .70 crores as a result of the inactivity caused by the imposition of curfew (as given in the data)

Our data supports that the Meerut riots which took place in September 1982 were also caused by vested interests from both communities to advance their own selfish interest. The events connected with the Mazar-Temple controversy reflects how petty-minded politicians most crookedly exploited a minor dispute between an individual and a trust in order to perpetuate their hold on the society.

Again, riots, but on a lower scale, took place in Malur Town, situated in the Kolar district of Karnataka in May 1983 following the alleged misbehaviour of a boy belonging to one community towards a girl of another community.

Suratkal in Mangalore also witnessed riots in 1998-99. They also started with a very trivial issue—Eve-teasing which ended in death of—many people.

During 1997, Coaimbatore saw communal violence, and the reason behind it was a traffic case. A member of a militant Muslim organisation was charged for breaking a traffic rule. He raised a hue and cry but the police officers pacified and let them go. On their way back, the traffic constable again booked them for violation of Traffic rule. They stabbed the constable who happened to be a Hindu and riots started which gave untold miseries to the people.

Seelampur riot which broke-out in January 1999 was due to a wooden piece landing on the cricket ground, which resulted in fighting, among boys and soon the public came out and started pelting stones.

c) Fomenting Communal Trouble: By Manipulating Religious Issues

The data collected has made it clear that sometimes provocation due to hurting of religious sentiments resulted in communal riots. In Srinagar the riots broke out in 1967 when some Muslim students were reported to have found torn pieces of the Quran in their college latrine. Again, minor riot took place in Tinsukia, an industrial town in upper Assam in March 1968, after a Muslim was alleged to have killed a cow.

The publication of an article containing defamatory remarks against Prophet Mohammed triggered communal riots in Bangalore and Mysore in December 1986.

Many a time, celebrations of religious festivals foment trouble. That was what exactly happened in Hyderabad in July 1981, when a Hindu religious procession played music outside a mosque to which the Muslims protested. The situation was already tense due to the alleged mass conversion of Harijans into the Muslim fold. Here it is interesting to note that our data have focused on instances where parochial elements played on the raw sentiments of the people for realising their myopic aspirations. The communal violence in Ahmedabad, and also in Pune and Solapur, in January and February 1982 respectively, had been the direct repercussion of the Meenakshipuram conversions.

From the data, Jamshedpur, an industrial city in southern Bihar, appears to be a communally–prone area. Major riot took place in Jamshedpur in April 1979, in which 117 people lost their lives and 333 people were injured. Communal rioting occurred when a Hindu religious procession led by some Janata Party members in the state assembly halted near a mosque.

The sullying of Muslim sacredness due to the intrusion of a pig into the Idgah during Id prayer apparently caused the 1980 communal killings in Moradabad. The ensuing altercation between the namazis and the Provincial Armed Constabulary (PAC) stationed there resulted in police firing. In order to camouflage their own criminal negligence and calculated apathy, the police gave and succeeded in giving a communal colour to the incident. The Moradabad incident had its repercussions in several other towns of the State and also in Delhi, Madhya Pradesh and Kashmir, causing about 180 deaths.

Again, religious celebrations became the cause of communal disturbances that took place in Hazaribagh in south Bihar in October 1983. The rioting occurred due to the attack on a Durga Puja procession.

Communal riots that took place in Amritsar, Patiala in April-May 1982, were the outcome of religious factors. The issue involved here was the demand for a total ban on smoking and cigarette sales in Amritsar. The demand was purely on the basis of religion as the use of tobacco is forbidden to Sikhs and Amritsar is considered by the Sikhs as a holy city.

But under no circumstances religious issues should be taken as single causative factor in communal violence. Political, economical and even personal issues incontrovertibly accompany it. Religion has become a cat's paw in the hands of unscrupulous elements. The spate of killings that occurred in Punjab in the 1980s had the streak of communalism committed by the Sikh militants with the intention to polarise the situation to their advantage. Hindu-Muslim communal disturbances that took place in Delhi-Meerut in 1987 were primarily politico-economic. The dispute about the Mandir-Masjid provided necessary outlet to the already simmering discontent—.

The communal forces of both sides manipulated the Faizabad court judgment in January 1986 for reopening of the Ram Janambhoomi Temple. The Babri Masjid Ramjanambhoomi temple involves deeper questions of identity and power much more than historical artifacts or places of worship.

It is to be noted that certain developments, like the concession given by the Rajiv Gandhi Government to Muslim fundamentalist forces in the Shah Bano controversy and the consequent reopening of the doors of the Babri Masjid for Hindus to worship, Muslim insurgency in Kashmir and Sikh terrorism in Punjab to a great extent had communalised the situation. It may be recalled here that the Bharatiya Janata Party (BJP) managed to add to its strength in the parliament in the 1989 election. It also managed to come to power in Madhya Pradesh, Rajasthan and Himachal Pradesh mainly on its own. At that time Bhartiya Janata Party was not entirely relying on the "Hindu platform" as political base. In the meantime on 5th August 1990, the Government of India headed by the Prime Minister Mr. Vishwanath Pratap Singh announced the decision to implement the controversial Mandal Commission report.

Bhartiya Janata Party viewed this announcement made by the government of Mr Vishwanath Pratap Singh as a threat to their political interest. The apprehension that the implementation of the

Mandal commission report would result in fragmentation of Hindus on caste lines resulted in intensifying the "Ramjanambhoomi" agitation. The Bhartiya Janata Party feared that cracks in Hindu unity would nullify its effort for the unity and hence would corrode its support base of upper caste Hindus in rural areas and in small and medium-sized towns.

Hence, the Bhartiya Janata Party raised the "Ramjanambhoomi" issue, hoping to arouse the emotions of all Hindus cutting across caste barriers in the name of "Hindutva". The Rath Yatra invariably became "Rakt" Yatra (journey of blood). Our data provides incidents of major rioting taking place at that time, though not exactly on its route. Perhaps, enough care was taken to prevent rioting on the route of the Toyota truck converted into a legendary `Rath' to avoid the accusation of inciting communal violence by the political opponents. From October 30th, 1990 the country witnessed unprecedented communal violence.

The demolition of the Babri Masjid on 6th December 1992, and the following rioting across the country reflect the acme of communal frenzy. The whole of Bombay (now Mumbai) was in the midst of communal carnage for more than a month from 7th December 1992 to January 1993. The first phase of rioting was the outcome of spontaneous reaction to the demolition coupled with biased acts of omissions and commissions on the part of the law and order machinery. Shiv Sena through provocative statements and "Maha Artis" systematically engineered the second phase of rioting. The Maha Artis, no doubt, provided a forum for communal forces. A variety of factors like rising unemployment and other stressful situations added to the flare up. The rivalry of political leaders, e.g., between Mr. Sharad Pawar the Congress leader, the ex-Chief Minister, and Mr.Sudhakar Naik, the then Congress Chief Minister of Maharastra also contributed to the communal violence.

In the post-freedom era, contrary to expectations communalism never became a thing of the past. Thousands of innocent people have suffered terribly. The demolition of Babri Masjid resulted in a series of mad communal killings. Communal violence was less during 1994 and 1995. A few riots that recurred in 1996 were spontaneous outbursts of violence on a smaller scale; hardly any instance of planned and organised ones. Significantly, violence was controlled quickly too. This, indeed, is a good sign. The Hindu communalists, launched *"Kashi" and "Mathura" temple movements,* which received only a lukewarm response. Similarly the Muslim leaders who had once aggressively launched the movement against the Shah Bano judgment are either quiet or marginalised. The common people it appears have realised the negative outcome of communal riots and consequently the political parties, it seems, have acknowledged the futility of getting any political mileage by engineering communal riots. Significantly, most of the communal riots are organised, planned and executed by the vested interests for deriving selfish gains.

However, it cannot be ignored, that Hindus and Muslims have deep-rooted prejudices against each other, which are taken advantage of by the communal fundamentalists. For instance, by mobilising the masses on communally sensitive issues, the communalists succeeded in inflaming the already existing prejudices. No efforts should be spared to remove stereotyped thinking. This in turn demands highlighting the history of communal relations with a secular perspective. History, interestingly, has periods both of confrontations and cooperation. Misrepresentation of the past not only corrupts our present but also weakens our future leaving us a prey to perpetual violence and conflicts. An openness of mind, a willingness to interact, to forgive and to forget, are the qualities that should be imbibed in the hearts of all Indians to wipe out the evils of communal violence from our country. This is all the more important in view of the fact that the effective participation of the people is needed in reducing the frequency and intensity of communal incidents.

Our data reflects that communal riots had taken place after the conversion of members of scheduled castes (Harijans) to Islam in Meenakshipuram district of Tamil Nadu in 1981. The outbursts of communal conflicts after the Meenakshipuram conversion episode indicate that caste and communal problems have become intertwined in Indian politics. The communal minded Hindus were offended by the conversion of a few Dalit families to Islam, as it was seen as adding to the number of Muslims. The Vishwa Hindu Parishad (VHP) exploiting the conversion issue launched in a calculated way the propaganda offensive thus intensifying communal discords in the country. The aggressive campaign conducted by the Vishwa Hindu Parishad on the question of conversion resulted in bloody riots in many parts of India. Communal riots in Ahmedabad in January 1982, and those in Pune and Solapur thereafter were the result of forceful campaign by the Vishwa Hindu Parishad. In Meerut riots (1982) too the hand of Vishwa Hindu Parishad was visible. The Vishwa Hindu Parishad's Ekatmata Yatra in 1985 to preach Hindu unity was designed as a means for spreading communalism.

d) Socio-political Issues: Another Variable in Communal Riots

Sometimes socio-political issues also flare-up communal violence. From the data, "language issue" appears as the instigating factor in the 1967 communal riots in Ranchi. The attempt to make Urdu, the second official language in Bihar gave rise to serious differences of opinion within the coalition government. Ultimately, violent communal riots broke out in Ranchi on August 24th, which continued till 28th August 1967. Mr. M.P. Sinha, then Chief-Minister of Bihar, gave the figure of those killed as 158; most of the victims were Muslims.

The sudden move to start a 10-minute Urdu newscast from the Bangalore station of Doordarshan had sparked off riots in Bangalore in October 1994. Unfortunately, "Urdu," a language originated in India has been wrongly made out to be the language of Muslim only. The introduction of a short Urdu news bulletin, an obvious attempt to influence the voting behavior of the minority community in the forthcoming state assembly elections, came in conflict with the strong feeling in Karnataka that the "primacy" of Kannada must be maintained at any cost. Those obsessed with the primacy of Kannada perceived the introduction of Urdu news bulletin as cutting into the primacy of Kannada language. However, from the moment the trouble started it was clear that apart from "linguistic sentiments" there was definitely a political overtone to the entire events.

As soon as the President's assent was given on the Aligarh Muslim University legislation, the Muslim League, in a number of towns in Uttar Pradesh organised demonstrations on January 11, 1972. According to the demonstrators, this act had taken away the minority character of the University. The demonstrations finally resulted in armed clashes between Hindus and Muslims in

Ferozabad and Benares, accompanied by arson and looting. Here the rioting was the outcome of perceived threat to minority rights.

Communal Riots: Varying in Intensity

During the last fifty years of India's independence, the country had witnessed and suffered the hardship of numerous communal riots. Some of these riots can be easily categorised as major riots, having a wider impact in terms of intensity (area-wise and duration-wise), number of victims (in terms of loss of life, loss of limb and loss of property). Communal rioting, which took place in Calcutta and other parts of West Bengal in 1964, can be treated as one of the earliest major communal riots that the country had experienced. Without giving a community-wise break-up, the then Union Home Minister, Mr. Gulzarilal Nanda stated that 208 people were killed in mob violence. He, however, hastened to add that another 56 persons had been killed as a result of police action. However, unofficial reports stated a large number of casualties. The total number of dead was cited as about 500 in Calcutta alone.

The 1964 disturbances at Rourkela (western Orissa), Jamshedpur (southern Bihar), and Raigarh (eastern Madhya Pradesh), also fall within the category of major riots. Union Home Ministry sources recorded 346 deaths, 458 injured till April 8th 1964 as a result of rioting at Rourkela, Jamshedpur and Raigarh.The loss of properties was estimated to be worth Rs. 4 lakhs in Rourkela alone.

Our data supports "political issues" as the primary factor responsible for communal riots in Hyderabad in September 1983. In terms of intensity and number of casualties, the Hyderabad riots can also be classified among the major ones.

The Ramjanambhoomi controversy surely caused much confusion in the minds of common man that was taken advantage of by the communalist forces. The communal disturbance that took place in Meerut in 1987 was one of the fiercest communal riots in independent India after the Ahmedabad riot of 1969 and the Bhiwandi Jalgaon riot in 1970. Some of the recent ferocious communal riots took place at Colonel Gunj (1989) in UP and in Sitamarhi (1992) in Bihar. The Bhagalpur rioting in 1989, definitely an out-come of the Ayodhya controversy, surpassed all previous records in so far as casualties and durations are concerned.

Our data reflect that Ramjanambhoomi agitation provoked communal violence in the mid-1980, especially, after the Faizabad court order, for unlocking and reopening the Ramjanambhoomi Temple, in 1986. Communal flare-ups in the mid-80's had taken a heavy toll of human life and property. For instance, communal rioting that followed in Meerut in 1987 recorded about 400 deaths. The 1989 Bhagalpur riots definitely a fall-out of Ramjanambhoomi controversy eclipsed all the previous records as far as casualties and duration are concerned. After Ramjanambhoomi Controversy the intensity of riots have come down drastically. Only Coaimbatore of Tamil Nadu experienced a high intensity riot, which was the work of militant organisation and not a natural riot.

In the year 2002, the riots, which occurred in Gujarat on 28th February, had surpassed all the records as far as casualties are concerned. The train burning incident occurred at Godhra in which 57 people including 25 women and 14 children were found dead in the burnt shell of the railway coach that had been carrying them from a Yagna at Ayodhya. After this incident the riots broke out in various towns and Talukas of Gujarat including Vadodara, Surat, Rajkot, Visnagar, Palanpur, Deesa, and Khedbrahma. These riots, which lasted for about 4-5 months, resulted in the deaths of thousands and injuries to many. There was also an extensive loss of property.

Other Factors Responsible for the Rise of Communalism in India

Communalism in India has developed due to many other factors. The main factors responsible for communal riots and disturbances are:

Disputes between Landlords and Tenants— Many times communal riot break out due to ordinary disputes between a landlord and a tenant. These ordinary disputes are sometimes exploited by vested interests, which may result in communal flare up. Police officers, irrespective of rank, should take such disputes seriously. Security proceedings should be initiated and they should be empowered to take timely action, which can prevent such a situation.

Eve Teasing—Eve teasing also sometimes results in communal tensions. Anyone indulging in such an unseemingly behaviour and trying to outrage the modesty of a girl belonging to another community is likely to be assaulted by the members of that particular community.

Objectionable Speeches—Leaders of communal parties sometimes make objectionable speeches. These speeches try to instigate and arouse the passions of different communities. Before giving these speeches, these speeches should be scrutinised and legal action should be taken. Even if a leader of a particular community provokes, abets or spreads hatred a case must be registered and investigated. These communal leaders often exploit certain situations for their own political gains. Such situations sometimes become the ultimate sources of all communal tensions and riots.

Objectionable Writings—Objectionable writings, published in periodicals, hurt the feelings of other community members. Whenever any objectionable writings are published, the authorities must take immediate action against such writings. These objectionable writings should be thoroughly examined and legal actions such as including the arrest of the editor or the writer concerned should be taken. Sometimes reports in newspapers giving detailed accounts of happenings and events accuse a particular community. Sometimes the way and the manner in which it is written arouse the passions of a particular community. Legal cells have been set up in almost all districts to examine the objectionable writing. Judges of the High court and the Supreme Court have probed every serious communal riot. The beliefs expressed by Hindu and Muslim communalists were brought into forefront by the Center for Rural Research and Industrial Development, (CRRID) Chandigarh; For example, Bhivandi riots of 1974 and Pune riots of 1982.

Disputes Over Places of Worship—Dispute over place of worship is very common. These matters may be dealt with on the basis of records or historical evidence. When it is not possible to sort out the matter through talks and deliberations, the best course is to refer the matter to Judiciary—whose verdict should be considered final and binding.

Clashing of Times of Prayers of Different Communities—Sometimes the times of prayers by different communities clash leading to communal tension. If "Aarti" is performed with the beating of drums or the ringing of bells or the playing of music at the same time as "Aazaan", by the Muslim Muzzazin for Namaz (Prayer), members of both the communities could resent. The solution to this can be that members of both communities should be called together to change the timings of one or both which should be agreeable to both communities. Mutual consultation and understanding and also respect for each other's religion will be helpful in diffusing communal tensions.

Desecration of Places of Worship—Sometimes some miscreants try to desecrate a place of worship or steal an idol which is held in high religious esteem. For example, in 1960s the misplacement and later recovery of "Muembarak", from the mosque in Srinagar sparked off great violence, between the religious and political leaders. Sometimes, throwing meat in the place of worship has caused serious tensions. Cases should be registered against such miscreants and culprits should be arrested.

Sexual Offences—Sometimes sexual offences, kidnappings and rapes may cause communal tension. Any crime committed by a member of a particular community against the other is likely to be exploited by vested interests.

Disturbances in Religious Processions/Functions—Sometimes religious disturbances occur during religious functions, processions such as Dussehra, Moharram or Gurupurv etc. Any mischief indulged in by mischief mongers can cause a large-scale conflagration. For example, during 1980s, in Moradabad at the time of Id prayers certain disturbances occurred. Prayers were disturbed when an animal allegedly entered the Id prayer area leading to death of several innocent persons. It seems the animal was pushed in deliberately to disturb the namaz.

Bangladeshi and Bihar Muslims—Sometimes Bihar Muslims and Bangladeshi refugees also cause serious problems giving rise to the problem of communal riot.

Visitors from Pakistan—Sometimes some Pakistan nationals who entered India and who have not gone back also cause some serious problems. Sometimes they furnish incomplete or false addresses of relations in India. They do not get their arrival or departure recorded.

Role of the Police—Police play a very important role in maintaining law and order. During riots the police must be impartial and honest. There should be no bias with regard to caste considerations. The police must take preventive action and issue prohibitory orders wherever necessary. They should use force to disperse unlawful assemblies which indulge in stabbing, killing etc.

Proper education is necessary for us to understand each other. Lack of education has been a major factor in escalating tensions. It is very important to educate people and bring the bad effects of communalism in front of them. Similarly they should also show people how the politicians are using the communal card for their own selfish gains or interests. National integration cannot be built with "brick and mortar" as said by a former President of India, S. Radhakrishnan. Religious tolerance is a must. Frequent lectures should be arranged and prominent secular-minded persons and religious leaders of different communities should be invited to address students as students are considered to be the future of our country. Educational institutions and proper education will prove useful in maintaining peace and communal harmony.

Communal Riots : 1950-2002
An Account

1950

Communal Riots in West Bengal and Assam[1]

Phase I

Immediate Cause: Trouble broke out in a number of districts in West Bengal on 24th January, due to the reports of alleged ill-treatment of Hindus in certain districts of East Bengal (Bangladesh) including Barisal, Jessore, Rajashahi and particularly in the neighbourhood districts of Khulna. Muslims were assaulted and their properties were looted and burnt. In these areas, forcible mass conversions to Islam, desecration of images of Hindu Gods, abductions of women, rape, and looting were said to have taken place.

- *Number of persons killed:* 50 (34 Muslims and 16 Hindus)
- *Number of persons injured:* 256 (146 Muslims and 110 Hindus)
- *Number of persons arrested:* 1,505 (1,339 Hindus and 166 Muslims)
- *Places affected:* Garabazar, Dum-Dum, Farashnagar, Ultadanga, Kanakurgachi, Murshidabad

Communal Riots in Assam

Immediate Cause: Trouble broke out on 24th January in several places in Assam due to the reports of alleged ill treatment of Hindus in certain districts of East Bengal (Bangladesh) including Barisal, Jessore and Rajashahi and particularly in the neighbourhood districts of Khulna.

- *Places affected:* Barpeta, Goalpara

Phase II

The disturbances in Calcutta and in Assam resumed once again on 26th and 27th March. Several persons were murdered in Howrah, Cossipore and in the suburbs of the city.

- *Number of persons arrested:* 214
- *Places affected:* Howrah, Cossipore and other suburbs of Calcutta, Bandel (25 miles from Calcutta), Goalpara, Kamrup and Cachar districts (Assam)

Note: In Bandel, which is 25 km. from Calcutta, A.H. Cameron, one of the leaders of the British Business Community in Calcutta and President of the Bengal and Associated Chambers of Commerce, was killed on March 20th while attempting to protect a Muslim bearer from a Hindu mob.

1961

Communal Riots in Jabalpur, Madhya Pradesh[2]

Immediate Cause: Trouble broke out on 4th February in Jabalpur, when rumour was spread that two young Muslims had assaulted a Hindu girl who had been later found dead. A rumour was also spread about the elopement of a Hindu girl with a Muslim boy. In a further outbreak of violence at Gurgawan (near Jabalpur) on 24th Feb., rioters locked 14 people in a house, including some children and later set fire to the house and burnt alive all the inmates.

The Real Cause: The real cause was something else. The Muslim boy was the son of a local bidi magnate who had gradually succeeded in establishing control over the local bidi industry. His Hindu competitors were very sore over this development. The *bidi* industry belonging to the Muslims in Jabalpur suffered heavily during the riots.

- *Number of persons dead*: 55
- *Number of persons injured:* 158
- *Number of persons arrested:* 1,003
- *Loss of properties*: A number of houses were raided and burnt. (The exact number of houses burnt is not available)
- *Places affected:* Jabalpur, Gurgawan and Bahdan, a village near Jabalpur

1962

Communal Riots in Malda District, West Bengal[3]

Immediate Cause: Trouble broke-out on 22nd March in Malda district, where-in Santhals armed with bows attacked a Muslim village in the district. (Immediate cause of the riot not available.)

- *Number of persons dead*: 14
- *Number of persons injured:* 64

1964

Communal Riots in Calcutta and other Parts of West Bengal[4]

Immediate Cause: Trouble broke out on 27th December in Calcutta when the holy relic of Prophet Mohammed from the Hazratbal Mosque in Kashmir was found missing. This led to serious riot in Khulna and Jessore districts of East Pakistan now Bangladesh. Their anger was mainly directed against the carelessness of the government and it had no trace of communal colour. Though the box was discovered within a week, the incident led to serious riots in Khulna in East Pakistan (now in Bangladesh), which caused panic among the Hindu population. They began migrating to India, carrying with them harrowing and sometimes exaggerated tales of their woes. This resulted in the atrocities committed against Muslims in Calcutta and other parts of West Bengal. The disturbances in Khulna began when a procession of 20,000 demonstrators entered the town, murdered the Hindus and looted their houses and burnt them. Few details of the riots were known as local newspapers were forbidden to publish any information about the friction between religious communities except those supplied by the government.

As hundreds of Hindu refugees fled to West Bengal to escape the riots, the disturbances began in Calcutta and in many rural areas of West Bengal. Some of the worst incidents occurred in the border districts. The disturbances broke out amongst the thousands of displaced persons from East Pakistan, but they were soon joined by the large criminal elements in the population, who burned and looted Muslim and Hindu's property indiscriminately.

- *Number of persons dead:* 208 (killed in mob-violence) and 56 (in police action). Unofficial reports gave the number of dead as about 500 in Calcutta alone

The riot occurred again in Calcutta and in Howrah on 18th March when students attacked schools and colleges, which had not closed in support of the demand for a judicial inquiry into the death of a student, killed in police firing.

- *Number of persons dead:* 21 (in Paragnas district)
- *Number of persons injured:* 105

- *Loss of properties:* The laboratories in the Scottish Church College were completely wrecked.
- *Places affected:* Calcutta, Howrah, Belghoria

Communal Riots In Bihar, Orissa and Madhya Pradesh[5]

Immediate Cause: The concentration of the bulk of the refugees in West Bengal, where 34,00,000 refugees had been settled since 1947, aroused fears that their presence would provoke new communal outbreak and therefore it was decided to disperse them. A conference of Ministers of the Central Government and the Governments of West Bengal, Orissa, Madhya Pradesh, Andhra Pradesh and Maharashtra agreed on 8th February to enlarge the area of the Dandakarnya project (a district in South-West Orissa, which was being developed to accommodate refugees) by addition of contiguous areas in Andhra Pradesh, Madhya Pradesh and Maharashtra. An unforeseen result of this policy was the spread of communal rioting to larger parts of Southern Bihar, Western Orissa and Eastern Madhya Pradesh as train-loads of destitute refugees passed through these states.

According to Gulzarilal Nanda, the then Union Home Minister, the right-wing Hindu organisation, Rashtriya Swayam Sevak Sangh, was believed to have been largely responsible for the disturbances. It's leader, M.S. Golwalkar, was arrested in Bihar on 23rd March and was expelled from the State.

The first outbreak of violence in Chakradharpur (Bihar) coincided with with the new outbreak in West Bengal on 16th March where Muslim shops were attacked and looted.

- *Number of persons dead:* 46 (In Rourkela, Jamshedpur and Raigarh)

From the towns, the rioting spread to the forest areas on the border of Bihar and Orissa, where Christian Adivasis raided Muslim villages as a reaction to the expulsion of tribal Christians from East Pakistan. On 29th March a police station was attacked in which the Muslims had taken refuge.

- *Number of persons dead:* 4
- *Number of persons injured:* 458
- *Loss of properties*: The properties worth Rs. 4,00,000 had been damaged at Rourkela.

On 18th March, shops were attacked at Jhargusuda in the Sambalpur district of Orissa (*Figures for exact number of shops damaged not given*). On 19th March, a violent mob set fire to a bus and two shops at Raigarh. 148 houses were burnt down in Jamshedpur.

- *Places affected:* Chakradharpur (Bihar), Jhargusuda in the Sambalpura district of Orissa, Sambalpura, Brajrajnagar, Rajnagpur, Sundargarh and Birmitrapur, Raigarh in Madhya Pradesh, Jamshedpur and Rourkela, and also the forest areas on the borders of Bihar and Orissa.

1965

Communal Riots in Udaipur, Rajasthan[6]

Immediate Cause: Trouble broke out on 19th July in Udaipur due to a minor scuffle between two neighbours, one Hindu, and the other a Sunni Muslim.

- *Number of persons dead.* 2
- *Number of persons injured:* 12
- *Loss of properties*: The *Loss of properties* was estimated to be about Rs. 12 lakhs.

1966

Communal Riots in Udaipur, Rajasthan[7]

Immediate Cause: Trouble broke out on 13th November in Udaipur due to a conflict between two wrestlers, one a Teli (a low caste Hindu) and the other a Kunjara (Muslims, who are professionally engaged in selling fruits and vegetables).

Real Cause: On both occasions the riot developed and the very same shops of the Bohras were burnt or looted in the old markets. The Bohras had absolutely no hand at any stage in the development of the riot. Both times the riots erupted due to a quarrel between a Hindu and a Sunni Muslim; but unfortunately the Bohras became the victims. The local Sunni Muslims were economically and socially backward and also temperamentally aggressive. Being low paid wage earners, they presented no challenge in the competitive market economy to the non-Muslim groups and had nothing to lose. The Bohras, on the other hand, were a potential business force in direct competition with the Hindu business elite in the open market. The tension between the two neighbours, essentially a private affair, provided an opportunity to settle business scores through violence in the streets.

- *Number of person dead:* 1
- *Loss of properties*: 86 shops were looted
- *Places affected:* Dhan Mandi, Mochiwara, Bara Bazaar and Moti Chohutta markets

1967

Communal Riots in Calcutta, West Bengal[8]

Immediate Cause: Trouble broke out over the dispute between Hindus and Sikhs over the right of access to a Hindu temple through a Sikh shrine. Following reports that their shrine had been desecrated; thousands of Sikhs, many of them armed, took part in protest march through the area on 29th March. A section of the demonstrators attacked and looted Hindu owned shops, whereupon the Hindus retaliated with stones.

- *Number of persons dead*: 11
- *Number of persons injured:* 100
- *Other details not available*

Communal Riots in Ranchi, Bihar[9]

Immediate Cause: A proposal to make Urdu the second official language in Bihar gave rise to serious differences inside the coalition government in the state. Karpuri Thakur (the then Deputy Chief Minister and Samyukta Socialist leader) on the other hand, said, on 2nd August that he would not attend meetings of the coordination committee of the United Front unless the Jana Sangh gave up its anti-Urdu policy. The General Secretary of the Jana Sangh, Deen Dayal Upadhyay, alleged, on 3rd August that the demand for a special status for Urdu was put forward by organisations which wanted to keep alive separatist feelings among Muslims, and said that his party would leave the Government if Urdu was made an official language. This dispute led to violent communal riots at Ranchi between 24th August and 28th August.

- *Number of persons dead:* 184 (19 Hindus and 164 Muslims)
- *Number of persons injured:* 100
- *Number of persons arrested:* 611 (409 Hindus and 102 Muslims)
- *Loss of properties:* 78 houses were affected by arson and 65 shops and business premises were affected by arson. 195 houses were affected by looting or damaged. 128 shops and business houses were affected by looting and some were damaged. 3 places of worship and 1 school were destroyed.

Communal Riots in Kashmir[10]

Immediate Cause: Trouble broke out in Srinagar during 24th August and 27th August due to the conversion of a Pandit (Brahmin) girl to Islam and her marriage to a Muslim. The girl's mother who brought a legal action in order to have the girl returned to her former home, alleged that she was below the legal age of marriage and that she had been abducted and forcibly converted and married. But the girl denied this herself. Commentators suggested that the agitation reflected the Pandit community's resentment at their loss of former privileged status. The Pandits' agitation for the return of the girl provoked counter demonstrations by Muslims on August 24th and several people were injured in clash between two communities. The rioting further spread on 26th August to Jammu, where troops were called in to maintain law and order. Further conflicts between Pandits and Muslims occurred on 27th August in Srinagar.

The riot also broke out in Srinagar on 3rd October, when Muslim students were reported to have found torn pieces of the holy book Quran in their college latrine, and therefore demonstrated in protest against the sacrilege.

- *Number of persons dead:* 3
- *Number of persons injured:* 162

Communal Riots in Malegaon, Maharashtra[11]

Immediate Cause: Trouble broke out in Malegaon on 25th September. (The immediate cause of the riot not available).

- *Number of persons dead:* 4
- *Other details not available*

1968

Communal Riots in Meerut, Uttar Pradesh[12]

Immediate Cause: Trouble broke out on 28th January in Meerut due to an attack by Hindus during a Muslim political meeting.

- *Number of persons dead*: 17
- *Other details not available*

Communal Riots in Karimganj, Assam[13]

Immediate Cause: Trouble broke out in Karimganj on 2nd March, over a minor incident involving a stray cow.

- *Number of persons dead:* 7
- *Number of persons injured*: 43
- *Number of persons arrested:* 233
- *Other details not available*

Communal Riots in Calcutta, West Bengal[14]

Immediate Cause: Trouble broke out on 14th March in Calcutta due to the quarrel between a Hindu and a Muslim.

- *Number of persons dead:* 3
- *Number of persons injured:* 9
- *Number of persons arrested:* 900
- *Other details not available*

Communal Riots in Allahabad, Uttar Pradesh[15]

Immediate Cause: Trouble broke out on 15th March in Allahabad during the celebration of the Hindu spring festival, Holi.

- *Number of persons dead*: 3
- *Loss of properties*: Houses and shops owned by Muslims were looted and burnt down. (The exact number of houses and shops burnt not available)

Communal Riots in Tinsukia, Assam [16]

Immediate Cause: Trouble broke out in Tinsukia on 30th March over the report that a Muslim had killed a cow, sacred to Hindus.

- *Number of persons injured:* 40
- *Loss of properties*: 3 houses were burnt down.

Communal Riots in Aurangabad, Maharashtra[17]

Immediate Cause: Trouble broke out on 8th June in Aurangabad over a report that a Muslim baker was reported to have killed a stray cow, which tried to eat some of the loaves of bread from his bakery shop. After hearing this, the Hindus ransacked the bakery shop and then looted Muslim shops and burnt them.

- *Number of persons dead*: 3
- *Loss of properties*: Many shops were looted and burnt (The exact number of shops looted are not available.)

Communal Riots in Nagpur, Maharashtra[18]

Immediate Cause: Trouble broke out in Nagpur on 10th June due to the differences over the payment of money between a barber and a customer belonging to different communities.

- *Number of persons dead:* 29
- *Loss of properties:* A cinema hall (theatre) and about 150 houses were burnt down.

1969

Communal Riots in Ahmedabad, Gujarat[19]

Immediate Cause: Trouble broke out on 18th September in Ahmedabad when some Hindu Sadhus and Muslims clashed near the Jagannath temple situated at the end of Jamalpur area thickly populated by Muslims. The clash was sparked off due to a commotion caused by a Muslim woman with two children. As happened every day, at about 3 p.m., a herd of cows were returning to the temple led by two Sadhus, who were quite familiar with the Muslims of the area. One of them, a dwarf, had always been an object of fun for the Muslim Youths of the locality. The sight of the crowd disturbed a cow, which in fright hurt the woman who was with her two children. Angered by this, the lady complained to the Sadhus. About the same time some Muslim youths were making fun of the short stature Sadhu, who in anger lifted his rod, which accidentally touched a Muslim woman standing behind him. Annoyed, the woman shouted at the Sadhu. In this atmosphere of tension and commotion, a scuffle developed between the youths and the Sadhus. Later, this incident sparked off major riots in Ahmedabad and other places in Gujarat.

- *Number of persons dead:* 512 (officially) 24 (Hindus) 430 (Muslims) and 58 (others) 600 (unofficially)
- *Number of persons injured:* 561 (officially) 232 (Hindus) and 329 (Muslims) 1,084 (unofficially)
- *Number of persons arrested:* under Section 151 Cr.P.C. (1898): 282 (Hindus) 515 (Muslims); under Section 188 of I.P.C. 666 (Hindus), 214 (Muslims); For specified offences 102 (Hindus) and 32 (Muslims).
- *Loss of properties:* 3,969 dwellings and 2,317 shops were destroyed. About 6,000 families lost their belongings and shelters. The value of property destroyed ran into crores of rupees. The total *Loss of properties* is estimated to be about Rs. 4,23,24,069.54. The number of religious places destroyed or damaged was 37 Mosques, 50 Darghas, 6 Kabrasthans and 3 temples.
- *The damages to Hindu properties:* 75,85,845
- *The damages to Muslim properties:* 3,47,38,224
- *Areas affected:* Khokhara, Mehmadavad, Amaravadi, Raipur, Rakhiyal, Bapunagar, Chamanpura and New Mental Hospital Colony. The nearby Villages Sabarmati and Ranip were also affected.[20]

Real Cause: Real cause of the Riot in Ahmedabad: Before the riot in Ahmedabad, a split had taken place in the Congress. Mrs. Indira Gandhi wanted to assert her position and so in order to assert her position she nationalised all the important banks in the country. This was an important backdrop to the communal riots in Ahmedabad. When she nationalised the banks, her intention was to over ride the other sections in the Congress and establish her leadership. She won massive support but she got isolated from the elite who immediately raised the slogan that she was taking the country towards communism and this must be fought out. The right wing forces took the whole thing very alarmingly, believing and propagating that it was a step towards communism, which could be stopped only by playing the communal card. Preparations were made for riot in Ahmedabad and some other parts of the country just to communalise the whole atmosphere.

Communal Riots in Ahmedabad and other Places in Gujarat[21]

Immediate Cause: The riot, which occurred in Ahmedabad between 18th and 24th September 1969, was one of the worst outbreak of communal rioting in India after independence. The violence began when a herd of cows belonging to a Hindu temple was driven past by a mosque and knocked down a number of Muslims, seriously hurting some children. The Muslims chased the cows to the temple and a fight took place. From Ahmedabad, the riots spread to other areas of the state, like Baroda and Mehsana.

Baroda[22]

- *Number of persons dead*: 7
- *Number of persons injured:* 44
- *Loss of properties*: The total Loss of properties suffered by Muslims was Rs. 33,26,006 and by Hindus was Rs. 4,58,210
- *Number of persons arrested:* 2,381
- *Loss of property*: Many shops and trains were attacked looted and burnt.

Note: According to Hitendra Desai; Home minister of Gujarat, there had actually been a much smaller number of communal disturbances, including minor incidents like stone throwing in Gujarat than in other states. 29 incidents occurred in Gujarat between 1963 and 1968 as compared with 572 in Bihar, 589 in Maharashtra, 133 in Uttar Pradesh, 375 in West Bengal and 84 in Andhra Pradesh, all between 1964 and 1968.

1970

Communal Riots in Bhiwandi, Jalgaon, Thana and Kalyan, Maharashtra[23]

Bhiwandi

Immediate Cause: Shiv Jayanti processions were taken out on 7th May in the Thane district in four places namely, Wada, Thana, Kalyan and Bhiwandi. The trouble broke out when the Shiv Jayanti procession was passing through the Bhusar Mohalla-Old Thane road. As a result of the propaganda carried on by the R.U.M. a number of persons came from the nearby villages to participate in the Shiv Jayanti procession. The Muslim parties have alleged that these villagers carried lathis to which Bhagwa flags were tied, indulged in shouting provocative and abusive anti-Muslim slogans and some of them threatened the Muslims and even damaged their properties.

- *Number of persons dead:* 78. 17 (Hindus) 59 (Muslims) 2 (unidentified)
- *Number of persons injured:* 335
- *Number of persons arrested:* In Cognisable cases*:* 21 (Hindus) 901 (Muslims)
- *For breaches of curfew and prohibitory orders:* 323 (Hindus) 1,282 (Muslims)
- *Loss of properties:* The total *Loss of properties* was estimated to be Rs. 1,53,20,163.

Jalgaon

Immediate Cause: Trouble broke out around 2.45 p.m. on 8th May near a "pan" shop at Rath Chowk when a Muslim, Abdul Hameed Shaikh Gulab, who had gone to purchase "pan" was assaulted by some Hindus. He ran away and hid in his house situated in Maniyar Wada, a part of Koli Peth. In a short while a Hindu mob gathered outside his house and started stoning his house and other Muslim houses and some Muslims were assaulted and injured.

- *Number of persons dead*: 43 (1 was a Hindu)
- *Number of persons injured:* 47
- *Loss of properties*: Total Loss of properties was estimated to be around Rs. 34,74,722.

Thana and Kalyan

After 11th May the situation improved in Bhiwandi and Jalgaon, but violence spread to the neighbouring towns of Thana and Kalyan, and in the villages near by.

- *Number of persons dead*: 14
- *Loss of properties*: Mosques and temples were burnt down.

Note: Yashwantrao B. Chavan, the then Union Home Minister, stated in the Lok Sabha on 12th May that the majority of people killed in the riots were Muslims, and that nearly all the houses which were burnt down, belonged to Muslims.

Real Cause of the Riot in Bhiwandi in May 1970: The Bhiwandi riot was a fall out of the Ahmedabad riot in 1969. There was a communally surcharged atmosphere during that time and the Hindu communalists wanted to create a base for themselves in Maharashtra. Press reports attributed the riots to Hindu communalist organisations, the Rashtriya Swayam Sevak Sangh and Shiv Sena, whose members were alleged to have played a leading role in it.

Communal Riots in Mumbai, Maharashtra[24]

Immediate Cause: Communal riot which broke out in Bhivandi spread to Mumbai on 24th August. (The Immediate cause of the riot not available)

- *Number of person dead:* 1
- *Number of persons injured:* 7

1971

Communal Riots in Aligarh, Uttar Pradesh[25]

Immediate Cause: Trouble that broke out in 1971 was due to the consequences of an agitation demanding that the Aligarh Muslim University be declared a Muslim University. This agitation created a violent reaction in the town that culminated in communal violence. (The exact date not available)

- *Other details not available*

Communal Riots in Tellicherry[26]

Immediate Cause: The background of the disturbances was prepared by political parties. Political agitations and propaganda had the effect of creating communal hatred and tension which led to the disturbances. The first phase of the disturbances was pre-planned by the Hindu communalists. The second phase was of the nature of retaliation by Muslims and third was of the nature of retaliation by the Hindus. A Kalasam procession was taken out with the difference that people who earlier used to organise the procession kept away this year. It was organised by others who were seeking encounter with others. Before the procession started one organiser, Mattangot Raghu made a speech to the following effect that Kalasam was going to start. The Kalasam would go along Chirrakkara, T.C. Mukku, O.V. Road, Mukunda Mallar Road to Narangppuram. There would be beating of drums before the Mosques. That was the usual practice and they are going to resist anyone who was going to attack them.

- *Number of persons killed:* Hindus were victims in 89 incidents and Muslims were victims in 480 incidents.
- *Loss of properties:* 72 shops and 4 houses belonging to Hindus were looted and 3 places of worship were damaged. 247 houses of Muslims were attacked and looted. 147 shops belonging to Muslims were damaged and 63 Mosques and Madrasas were damaged. The remaining cases included the attack on 3 schools belonging to Muslims, 1 school belonging to Hindus and damage to or destruction of 3 motor cars, 3 lorries, 3 country boats, 1 motorcycle, 1 bicycle and other moveables belonging to Muslims and 2 cases of attack on the police party near Mattambaram Mosque.

1972

Communal Riots in Ferozabad and Benares, Uttar Pradesh[27]

Immediate Cause: The Muslim League party in Uttar Pradesh organised demonstrations in many towns on 16th June as a protest against the Aligarh Muslim University Act, which had received the President's assent on the previous day. Opponents of the Act maintained that the new regulations destroyed the minority character of the University (the only Muslim University in India) and violated the constitutional right of religious minorities to establish and administer their own educational institutions, and demanded that only Muslims should have an effective say in the administration of the university. The vice-chancellor of the university, Dr. Abdul Aleem, however, said on 11th June that the basic provisions of the act were retained, including special provision for Islamic Studies, and that by the new regulations, donors and former students would no longer be represented in the University Court and the executive council would minimize political interference by outsiders in the University's affairs.

The demonstrations on 16th June led to armed clashes between Hindus and Muslims in Ferozabad and Benares, accompanied by arson and looting.

- *Number of persons dead*: 23

1973

Communal Riots in Meerut, Uttar Pradesh[28]

Immediate Cause: Trouble broke out on 10th December in Meerut over an argument between a Hindu shopkeeper and a Muslim customer.

- *Number of persons dead*: 9
- *Number of persons injured:* 40
- *Number of persons arrested:* 600

The Guardian correspondent commented, "The clashes appeared to be instigated by political parties competing for the Muslim vote in the state election. A Right wing opposition party was believed to have started the riot, but the Hindu Nationalist Jana Sangh accused the Congress of starting it to show that only the Congress Government could protect the Muslims.

1974

Communal Riots in Delhi[29]

Immediate Cause: Trouble broke out on 5th May in Old Delhi due to the quarrel between the armed Hindu and Muslim mobs who fought in the streets for eight hours.

- *Number of persons dead:* 10
- *Number of persons injured:* 300
- *Loss of properties:* 100 shops and offices were destroyed
- *Other details not available*

1975

Communal Riots in Muppala Village, Guntur District, Andhra Pradesh[30]

Immediate Cause: Trouble broke out on 17th April in Muppala village due to the dispute over the rights of the passage in front of a temple.

- *Number of persons dead*: 10
- *Number of persons injured:* 8

1977

Communal Riots in Varanasi, Uttar Pradesh[31]

Immediate Cause: Trouble broke out on 1st October, in Varanasi when a few students of the local Anglo-Bengali college and a few young men from the adjoining locality of Muslim weavers clashed over a question of whether the spreading of the yarn by weaver boys on a part of the playground is broken on the side of the residential area of the Muslim weavers. The clash on the fateful day began with some of the weavers being beaten up by the students and driven off the field. The weavers later beat up some of the students and drove them to their classrooms. Later the police sub-inspector along with a few constables came. Altercations took place between the policemen and the youths of the weaver community. The sub-inspector was beaten up. Later, the policemen looted a large number of houses, burnt down many of them and beat them up during the immersion procession of Goddess Durga.

Trouble broke out again on 22nd October. A procession was taken out from the Hindu area behind Madanpura and led through the old route passing through a lane coming out on the main road. But the boys installed another idol of Durga on the night of 22nd October and on 23rd October they made it widely known that they intended to take the procession of the idol through Muslim areas.

- *Number of persons dead*: 5
- *Loss of properties:* 2 graveyard domes and 3 Mosques were completely destroyed.
- *Place affected:* Madanpura.

1978

Communal Riots in Sambhal Town Moradabad District, Uttar Pradesh[32]

Immediate Cause: Trouble broke out on 29th March in Moradabad district when a particular community took out a procession. Firearms and daggers were freely used in the rioting.

- *Number of persons dead*: 15
- 9 persons were burnt alive by a violent mob that razed a Khandsari factory in the town
- *Loss of properties:* 100 shops were damaged.

Communal Riots in Mattan, Anantnag District, Jammu and Kashmir[33]

Immediate Cause: Trouble broke out on 29th July in Mattan when someone hoisted the *waqf* flag in a compound adjoining the ancient sun temple. This was objected to by the Mahant of the Amarnath cave shrine, Swami Krishnand Saraswati, who insisted that the flag should be removed before the scheduled annual pilgrimage to the cave through Mattan. On 29th July following the removal of the flag by the authorities, a protest demonstration was organised. The crowd turned violent and stoned the police and the police retaliated.

- *Number of persons dead*: 3
- *Number of persons injured:* 30
- *Number of persons arrested*: 50

Communal Riots in Hyderabad, Andhra Pradesh[34]

Immediate Cause: Trouble broke out on 28th August in Hyderabad when a quarrel between a pan shop owner and four customers sparked off the clashes between two sections of communities. Army was called in to quell the riot.

- *Number of person dead:* 1
- *Number of persons injured:* 85
- *Number of persons arrested:* 150
- *Loss of properties:* 20 houses, shops and hotels were burnt.

Communal Riots in Chindwara District, Madhya Pradesh[35]

Immediate Cause: Trouble broke out on 3rd September in Chindwara district during a religious festival at Pandurna.

- *Number of person dead:* 1
- *Number of persons injured: Several (The exact Number of persons injured not available)*
- *Other details not available*

Communal Riots in Aligarh, Uttar Pradesh[36]

Immediate Cause: Trouble broke out in Aligarh after reports that Muslims allegedly had murdered a Hindu in Aligarh.

(The exact date of the out-break of the communal riot not available)

- *Number of persons dead*: 12 (Muslims)
- *Loss of properties*: Muslim shops and houses were burnt down.

Communal Riots in Adoni, Andhra Pradesh[37]

Immediate Cause: Trouble broke out on 12th October after a Hindu religious procession was stoned while passing through a mosque.

- *Number of persons dead*: 2

Communal Riots in Aligarh, Uttar Pradesh[38]

Immediate Cause: Trouble broke out on 6th November in Aligarh, due to a rumour alleging that some Muslims had killed a Hindu.

Number of persons dead: 16 (3 persons died in stabbing incidents, 3 were killed due to the explosions while manufacturing bombs and 10 were shot dead by the police).

1979

Communal Riots in Jamshedpur, Bihar[39]

Immediate Cause: Trouble broke out on 11th April in Jamshedpur. The Jhanda of Sonaram Manjihi of Dimna Basti Akhara was taken out at about 8.00 a.m. and reached the New Purulia road at about 9.15 a.m. After the procession had moved further up to the Yadava petrol pump on the New Purulia road, it got stalled and demand was raised for the release of B.K. Trivedi and other persons who were arrested. Inspite of the District Collector making the best possible efforts to get the procession moved and cleared through the new Purulia road, the procession was held up with the result that communal disturbances flared up This led to one of the worst communal riots in the industrial city of Jamshedpur and it was caused when a Hindu religious procession led by members of Janata Party of State Assembly halted near a mosque. These riots resulted in killing, arson and looting on a large scale.

- *Number of persons dead*: 117
- *Number of persons injured:* 333
- *Number of persons arrested:* 1,215
- *Loss of properties:* 772 houses and shops were burnt down.

Note: After the Jamshedpur riots, *the Hindu* correspondent wrote on April 14, 1979: "One thing is clear and established beyond doubt: the conflagration, clashes, carnage and widespread arson were not a sudden eruption.... Contractors, goons and musclemen who inhabit the densely populated and squalid areas, which have sprung up on the fringes of the industrial township, dominate Jamshedpur. That the whole operation was meticulously planned is established by the grim fact that gangsters, goons, musclemen and sophisticated arms were being smuggled into Jamshedpur, days and weeks before the holocaust began".

Communal Riots in Purnea District, Bihar[40]

Immediate Cause: Trouble broke out on 4th July in twelve villages in the Purnea district of Bihar, which continued up to 7th July. *Immediate cause and the communities involved in the conflict not available.*

- *Number of persons dead*: 30
- *Number of persons injured:* 100

Communal Riots in Jamshedpur, Bihar[41]

Immediate Cause: Trouble broke out again between August 28th and August 29th in Jamshedpur. *The Immediate cause and communities involved in the riot not given.*

- *Number of persons dead*: 10 (officially); 18 (unofficially)
- *Number of persons injured:* 50

Communal Riots in Nadia District, West Bengal[42]

Immediate Cause: Trouble broke out on 21st June between Hindus and Muslims. The riot between Hindus and Muslims the first of its kind in West Bengal for many years, was reported to have been caused by an increase in armed robberies in the area, for which each community blamed the other.

- *Number of persons dead*: 28
- *Loss of properties:* 400 houses in 12 villages were burnt down
- *Places affected:* Nadia and Chapra districts, Krishna nagar

Communal Riots in Hyderabad, Andhra Pradesh[43]

Immediate Cause: Trouble broke out on 23rd November in Hyderabad. The trouble sparked off when some Muslims refused to observe hartal in protest against the seizure of the Kaaba mosque in Mecca.

- *Number of persons injured:* 100
- *Number of persons arrested:* 1,425
- *Loss of properties:* The *Loss of properties* was estimated to be around Rs. 5 million
- *Places affected:* Gouliguda and Charminar

1980

Communal Riots in Giridih, Bihar[44]

Immediate Cause: Trouble broke out on 12th February between two communities over the quarrel between two boys.

The exact cause and the communities involved in the conflict not available.

- *Number of persons injured:* 2
- *Loss of properties:* 6 shops were burnt down.

Communal Riots in Jalgaon, Maharashtra[45]

Immediate Cause: Trouble broke out on 13th July in Jalgaon due to an altercation between Harijan and a person belonging to minority community.

- *Number of persons dead*: 4

- *Number of persons injured:* 58 (28 injured in stone throwing and 30 in police firing)

(The Jalgaon Deputy Superintendent of Police S.S. Thakur gave the break up of the policemen injured—2 police inspectors, 1 sub-inspector and 25 constables.)

- *Loss of properties:* 2 houses were burnt down
- *Places affected:* Balirampeth, Katyafile and Senipeth

Communal Riots in Delhi[46]

Immediate Cause: Trouble broke out on 13th August in a local teashop between two communities on Punchkuin road.

(Immediate cause and communities involved in the conflict not available)

- *Number of persons injured:* 12

Communal Riots in Moradabad, Uttar Pradesh and Other Places[47]

Immediate Cause: Trouble broke out on 13th August, in Mordabad on the day of EID, when some 80,000 Muslims had gathered at Idgah for prayers. A pig suddenly entered the mosque violating the sanctity of the mosque. This made the Muslims angry who thought that this was an act done by the Hindus. Muslims put the blame on the Provincial Armed Constabulary who were posted there to guard and maintain law and order. They asked Provincial Armed Constabulary to remove the pig but they refused to do so saying it was not their job. An altercation between the congregation and Provincial Armed Constabulary (PAC) stationed there developed into a clash.

- *Number of persons dead:* 119
- *Number of persons injured:* 200
- *Number of persons arrested:* Several (exact figures were not given)
- *Loss of property:* The Galshahid police post was burnt down. A mob also burnt some houses in Ramtilaiya on the outskirts of Moradabad. A train running between Moradabad and Gajraula was attacked.
- *Places affected:* Galshahid, Faizganj, Deputyganj and Ramtilaiya situated on the outskirts of Moradabad.

The Moradabad incidents had their echo in several other towns of the state.

Communal Riots in Meerut, Uttar Pradesh[48]

Immediate Cause: Trouble broke out on 14th August in Meerut when a protest procession was taken out against the Moradabad incident. Some of the demonstrators attacked policemen and civilians with knives.

Other details not available

Communal Riots in Rampur, Uttar Pradesh

Immediate Cause: Trouble broke out in Rampur in reaction to the Moradabad incident.

- *Number of persons dead:* 1
- *Number of persons injured*: 1
- *Number of persons arrested:* 4
- *Loss of properties:* 12 houses were burnt down
- *Place affected:* Civil Lines area

Communal Riots in Aligarh, Uttar Pradesh[49]

Immediate Cause: Trouble broke out on 16th August in Aligarh in protest against the Moradabad incident.

- *Number of persons dead*: 2
- *Number of persons injured:* 5
- *Place affected*: Upperkot

Communal Riots in Barailly, Uttar Pradesh[50]

Immediate Cause: Trouble broke out in Barailly in reaction against the Moradabad incident.

- *Number of persons dead:* 1
- *Number of persons arrested:* 50
- *Ammunitions recovered:* 121 factory-made and 13 country-made firearms

Communal Riots in Allahabad, Uttar Pradesh[51]

Immediate Cause: Trouble broke out on 15th August in Allahabad in protest against the Moradabad incident.

- *Number of persons dead:* 1
- *Number of persons injured*: 1

- *Number of persons arrested:* 679
- *Ammunitions recovered:* 503 foreign arms, 12 bombs, 3 guns, 45 knives and 5 pistols

Communal Riots in Sambhal, Bihar[52]

Immediate Cause: Trouble broke out on 15th August in Sambhal in Bihar when a procession was taken out in protest against the Moradabad incidents.

Other details not available

Communal Riots in Walled City, Ahmedabad[53]

Immediate Cause: Trouble broke out on 16th August in walled city.

The Immediate cause and the communities involved in the conflict not available.

- *Number of persons dead:* 2
- *Number of persons injured:* Several (Exact figures not available)
- *Places affected:* Chandni Chowk, Kamla Market, Turkman Gate, Lahori Gate, Houz Khas and Jama Masjid

Communal Riots in Mhow, Madhya Pradesh[54]

Immediate Cause: Trouble broke out on 15th August in Mhow when some students in a procession wanted to enter a locality where the majority of residents belonging to a minority community had given a call for a black day to protest against the Moradabad incident. The procession was obstructed by the residents resulting in stone throwing followed by a series of clashes in various parts of the town.

- *Number of persons dead:* 3
- *Number of persons injured:* 34

Communal Riot in Jammu and Kashmir[55]

Immediate Cause: Trouble broke out in Jammu and Kashmir in protest against the Moradabad incidents.

The exact date of the riot not available

- *Number of persons arrested:* 2,000. (The arrested persons included Jamat-e-Islami party MLA Sayed Ali Shah Geelani. It is to be noted that Jamat-e-Islami was recently accused of fomenting trouble and creating disharmony in the state.)

Communal Riots in Devangere, Karnataka[56]

Immediate Cause: Trouble broke out on 18th September in Devangare, a textile town 200 kms away from Bangalore, due to the clashes between two warring groups, The long standing enmity between two communities was said to be the cause of the trouble.

The communities involved in the conflict not available.

- *Number of person dead:* 1
- *Number of persons injured:* 3

Communal Riots in Virudhunagar, Ramnad District, Tamil Nadu [57]

Immediate Cause: Trouble broke out on 20th October during the religious procession that was taken out as part of the Mahara Nombu festival. The police fired in order to control the clash involving three communities.

- *Number of persons injured:* 14
- *Other details not available*

Communal Riots in Moradabad, Uttar Pradesh[58]

The violence again occurred in Moradabad on 26th October.

Immediate cause and the communities involved in the conflict not available.

- *Number of persons dead:* 16
- *Number of persons arrested:* 150

Communal Riots in Saharanpur, Uttar Pradesh[59]

Immediate Cause: Trouble broke out in Saharanpur during the Dussehra and Id celebrations. Curfew was imposed on Mallipur village, which is situated in Saharanpur district.

- *Number of persons dead:* 2

Communal Riots in Godhra, Panch Mahal District, Gujarat[60]

Immediate Cause: Trouble broke out on 29th October in Zahumpura, when two hawkers (One Sindhi and the other Ghanchi Muslim) quarreled with each other on the positioning of their handcarts. They hurled abuses and started beating each other. Soon the Sindhi crowd and the Ghanchi Muslims gathered from nearby and within a short time, violence broke out between the two communities.

- *Number of persons dead*: 5
- *Loss of properties:* The total number of properties burnt on 29th October was 230, (116 belonged to the Muslims and 114 belonged to Sindhis). On 30th October according to Advocate Rashid, a Ghanchi Muslim leader, the Badshahbawa and Chamanpura mosques were damaged. In Baharpura the Iqbal Union school was attacked and 5 of its rooms were demolished by a Sindhi mob on 30th October. The rooms were razed to the ground.
- *Places affected:* Zahunpura, Single Falia locality and Baharpura

Communal Riots in Cuttack, Orissa[61]

Immediate Cause: Trouble broke out on 10th November in Cuttack over the differences in the method of Godess Kali immersion processions.

- *Loss of properties:* 6 shops were ransacked and looted by miscreants
- *Places affected:* Chaudhary Bazaar in Cuttack and Telenga Bazaar

1981

Communal Riots in Godhra, Panch Mahal District, Gujarat[62]

Immediate Cause: Trouble broke out on 29th March in Godhra. The Sindhis collected funds for construction of trade premises of their fellow members. The scheme was to rebuild concrete constructions for converting the old wooden cabins into the pucca shops for Sindhis near railway station. Sindhi panchayat had collective permission for construction. This was resented by Muslims because a Bohra trader was denied similar permission on the grounds of road widening plans. Before riots, the whole scheme was dropped by Muincipal authorities but after riots it was approved, leaving out the sole Bohra buisnessman on untenable grounds. Nuruddin, the Bohra businessman, was ready to give up 15 feet for road widening, but in vain. Nuruddin's shop was originally situated on a disputed piece of land. A Parsi, was given the land on lease for 99 years by a Hindu temple trust after taking back the land wanted to construct a temple. The trust approached Muincipality for permission. Sindhis came out with an idea to construct a Gurudwara on the same land for the benefit of many. Thus the real business or economic issues were hidden behind religious ones.

- *Loss of properties:* Sindhi shops were looted.

Communal Riots in Biharsharif, Bihar[63, 64]

Immediate Cause: The real cause of the riot was a dispute between the Muslims and the Yadavas over a cemetery land. Towards the end of 1980, a dispute over a piece of cemetery land was going on between the Muslims and Yadavas (a dominant agricultural community) at a place called Gagrdivan. According to Azmat Hussain Khan, a lecturer in history from Biharsharif, the land on a hillock belonged to the Muslims, but the Yadavas were claiming it as their own. The Yadavas, according to Hussain, came in strength during night, constructed a temple overnight and covered it with cow dung to hide it from others. As the land was a grazing ground for animals, cowdung heaps were a normal sight. The plan was to 'discover' the temple a few months later in order to claim the land. However, the Muslims noticed it a month later and a pitched battle was fought between the two groups using bombs and bullets. However the police brought the situation under control. Apart from this land dispute there is a political dimension of the conflict between Rashtriya Sevak Sangh and Communist Party of India, which has an important stronghold.

The drunken brawl in a toddy shop on 30th April was merely an excuse. The Yadavas, who wanted to sabotage the district authorities' attempt to settle the graveyard dispute, came in conflict with the Muslims, and the Rashtriya Swayam Sevak Sangh was waiting in the wings to start the massacre. Soon after the brawl the town was bristling with rumours, and thus killing and looting started.

- *Number of persons dead*: 47 (officially), 150-200 (unofficially)
- *Number of persons injured:* 68
- *Number of persons arrested:* 550 (5 were well known office-bearers of the Rashtriya Swayam Sevak Sangh.)
- *Loss of properties*: 12 houses were completely burnt down.
- *Places affected:* Alinagar, Teli Mohalla and Gulni village

Communal Riots in Lucknow, Uttar Pradesh[65]

Immediate Cause: Trouble broke out on 11th May in Lucknow when police fired to disperse two groups of vegetable sellers belonging to two different communities. Trouble also began when two young men quarrelled at a ration shop in the Naya Gaon area. Soon after, supporters of the two boys clashed near the shop. *Communities involved in the riots not available.*

- *Number of persons injured:* 34
- *Number of persons arrested:* 25
- *Loss of properties:* In Mazirabad market, rioters stoned and looted shops.(The exact number of shops stoned and looted not available)

Communal Riots in Aligarh, Uttar Pradesh[66]

Immediate Cause: Trouble broke out on 12th May in the Aligarh Muslim university campus. The hostel accommodation in Aligarh Muslim University campus is woefully short. While the total accommodation available is far less than 4,000 seats, not less than 9,000 students are residing in the hostels. Thus overcrowding has led to certain serious problems. The authorities do not have a proper record of accommodation. Many students do not pay for the hostel accommodation and quite often bad characters live in hostels.

Other details not available

Communal Riots in Hyderabad, Andhra Pradesh [67]

Immediate Cause: Trouble broke out on 22nd May in Hyderabad due to the clashes between two communities.

Immediate cause and the communities involved not available.

- *Number of persons injured:* 6
- *Number of persons arrested:* 25
- *Places affected:* Sayeedabad and Yakapura

Communal Riots in Dhoraji town, Gujarat [68]

Immediate Cause: Trouble broke out on 13th June in Dhoraji town when a 2,000 strong mob turned violent while protesting against the local civic body's alleged removal of building materials from a place of worship.

- *Number of person dead:* 1
- *Number of persons injured:* 8
- *Loss of properties:* 65 houses, 1 hospital, 37 cabin shops and 25, 'pucca' shops and 5 vehicles were destroyed.

Communal Riots in Godhra, Gujarat[69]

Immediate Cause: Trouble broke out on 18th June in Godhra when there was an incidence of mob violence near civil hospital; Ganchi and Hindu boys had clashed over an issue of dairy-milk queue.

Other details not available

Communal Riots in Hyderabad, Andhra Pradesh[70]

Immediate Cause: Trouble broke out on 12th July in Hyderabad when a Muslim conference was being held in the city. Besides this, the trouble was also aggravated by the report of mass conversions of Harijans to Islam. When the Hindu religious procession played music outside a mosque on 12th July, the Muslims protested and fighting broke out which continued till 19th July.

- *Number of persons dead*: 28
- *Number of persons injured:* 250 (in stabbing)
- *Number of persons arrested:* 1,300 persons were arrested under the National Securities Act. Among them were BJP leaders and 5 Majilis-e-Ittehdul-Nuslemeen leaders.

Communal Riots in Godhra[71]

Trouble broke out on 21st August in Godhra when rumours were spread that the attacks were planned against the Muslims. It was feared that the curfew would be imposed resulting in prevention of Id celebrations. There was a strong rumour in the city that the Muslim houses would be attacked while Muslim go for namaaz. It is alleged that one police inspector Bhogal entered the Mosque with his men to beat up the *namazis*. The police entered with shoes on and they insulted the Quran. Police entered at three places of worship and beat up or arrested the inmates. This situation was going on for almost a year and people on either side were tired of tension, riot and curfews. Both communities had suffered heavily for long and some mutual understanding was necessary to strike a formulae for peace. By September 1981, they had arrived at a settlement and no major skirmishes were reported. The communal tension and riots in Godhra were preceded by communal politics involving economic competition and petty trade rivalries.

- *Number of persons arrested:* 23 (Muslims)

Reace Cause: The real cause of the riot in Godhara in 1980-81 was due to conflict of interests between local Sindhi and Ghanchi traders with Municipal politics thrown in. Sindhis had come to this town after partition and were a community of petty traders. The Ghanchi Muslims are a very old Muslim community of Godhra and apart from cultivation, they had taken to transport business and owned a large part of fleet of trucks in the town. Since the days of partition, intense animosity existed between Sindhis and Ghanchis and so even through there was long intervals of communal peace, it often got disturbed by violent clashes over positioning of stall boards or vendors' carts.

Communal Riots in Ahmedabad, Gujarat[72]

Immediate Cause: Trouble broke out on 24th August in Ahmedabad when two groups clashed in Sarjapura area during Janmashtami celebration.

- *Number of persons arrested:* 110
- *Loss of properties:* 10 shops were set ablaze.

Communal Riots in Moradabad, Uttar Pradesh[73]

Immediate Cause: Trouble broke out in the Garikhana locality when miscreants threw explosives at a congregation in a place of worship in Moradabad in Uttar Pradesh.

The exact date not available

Other details not given.

Communal Riots in Baroda, Gujarat[74]

Immediate Cause: Trouble broke out on 13th September in Baroda when dirty water was thrown on a *"Ganesh visarjan"* procession, from the top of some buildings in the Wadi area, which immediately led to the riot, which spread to other localities in the area.

Real Cause: Baroda riots were not only between Hindus and Muslims, but were mainly backed by Bhoi and Muslim anti-social or underworld elements and backed by rival political factions in ruling party as well as the opposition parties. The Baroda riots have their roots in the clashes that originated out of the shifting nature of and brutal competition between ruling liquor dons of socio-economically more or less at par communities of Bhois/Kahars, Muslims and Marathas.

- *Number of persons dead*: 5
- *Number of persons injured:* 30

Communal Riots in Chomu town, Rajasthan[75]

Immediate Cause: Trouble broke out on 3rd October in Chomu town over the dispute of land. The authorities had ear-marked the land for Munsif magistrates court, but Muslims claimed it as part of a graveyard. To establish their claim, Muslims raised a wall around the area that was immediately pulled down by Hindus.

- *Number of persons injured*: 3
- *Number of persons arrested:* 28

Communal Riots in Patiala, Punjab[76]

Immediate Cause: Trouble broke out on 17th October in Patiala when a few volunteers of the Hindu Raksha Samiti, had given a call for a hartal. They tried to get the shops of members of the Akali Jatha closed. The hartal was in protest against the shooting incident at Chandigarh on 16th October.

Other details not available.

1982

Communal Riots in Ahmedabad, Gujarat[77]

Immediate Cause: Trouble broke out on 10th January and which continued till 12th January in Daryapur. A quarrel between two groups on Kite-flying soon led to stone-throwing.

- *Number of persons dead*: 7 (6 Hindus)
- *Places affected:* Daryapur, Kalupur, Changiz Pole

Real Cause: As usual the kite-flying incident was merely a spark. Systematic efforts were being made for a long time to build up communal tensions in the city. Sometime before, several branches of the Vishwa Hindu Parishad (VHP) actively supported by the Rashtriya Swayam Sevak Sangh were formed in Ahmedabad. The Vishwa Hindu Parishad was carrying out its violent campaign against the conversion of Harijans to Islam and its activists were collecting funds in a big way. A large number of leaflets in Gujarati condemning the conversion of some Harijans to Islam and appealing for funds, for saving the Hindu culture were also distributed.

Communal Riots in Solhapur, Maharashtra[78]

Immediate Cause: Trouble broke out on 15th February in Solhapur at 8 p.m. when the procession taken out by the Vishwa Hindu Parishad was coming to an end. In the beginning it remained peaceful, but according to eye witnesses when it came near the Punjab Talim mosque, a usual trouble spot during the Ganesh festival, some miscreants from the procession started shouting provocative slogans: *"Ek dhakka aur do, pakistan tod do. Vande mataram gana hoga nahin to Hindustan chhodna hoga. yeh desh Hinduon ka, nahin kisi ke bap ka."* Soon, properties belonging to the Muslims were damaged in Tilak Chowk and therefore the Muslims retaliated.

- *Number of persons dead*: 12
- *Number of persons injured:* 8 (4 in stabbing incidents and 4 in police firing)
- *Loss of properties:* A hand-cart, a cold-drink shop and a pan shop belonging to Muslims were burnt down. 3 shops belonging to Hindus were burnt down.
- *Places affected:* Tilak Chowk, Shukrawar Peth and Guruwar peth

Communal Riots in Pune, Maharashtra[79]

Immediate Cause: Trouble broke out on 15th February in Pune after the Vishwa Hindu Parishad had announced its intention to take out a procession. The procession carried the potraits of Dr. Ambedkar, Mahatma Phule and Mahatma Gandhi along with that of Golwalkar and a copy of Manusmriti. According to Baba Adhav, a prominent social worker from Pune, the processionists were shouting extremely filthy slogans to provoke Muslims. The procession changed its route and entered a Muslim locality. Then passing through Deccan Gymkhana, the miscreants in the procession attacked properties belonging to Muslims.

- *Loss of properties:* 2 Muslim (Irani) hotels were burnt down. 1shop belonging to Bohra Muslim was completely burnt down. According to the owner of one of the shop, he suffered a loss of about Rs. 4 akhs. Also, many Muslim shops were stoned and damaged.

Reace Cause: The real cause of the riots in Pune and Solapur was the campaign by the Vishwa Hindu Parishad for Hindu unity, and against the conversion of some Harijans to Islam. Also, the last major riot that occurred was in 1967, in which 12 persons were killed. Vishwa Hindu Parishad also started collecting funds for their own party but the real intention was to harangue the Hindus on the Meenakshipuram conversions and to awaken them to the "danger lurking over their heads of being reduced to a minority in their own country".

Communal Riots in Nabha, Patiala District, Punjab[80]

Immediate Cause: Trouble broke out on 1st May in Nabha, after an act of sacrilege before the temple in Amritsar. It started when brickbats were thrown at a procession being taken out to protest against the sacrilege inside a place of worship. The processionists retaliated forcing the police to swing into action, which led to an exchange of brick–batting, when the processionists after re-grouping once again reached another place of worship. The secessionist Dal Khalsa claimed responsibility for this act.

- *Number of persons injured:* 32

Note: The State banned the sale of meat, tobacco and liquor in the vicinity of place of worship. Press Trust India reported that tension mounted at Anandpur Sahib following the recovery of a few packets of bidis and cigarettes in the *kesgarah* Sahib Gurudwara, which is among the five supreme seats in the Sikh religion.

Communal Riots in Meerut, Uttar Pradesh[81]

Immediate Cause: Trouble broke out on 30th September in Meerut. The riot was the result of a Temple-Mazar controversy. In the commercial locality of Shahgang, there is a peepal tree under which is located a shop of a beetle merchant and a water hut (piao). Behind this piao is a well which is enclosed by high walls. Near this well there are three shops owned by a trust. Adjacent to the well is a house of a Muslim advocate, Qazi Zaheeruddin. The dispute arose between the Trust and Qazi Zaheeruddin. The Hindus and Muslims put counter-claims forward. The Hindus asserted that originally there was a temple under the tree; and the Muslims insisted that the place had a tomb of a Muslim saint. To assert their right, the Hindus started having evening prayers (*aarti*) with the playing of gong and conch shell. A *ghanta* (huge bell) was also installed there. As a result tension began to mount.

On Bakr-id (28th September), the Shahar Qazi Zainul Abidin declared that the Id prayers would not be held at Idgah but would be held in Mosques in different Mohallas and that Muslims would wear black badges in protest against the removal of the seal. Black flags were also hoisted on some Muslim houses. Hindus now started the campaign to hoist saffron coloured flags. Soon the situation went out of control and hell was let loose from 30th September to 2nd October. The Muslims declared that they would demonstrate their protest by wearing black badges. The situation went out of control, and the police had to intervene. Several people got killed in the firing by the PAC (Provincial Armed Constabulary).

Real Cause: A look at the genesis of the riot shows it to be political rather than economic. The high percentage of Muslim population (49%) makes them very important. Their support along with the Harijan votes to any political party becomes crucial. Hence a conscious attempt to woo the Harijans was being made by the Bhartiya Janata Party.

To understand the genesis of this riot, it is necessary to know what happened immediately before in Meerut. The Rashtriya Swayam Sevak chief, Balasaheb Deoras visited Meerut in January 1982. Tension began to mount after Balasaheb's visit to the city. The Mazar-temple controversy began to assume serious proportions from the month of April 1982. Also during the month of August and September the activists of Bhartiya Janata Party and Vishwa Hindu Parishad were quite prejudicial to the cause of communal peace in Meerut.

- *Number of persons dead:* 100 (90 Muslims 10 Hindus), out of which 42 were killed in PAC bullets.

- *Number of persons killed in police-firing:* 7 Hindus and 24 Muslims (8 in police-firing)
- *Number of persons injured:* 53 Hindus and 27 Muslims received injuries.
- *Loss of properties:* 35 Hindu and 126 Muslim houses and 3 mosques were damaged. Properties worth Rs. 28 lakhs was damaged.
- *Ammunitions recovered:* 31 knives, 1,599 sharp weapons, 10 country-made revolvers, 28 bombs, 27 litres of acid, 16 kg. of potash and 150 kg of other bomb-making materials.

Communal Riots in Baroda, Gujarat[82]

Immediate Cause: Trouble broke out on 22nd October in Baroda. According to the Deputy Mayor of Baroda, Sayyed Nisar Bapu, riot broke out when a person in Navapura locality was brutally stabbed. Sporadic clashes occurred and curfew was clamped. The Muslims, therefore, decided not to install 'Tazias' (Imitation of Imams Hussain's tomb in Kerbala, Iraq) in view of the communal tension. However, Prabodh Rawal, the Home Minister of Gujarat, persuaded the Muslims to go ahead with the installation of 'Tazias' and assured them that no harm would come to them.

On this assurance, the Muslims installed Tazias the following day and strangely enough the police, Bapu said, fell upon them on the pretext that they were breaking curfew. Either the police did not obey the Home Minister or the Home Minister never instructed the police to allow the Muslims to install Tazias.

- *Number of persons dead:* 7 (6 in stabbing incidents and 1 killed in police firing)
- *Number of persons injured*: 55
- *Number of persons arrested:* 622 (540 Muslims)
- *Loss of properties:* 31 properties were burnt down
- *Places affected:* Navapura, Bahucharwada, Panigate area and Nalbandwada in Mughalwada locality.

Note: Trouble broke out in Baroda in the wake of the most cataclysmic riot in Ahmedabad in 1969 and it was here again in September 1981 that communal riot erupted.

Real Cause of riot in Baroda in October: Until 1977, some Muslims had the monopoly of illicit liquor business. But by 1982 it was taken over by the Kahars (a schedule caste community) and one Shiva Kahar was now in absolute command of the business. It was alleged by some social workers in Baroda city that liquor worth one lakh of rupees was sold every day and *'hafta'* totalling Rs. 60 lakhs per year was paid to the police officials and political bosses. Shiva Kahar was said to have very close relationship with police officials and some important political bosses of the ruling party enjoying their patronage. Due to Shiva Kahar many other members of the Kahar community were having a field day.[83]

Generally the festival of Dusshera was celebrated with great fanfare among the middle and upper castes like Patels, Desais, etc. However, that year the Kahars celebrated Dusshera very lavishly. Everywhere in the Kahar locality photographs of Shivaji were hung and real swords and spears were kept near the photographs on the occasion of this festival.

Shiva Kahar was arrested in May 1981—in connection with some group clashes. However, he was provided with all the comforts in jail. It was alleged by some social workers that even liquor was freely supplied to him through the connivance of the police. One Alam Shah Diwan, a social worker, lodged a protest with the city police chief in this regard and the then District Superintendent of Police stopped these facilities to Shiva Kahar. This roused the ire of Shiva Kahar who swore to take revenge. He was only waiting for an opportunity to seek revenge on Muslims (specially those who were his rivals); and in his stronghold Bahucharwada (Panigate area), he destroyed every Muslim hut.

Communal Riots in Meenakshipuram, Tamil Nadu[84]

Immediate Cause: At Meenakshipuram an improvised mosque built 16 months earlier, where most of the Harijans of the village embraced Islam was completely gutted shortly after communal frenzy.

- *Number of persons dead:* 1,026 (876 persons were Muslims and 150 Hindus)
- *Number of persons arrested:* 2,000 (1,100 were Hindus and 900 Muslims)
- *Loss of properties:* 3,932 houses were burnt to ashes and 891 shops were looted and burnt. 3,000 power looms were looted and burned. Also, 37 mosques, 7 madrasas, 8 tombs and 5 Shia Imambaras were destroyed. The number of Hindu houses gutted completely is not exactly known, but it is estimated that more than 300 Hindu houses were completely gutted.

Communal Riots in Puliangudi, Tirunelveli District, Tamil Nadu[85]

Immediate Cause: Trouble broke out in June over the question of entry of a Hindu propaganda van 'Gnana Ratham' of the Vishwa Hindu Parishad. Muslims and converted Harijans in Puliangudi had clashed with members of the Thevar community on the issue.

Exact date not available.

- *Number of persons dead*: 7

Communal Riots in Settur, Tamil Nadu[86]

Immediate Cause: Trouble broke out on 6th July in Settur following an alleged kidnapping of a Harijan boy and an attack on another boy. *The community of the other person is not available.*

- *Number of persons dead*: 2
- *Number of persons injured:* 5

Communal Riots in Ahmedabad, Gujarat[87]

Immediate Cause: Trouble broke out on 22nd August in Ratiyawada following a quarrel between two communities. Some unknown person who was gambling in a church compound picked up a quarrel with the people of the locality who had objected to their activities, which led to a minor quarrel and which turned into a pitched battle between the two communities for half an hour.

- *Number of persons injured:* Several (The communities involved in the riot and the exact number of persons injured were not available.)

Communal Riots in Bellur, Nagamangla[88]

Immediate Cause: Trouble broke out on 21st October in Bellur. While members of one community were attending a function at a place of worship, they were allegedly attacked by people of another community with stones, resulting in a clash.

- *Number of persons arrested:* 50
- *Loss of properties:* 4 haystacks, 5 shops and one four-wheeler were set on fire, while 3 houses were ransacked and looted.

Communal Riots in Sankarankoil taluk, Tirunelveli District and Muthuswamipuram, Tamil Nadu[89]

Immediate Cause: The Meenakshipuram conversions led to riot in the Sankarankoil taluk which later spread to Muthuswamipuram. *The exact date not available.*

- *Number of persons dead*: 9
- *Loss of properties:* 30 Harijan huts were burnt down.

Communal Riots in Meerut, Uttar Pradesh[90]

Immediate Cause: Trouble broke out on 6th September over a dispute about the closure of a place of worship in the Shahghasa area, which led to the riots. Tension in Shahghasa area, according to police officers was building up because of a dispute of Shiva temple and a Mazar in the Shahghasa in two adjoining buildings. As a precautionary measure, armed policemen were posted there, but in August when a group of people offered prayers before the Shiva temple, there was tension. After 10 p.m. on 6th September some people fired crackers in the area, which produced a chain of reactions leading to riots.

- *Number of persons dead*: 11
- *Number of persons injured:* 24
- *Places affected:* Shahghasa, Lisadi Gate, Sabum Godam area, Sadar Bazar and Bhumia ka pul

Communal Riots in Bangalore, Karnataka[91]

Immediate Cause: Trouble broke out on 10th September in Bangalore when the demolition of a Muslim place of worship by the Banglore Development Authority (BDA) at Viveknagar resulted in a violent protest and therefore the police had to open fire. The flashpoint appeared when a policeman threw a copy of the Quran along with other things into a lorry.

- *Number of person dead:* 1

Communal Riots in Vadodara, Gujarat

The exact date, the cause and the communities involved in the conflict are not available.

- *Number of persons dead:* 7 (6 in stabbing and 1 by police bullet)
- *Number of persons injured:* 55
- *Number of persons arrested:* 622

1983

Communal Riots in Rajouri, Jammu and Kashmir[92]

Immediate Cause: Trouble broke out on 9th March in Rajouri when a group of people seriously stabbed a spiritual leader, Baba Ram Dass.

- *Number of persons injured:* 14
- *Loss of properties:* Several shops were looted. (The exact number of *Loss of properties* is not available)

Communal Riots in Malur Town, Kolar District, Karnataka[93]

Immediate Cause: Trouble broke out on 13th May in Malur town following the alleged misbehaviour of a boy belonging to one community towards a girl of another community.

- *Number of persons dead:* 5
- *Number of persons injured:* 50 (45 policemen)

Communal Riots in Nalanda, Bihar[94]

Immediate Cause: Trouble broke out on 29th May in Nalanda when the police opened fire at Katra locality under Biharsharif in self-defence when a posse of armed policemen, led by the District Magistrate and Superintendent of Police, Nalanda, who had gone to disperse clashing groups of two communities near a religious place, was attacked with lethal weapons.

- *Number of persons dead:* 2
- *Number of persons injured:* 2
- *Number of persons arrested:* 15
- *Loss of properties:* The car of the District Magistrate and jeep of the Superintendent was damaged.
- *Ammunitions Recovered:* Huge quantity of bombs, live cartridges and weapons.
- *Place affected:* Katra locality.

Communal Riots in Malegaon, Maharashtra[95]

Immediate Cause: Trouble broke out in Malegaon on 26th June over the bursting of crackers near a place of worship after Indian victory in the Prudential World Cup cricket.

- *Number of persons dead:* 4
- *Number of persons injured:* 30
- *Number of persons arrested:* 500

Communal Riots in Hyderabad, Andhra Pradesh[96]

Immediate Cause: Trouble broke out on 7th September in Hyderabad during the Ganeshutsava celebrations, in which the role of Vishwa Hindu Parishad was very obvious. It was in the highly charged atmosphere that certain incidents occurred. A Muslim belonging to the Charminar area threw a stone at a temple near one of the Minars while coming out of a Mosque on 7th September. Tension was created due to this incident and revenge for this desecration was sought to be taken by desecrating a mosque elsewhere. On 8th September, the mosque in the compound of a factory was desecrated. The fans were damaged and the copies of the Qoran were thrown into an ablution tank.

Real Cause: Hyderabad, until the police action in 1948, was ruled by the Nizam. The Muslim ruling class was feudal in nature and was totally ruined after the abolition of the Nizam's rule. Along with it, all those Muslims who were dependent on the feudal system were also ruined. Those who could, fled to Pakistan. But those left behind were utter destitutes. The old city of Hyderabad was full of such Muslims and ever since it has been a hot-bed of communal conflicts.

The bitter memories continued to persist among both Hindus and Muslims. During the Nizam's rule there existed poor people both among Hindus as well as Muslims. While the Muslim poor took solace in the fact that their co-religionists were ruling, the Hindu poor cursed the Muslim rulers for their fate. Such feelings were quite widespread among the petty bourgeois Hindus in Hyderabad. The communal organisations played on those feelings whenever it suited them. The Hindu Bhartiya Janata Party, Arya Samaj and Vishwa Hindu Parishad, and the Muslim Majlis-e-Ittihadul Muslemin mainly appealed to communal sentiments and brought communal tensions to the threshold of communal violence on the eve of elections or religious festivals.

The primary factor for the riots was political. In the old city, due to the mixed population of Hindus and Muslims, there was tough competition between the Bhartiya Janata Party and Majlis-e-Ittihadul Muslemin. Communal riot also erupted during the Assembly elections in April 1983. The main parties responsible for the riots were the Bhartiya Janata Party and the Majlis-e-Ittihadul Muslemin.

- *Number of persons dead*: 45 (officially), 70 (unofficially)
- *Number of persons injured:* 150 (officially), 200 (unofficially)

Communal Riots in Hyderabad, Andhra Pradesh[97] (Second Stage)

Immediate Cause: Trouble broke out on 9th September in Hyderabad when a *"Bandh"* called by the Muslim Muttehda Mohaz in Hyderabad took a violent turn. The *Bandh* was called to express resentment against the alleged desecration of a place of worship inside the state-owned Allwyn factory in north-west Hyderabad on 7th September.

Number of persons dead: 45 (12 killed in stabbing incidents, 2 in police firing and 3 attacked by lathis and stones)

- *Number of persons injured:* 150
- *Number of persons arrested:* 300 (3 Members of Legislative Assembly belonging to Majlis-e-Ittibadul Muslemin)
- *Loss of properties*: The *Loss of properties* was estimated to be about Rs. 2 lakhs.
- *Places affected:* Saroornagar, Moghulpura, Begumbazar, Chowk areas, Dabirpura, Saidabad, Ghodeki Khabar, Malepally and Charminar.

Communal Riots in Kadri town, Anantapur District, Andhra Pradesh[98]

Immediate Cause: Trouble broke out on 21st September in Kadri town in Anantapur district when police fired to quell a rioting mob, which stoned a Ganesh procession at Anantapur district

- *Number of persons dead*: 2
- *Number of persons injured:* 14
- *Loss of properties:* The *Loss of properties* was estimated to be around Rs. 2 lakhs

Communal Riots in Hyderabad, Andhra Pradesh[99]

Immediate Cause: Trouble broke out on 25th September in the old city of Hyderabad.

Immediate Cause and the communities involved in the conflict not available.

- *Number of persons arrested:* 45
- *Place affected*: Gowliguda

Communal Riots in Karmala town, Solapur District, Maharashtra[100]

Immediate Cause: Trouble broke out on 16th October when the Dussehra procession was heavily stoned near a place of worship forcing the police to fire several rounds to disperse the unruly mobs, which attacked shops and houses.

- *Number of persons dead*: 7
- *Loss of properties:* Shops and houses were attacked. (The exact number of shops and houses attacked are not available)

Communal Riots in Hazaribagh, Bihar[101]

Immediate Cause: Trouble broke out on 17th October in Hazaribagh when the Durga puja procession was attacked by anti-social elements near Juma Masjid road. According to eyewitness accounts, there was no immediate provocation for the attack. As the procession was crossing from the mosque side, missiles were thrown on the procession. Anti-social elements resorted to heavy stone throwing, damaging the idol and injuring many people.

- *Number of persons dead*: 2
- *Number of persons arrested:* 100

1984

Communal Riots in Amritsar, Punjab[102]

Immediate Cause: Trouble broke out on 14th February which continued till 8th March in Amritsar after violent clashes occurred between Hindus and Sikhs, following an attempt by some Hindus to impose a general strike to protest against what they saw as the appeasement of the Sikh community by the Central authorities.

- Number of persons dead: 2,733 (officially)
- *Other details not available*

Communal Riots in Panipat, Haryana[103]

Immediate Cause: Trouble broke out on 19th February in the town of Panipat in Haryana when a large group of Hindus attacked and burnt houses and shops belonging to Sikh community.

The Immediate cause of the riot not available.

- *Number of persons dead*: 9 (Sikhs)

Communal Riots in Gurdaspur District, Punjab[104]

Immediate Cause: Trouble broke out on 21st February, when Sikhs on motorcycle armed with submachine guns raided two adjoining villages in the Gurdaspur district of Punjab.

- *Number of persons dead*: 9 (Hindus)

Note: On 23rd March, Sikh gunmen killed a Hindu village leader who was due to appear as a witness for the prosecution in a trial in which a group of Sikhs was charged with the murder of four policemen.

Communal Riots in Amristar, Punjab[105]

Immediate Cause: Trouble broke out on 2nd April in Amritsar in Punjab when Harbans Lal Khanna, President of the Amritsar branch of the Bhartiya Janata Party, was killed by a previously little known group called the Dashmesh Regiment. The same group later claimed responsibility for the murder on 3rd April in Chandigarh of V.N. Tiwari, a Hindu and Congress (I) member of the Rajya Sabha.

- *Number of persons dead:* 10 (Hindus); and a policemen died in subsequent disturbances

Communal Riots in Jallundur, Punjab[106]

Immediate Cause: Trouble broke out on 12th May in Jallundur when Ramesh Chander, a Hindu newspaper editor, was killed. The Dashmesh Regiment claimed responsibility for the murder and added that whosoever speaks or writes against Sant Jarnail Singh Bhindranwale would be answered with bullets. (In 1981 a warrant had been issued for the arrest of Sant Bhindranwale in connection with the shooting of Chander's father, Lal Jagat Narain, also a critic of Sikh militancy.)

The Hindu population of Jallundur reacted angrily to the death of Chander.

Later the disturbances spread to Haryana and large parts of northern India were called for a "Bandh" on 15th May as many Hindus responded to a strike call to protest over the murder.

- *Number of persons dead*: 8

- *Loss of properties*: A Sikh library, some Sikh shops and some buses were burnt down.

Communal Riots in Aurangabad, Maharashtra[107]

Immediate Cause: Trouble broke out on 17th May in Aurangabad in Maharashtra, just a day before the Muslim Eid. A large crowd gathered outside the court where a petition challenging the election of the Mayor was coming up for hearing. An alert administration would not have allowed such a huge crowd to gather there, especially when tempers of the Shiv Sena were frayed. Right outside the court, Mr Chaggan Bhujbal, the Sena leader notorious for communal outbursts was threatening that the whole city of Aurangabad would burn if the judgement went against them. (*i.e.* if the mayoral election as not set aside.)

- *Number of persons dead:* 5 (4 Hindus and 1 Muslim)
- *Number of persons injured:* 136 (18 Muslims) 85 (in stabbing incidents)
- *Loss of properties:* A cloth shop, a house, 2 godowns, a religious place, a country liquor shop and a rickshaw woro cot on firc./
- *Places affected:* Baujipura, Jinsi, Kaisar colony, Chistiya colony, Indira Nagar, Sector number-7 in Cidco, Lota Karanja, Shahganj, Mulmuchi Bazar, Gandhi Chowk, Roshan Gate, Kasari Bazar, Aurangpura and Gulmandi. Stabbing incidents also took place in Jijmata Colony, Nehru Bhavan, Juna Bazar, Khara Runwa, Rangar Galli, Kaisar Colony and Jinsi.

Communal Riots in Bhiwandi, Thane and Bombay, Maharashtra[108]

Immediate Cause: Trouble broke out on 17th May in Bhiwandi in Thane district when stone throwing incidents occurred and sporadic localized Bandh was called in parts of Bombay (now called Mumbai) and in its suburbs by Shiv Sainiks, in protest against the alleged garlanding of a portrait of their chief, Bal Thackeray with *chappals* in Parbhani district. On the other hand, alleged remarks of Thackeray at a meeting on Prophet Mohammad, reported by a section of the Urdu press, were highly resented by the Muslim community. According to the Maharashtra Chief Minister, Vasantrao Patil, the trouble broke out on 17th May, when one group, which sought to put up its flag near a Shiv Sena office, was opposed. He said that a temporary truce had been declared when both police and citizens intervened. But around midnight, trouble started again and went on throughout the night with the mob indulging in arson and stone throwing.

Real Cause: Bhiwandi, a thriving centre of powerloom industry naturally attracted a large number of Muslim expert weavers from UP. These Muslims or at least some of them, through enterprise and hard work, had purchased looms and started their own businesses. Usually Marwaris or Gujaratis who were the financial magnates financed them. Maharashtrians on the other hand, hardly owned any loom out of more than two lakh looms operating in the town and this situation caused tension. This underlying tension was taken advantage of by rabid communalists for generating violence.

- *Number of persons dead*: 226
- *Number of persons injured:* 150
- *Loss of properties*: 500 huts were burnt down in Bhiwandi and reduced to ashes. In Mumbai 3 lorries were burnt down. According to the UNI Report on 7th June the loss to public and private property as well as business establishments in Bhiwandi and in Thane towns were Rs. 2,000 million.
- *Places affected:* Byculla, Nagpada, Pydhonie, Dongri, V.P. Road, Bhandup, Govandi, Jogeshwari and Kherwadi.

Communal Riots in Kherwadi, Maharashtra[109]

Immediate Cause: Trouble broke out on 24th June in Kherwadi when Hindus began street protests over the arrest of Bal Saheb Thackeray of the Shiv-Sena who had made an apparently provocative speech.

- *Number of persons dead*: 4

Communal Riots at Sadar Bazar, Delhi[110]

Immediate Cause: Trouble broke out on 6th July when a man riding a cycle who belonged to one community hit a man of another community who, along with his brother, retaliated by stabbing the cyclist. *The identity of the person not known.*

- Number of person injured: 1
- *Number of persons arrested:* 8
- *Places affected:* Gali Jatan, Gali Teliyan and Sadar Bazar.

Communal Riots in Hyderabad, Andhra Pradesh[111]

Immediate Cause: Trouble broke out on 9th September in Hyderabad during a Hindu religious procession.

- *Number of persons dead*: 19

Communal Riots in Sendhwa Town, Madhya Pradesh[112]

Immediate Cause: Trouble broke out on 10th September in Sendhwa during a Ganpati immersion procession. When the procession was passing along a three-storeyed lodge, a sizeable section of the processionists turned towards the building and resorted to heavy brick-batting.

- *Number of persons dead*: 4

Communal Riots in Mankachar town, Dhubri District, Assam[113]

Immediate Cause: Trouble broke out on 4th October in Mankachar town when they were taking out the procession with the image of Durga for immersion.

- *Number of persons dead*: 2
- *Number of persons injured:* 9

Communal Riots in Nagda town, Ujjain District, Madhya Pradesh[114]

Immediate Cause: Trouble broke out on 5th October in Nagda town on the occasion of the Durga immersion procession. The clashes broke out when the Durga procession, passing through the main thoroughfare of the town to the immersion ghats was stoned.

- *Number of persons dead*: 3
- *Other details not available*

Communal Riots in Belgaum, Karnataka[115]

Immediate Cause: Trouble broke out on 5th October in Belgaum when a man of "unsound mind" desecrated the place of worship.

Real Cause: This was the culmination of a controversy over the naming of a particular square in the Market. The Muslims had been referring to it as the Jinnah chowk and the Hindus wanted it named as Veer Savarkar chowk. At one of the meetings convened by the divisional commissioner, both the groups agreed to name it as the Maulana Azaad chowk. But the government turned down this suggestion on the ground that the naming of streets, squares and similar things should be taken up only after the local bodies were constituted to build up.

- *Loss of properties:* Several shops were looted and then set on fire

Post-Indira Gandhi assassination killing in Delhi and other places[116]

Immediate Cause: Trouble broke out on 31st October in Delhi, following Mrs. Indira Gandhi's assassination.

- *Number of persons dead*: 2,000
- *Loss of properties:* The Loss of properties is estimated to be around Rs. 200 million.

1985

Communal Riots in Ahmedabad, Gujarat[117]

Immediate Cause: Trouble broke out on 18th March in Ahmedabad after the success of "Bandh" declared in Ahmedabad city against the anti-reservation campaign.

- *Number of persons dead:* 19. (14 in Police firing and 5 in stabbing incidents)
- *Number of persons injured:* 52
- *Loss of properties:* The *Loss of properties* is estimated to be worth Rs. 3 crores.

Communal Riots in Ahmedabad, Gujarat[118]

Immediate Cause: Trouble broke out in Ahmedabad on 10th June when Jagannath Rath Yatra was taken out in a tense communal atmosphere in the teeth of government opposition. They were carrying stones, lathis, trishuls and other weapons. They were carrying kerosenes as well. They were shouting anti-Muslim slogans to provoke Muslims. On the same day *Id-ul-Fitre* festival was celebrated. The communal tensions became so sharp that a clash followed.

- *Number of persons dead*: 8
- *Number of persons injured:* 12

Note: The anti-reservation campaign, Shah Bano agitation campaign and the intense rivalry between different liquor gangs played an important role in the outbreak of communal riots.

1986

Communal Riots in Jammu and Kashmir[119]

Immediate Cause: Trouble broke out on 1st February in Jammu and Kashmir due to a district court order permitting Hindus to worship on a site claimed as a shrine by Muslims at Ayodhya in Uttar Pradesh. This was the alleged cause of a breakdown in law and order in a number of Indian States, leading to the fall of the State government in Jammu and Kashmir.

- *Number of persons injured:* 200 (including 97 policemen, when Hindus attacked a police station in response to an earlier demonstration by Muslims some of whom had been chanting pro-Pakistan slogans).

Communal Riotc in Dclhi[120]

Immediate Cause: Trouble broke out on 14th February in Delhi when the police fired on a mob when it attacked a place of worship at Lal Kuan. The rioting was a sequel to the protest day called by several groups. The protest was against a Faizabad court order for reopening the Ramjanambhoomi.

- *Number of person dead:* 1
- *Number of persons injured:* 26
- *Number of persons arrested:* 60
- *Loss of property:* More than 30 vehicles, including several Delhi Transport Corporation buses were damaged in stone-throwing incidents
- *Places affected:* Lal Kuan, Farash Khana area from Jama Masjid to Asaf Ali Road and from Daryaganj to Kamala Market were affected by the riot.

Communal Riots in Sehore, Madhya Pradesh[121]

Immediate Cause: Trouble broke out on 17th February in Sehore in Madhya Pradesh in the wake of the Ram Janambhoomi judgement. A protest march against the Faizabad court order to open the doors of the Ram Janambhoomi triggered off the tension.

- *Number of persons dead*: 6
- *Number of persons arrested:* 100
- *Loss of properties*: 3 houses were burnt down

Communal Riots in Batala, Punjab[122]

Immediate Cause: Trouble broke out on 19th February in Batala due to an attack by Sikh extremists on Hindus. The members of the All India Sikh Students Federation clashed with members of Shiv Sena, who were protesting against the assassination of a local branch president.

- *Number of persons dead*: 6 (Hindus)
- *Other details not available*

Communal Riots in Calcutta, West Bengal[123]

Immediate Cause: Trouble broke out on 23rd March in Calcutta as two groups clashed at Beniapukur in East Calcutta when an old women was knocked down by a cyclist.(The identity of the old woman and the cyclist not known.)

- *Number of persons injured:* 8
- *Number of persons arrested:* 20
- *Loss of property*: According to the Municipal Affairs Minister, Prasant Sur, a religious place of worship was damaged

Communal Riots in Ludhiana, Punjab[124]

Immediate Cause: Trouble broke out on 28th March in Ludhiana when the Sikh militants, disguised as police officers and riding motorcycles, fired indiscriminately on crowds in a park in the Hindu majority city.

- *Number of persons dead*: 13
- *Other details not available*

Communal Riots in Nasik, Nanded and Panvel, Maharashtra[125]

Immediate Cause: Trouble broke out on 10th May in Nasik. On 8th May Police Inspector Gaikwad called the peace committee meeting in which along with 4 prominent Muslims the Shiv Sena chief Rajendra Bagul and representatives of the Rashtriay Swayam

Sevak Sangh, Bhartiya Janata Party, Hindu Ekta Andolan and the Congress(I) were present. Muslims would welcome the processionists with Sharbat and cold water. The procession was to start at 2.00 p.m. from Hamid chowk but no one had arrived up to 3.30 p.m. on 10th May. At 4.00 p.m. a group of Shiv Sena and a group of Bahujana Yuwa Sanghatna entered the chowk. There was a minor scuffle between the Sena and Bahujan Sanghathna on this issue. While the scuffle was on some groups of Shiv Sena youth entered lanes and by-lanes and began to dance with swords in hands and shouted provocative slogans in front of Muslim houses. It is alleged that at about 6.10 p.m. the Sena chief Bagul went to a Mandir on a main road in Hamid chowk and after puja raised his both hands holding coconut which was treated as a signal by its volunteers and started attacking the houses and shops of Muslims.

- *Number of persons killed:* 8 (4 Hindus and 3 Muslims and 1 was killed in stabbing incidents)
- *Number of persons injured:* 65 (unofficially 72)
- *Number of persons arrested:* 200

Communal Riots in Panvel, Maharashtra[126]

Immediate Cause: Trouble broke out on 10th May in Panvel when the Shiv Jayanti procession reached near a narrow junction known as Muslim Naka Masjid. According to Mr Maste (leader of the Peasants and Workers Party, some of the processionists who had come from outside tried to change the route, entered a lane near the mosque and began shouting obscene slogans like Lungi Uthao, Pungi Bajao aimed at some Muslims. This went on for a couple of minutes and some processionists also threw Gulal inside the mosque when some stones were thrown on the procession. There was panic and the people began running helter and skelter.

- *Number of persons dead:* 3 (2 Muslims were stabbed)
- *Loss of properties:* The loss of properties was estimated to be around Rs. 1 crore.

Communal Riots in Nanded, Maharashtra[127]

Immediate Cause: Trouble broke out on 10th May on the day of Shiv Jayanti in Nanded. The Shiv Jayanti procession was joined by many Muslim leaders. However there were some communal elements who shouted provocative slogans in front of two Mosques in the route. The slogan shouted was "Pakistan Todo".

- *Number of persons injured:* 2 (policemen in stabbing incidents)
- *Loss of properties:* 30-40 shops (belonging to minorities) were burnt down. one S.T. bus and Muincipal truck were set ablaze.

Communal Riots in Aurangabad, Maharashtra[128]

Immediate Cause: Trouble broke out on 20th May in Aurangabad due to a green flag hoisted on a tree in a temple in Gulmand.

- *Number of persons injured:* 21
- *Number of persons arrested:* 45
- *Loss of properties:* A truck, two auto-rickshaws and two mopeds were destroyed

Communal Riots in Allahabad, Uttar Pradesh[129]

Immediate Cause: Trouble broke out on 15th June in Allahabad when negotiations were still going on between two communities over the setting up of temporary shops beside a shrine. When the negotiations almost had concluded, a mob of about 300 surrounded a police post and started throwing stones and bottles.

- *Number of persons dead:* 6
- *Number of persons injured:* 27
- *Number of persons arrested:* 88
- *Ammunitions Recovered:* 4 live-bombs, a sword and a gun were recovered.

Communal Riots in Ahmedabad, Gujarat[130]

Immediate Cause: Trouble broke out on 9th July when the Jagganath Rath Yatra procession was stoned.

- *Number of persons dead:* 11
- *Other details not available*

Communal Riots in Ahmedabad, Baroda and Broach, Gujarat[131]

Immediate Cause: Trouble broke on 12th July in Baroda and Broach due to a call for "Gujarat Bandh". The one day *bandh* was called by religious organisations including the Vishwa Hindu Parishad, to protest against the attack on the *Rath Yatra* which took place on 9th July.

- *Number of persons dead*: 40
- *Number of persons injured:* 250
- *Number of persons arrested:* 6
- *Places affected:* Meghaninagar, Navrangapura, Paldi, Shahi Baug and Haveli police station areas.

Communal Riots in Ahmedabad, Wadi town, Nadiad town and Baroda, Gujarat[132]

Immediate Cause: Trouble broke out in various parts of Gujarat when the mob protested against the attack on the "Rath Yatra".

- *Number of persons dead*: 18
- *Number of persons injured:* 14

Communal Riots in Ramanagaram, Karnataka[133]

Immediate Cause: Trouble broke on 24th July, in Ramnagaram when a temple procession was attacked while passing beside a mosque.

- *Number of persons dead*: 4 (1 in police firing)
- *Number of persons injured:* 15
- *Loss of properties:* 8 shops and a car were burnt down

Communal Riots in Delhi[134]

Immediate Cause: Trouble broke out on 26th July in West Delhi due to the gunning down of 15 bus passengers in Punjab.

- *Number of persons dead*: 5
- *Number of persons injured:* 50
- *Number of persons arrested:* 84
- *Places affected:* Tilak Nagar, Moti Nagar

Communal Riots in Baroda, Gujarat[135]

Immediate Cause: Trouble broke out in Baroda on 15th August to 15th September due to tensions which escalated on Ganpati Immersion day.

The exact cause of the riot not available

- *Number of persons dead*: 3
- *Number of persons injured:* 20

Communal Riots in Singoli village, Mandsaur District, Madhya Pradesh[136]

Immediate Cause: Trouble broke out on 19th August in Singoli village due to a clash between two communities.

- *Number of person dead:* 1
- *Other details not available*

Communal Riots in Khumban village, Punjab[137]

Immediate Cause: Trouble broke out on 25th October in Khumban village.

The Immediate cause and the communities involved not available.

- *Number of persons dead:* 8 (Hindus)

Communal Riots in Kishtwar town, Doda District Jammu and Kashmir[138]

Immediate Cause: Trouble broke out on 2nd November in Kishtwar when the clash occurred between two communities in a local cinema hall. The Jammu police had arrested some pro-Pakistani elements which was resented by members of one community who pelted stones at the Kishtwar police station and burnt it down.

No other details given.

Communal Riots in Amravati, Maharashtra[139]

Immediate Cause: Trouble broke out on 2nd and 3rd November in Amravati. The trouble started on the night of November 2nd. The triggering incident in this case was a petty quarrel over playing of cards near the Kholapuri Gate area by some Muslims. Before this there were Warud incidents in which 3 Hindus were killed in police firing. A call was given by Shiv Sena on 23rd October. The Muslims and Sindhis refused to down the shutters. This further raised the level of communal tension in Amravati. It was followed by Ghyaneshwar Karole objecting to five Muslim youths playing cards outside his house. One of them assaulted Karole with razor blade and a minor scuffle followed. The police was called and they managed to diffuse the tension. However the same evening, a Dalit girl was allegedly molested by a Muslim youth. A number of Dalit and Hindu women marched to the police station and demanded action against the culprits. This enraged the Hindu feelings. In the night of November 2nd, looting and burning started. The Hindus maintain that the Muslims attacked Hanuman Nagar shouting slogans like "Hindustan Murdabad","Allah Zindabad" and Muslims say that the slogans of "Jai Shivaji"rent the air whole night when their houses were being attacked.

- *Number of persons dead*: 7 (unofficially 9) out of which 6 (Muslims)
- *Number of persons injured:* 50
- *Number of persons arrested:* 537

Communal Riots in Majalgaon, Beed District, Maharashtra[140]

Immediate Cause: Trouble broke out on 22nd November during a religious procession.

- *Number of person dead:* 1
- *Number of persons injured:* 4

Communal Riots in Tanda village, Hoshiarpur District, Punjab[141]

Immediate Cause: Trouble broke out on 30th November in Punjab when the passengers, mainly Hindus, travelling in the bus were killed near Tanda village in Hoshiarpur district. Members of the Khalistan Liberation Force claimed responsibility for the killing. The attackers who had boarded the bus reportedly separated Sikhs from Hindus, and forced the Hindus to shout anti-Sikh slogans before shooting them.

- *Number of persons dead*: 24 (Hindus)

Communal Riots in Mysore, Karnataka[142]

Immediate Cause: Trouble broke out on 10th December in Mysore. Fanatics on either side were obviously waiting for an opportunity to vent their spleen over a Deccan Herald short story. This provided them with as good as an opportunity as they needed.

- *Number of persons dead*: 4
- *Number of persons injured:* 250 (75 policemen)
- *Number of persons arrested:* 800
- *Loss of properties:* 200 vehicles, 200 shops were looted and set on fire and 400 private homes were looted, burnt and damaged. The total loss of property was estimated to be Rs. 88 lakh

Communal Riots in Sukurhutoo village, Ranchi, Bihar[143]

Immediate Cause: Trouble broke out between two communities which gave rise to communal riot in Sukurhutoo village in Ranchi.
The exact date of the outbreak of the riot not available.

- *Number of persons killed:* 3
- Communities involved in the conflict and other details not given.

1987

Communal Riots in Ahmedabad, Gujarat[144]

Immediate Cause: Trouble broke out on 4th January in Ahmedabad over a kite-flying incident.
The exact cause of the riot not available.

- *Number of persons injured:* 18
- *Other details not available*

Communal Riots in Ujjain, Madhya Pradesh[145]

Immediate Cause: Trouble broke out on 1st February in Ujjain when two groups clashed during a religious procession.

- *Number of persons arrested:* 130
- *Places affected:* Topkhana and Daulatganj

Communal Riots in Ahmedabad, Gujarat[146]

Immediate Cause: Trouble broke out on 14th February in Ahmedabad on the arrest of Abdul Latif, considered to be the don of the underworld and who created history when he won all the five seats which he contested from the Muslim-dominated areas during the Ahmedabad municipal elections. When Latif was being taken to the court the mob started shouting slogans, became restive and started throwing stones at the police.

- *Number of persons dead*: 9
- *Number of persons injured:* 50
- *Loss of property:* Several shops, cars and scooters were burnt. *The exact number of shops, cars and scooters burnt not available.*

Communal Riots in Virpur, Nurpur and Patiya village, Khaira District, Gujarat[147]

Immediate Cause: Trouble broke out on 9th April when a religious procession was stoned.

- *Number of persons dead-* 6
- *Number of persons injured:* 50
- *Loss of property:* 60 shops and 50 houses were burnt down.

Communal Riots in Panchmahal District, Gujarat[148]

Immediate Cause: Trouble broke out on 13th April in five villages of Panchmahal district.

The exact and Immediate cause involved in the conflict not available.

- *Number of person injured:* 1
- *Other details not available*

Communal Riots in Nadiad town and Cambay, Gujarat[149]

Immediate Cause: Trouble broke out on 20th April in Nadiad and Cambay following tension after arson incidents. Curfew was imposed in Nadiad town and Cambay.

The exact and the Immediate cause involved in the conflict not available.

- *Number of persons arrested:* 50
- *Other details not available*

Communal Riots in Shahpur, Gujarat[150]

Immediate Cause: Trouble broke out on 26th April in Shahpur due to a quarrel between the youths of two communities which resulted in widespread arson in the area.

- *Number of persons dead:* 5 (2 by police bullets and 3 by stabbing)
- *Number of persons injured:* 10
- *Loss of properties*: Six vehicles and two shops were set ablaze.

Communal Riots in Meerut and other parts of Uttar Pradesh and Delhi[151]

Immediate Cause: Trouble broke out on 18th May in Meerut due to strained relations between Hindus and Muslims in Uttar Pradesh This was due to a district court order in February 1986—permitting Hindus to worship on a site claimed as a shrine by

Muslims at Ayodhaya in Eastern Uttar Pradesh. The Provincial Armed Constabulary, under the command of Tripathi, pulled out 34 young boys from Hashimpura and shot them dead by the side of a canal. Also, on 23rd May they shot dead about 67 Muslims coming out of the Mosque after the Friday prayer in a village six kilometers from Meerut city.

- *Number of persons dead*: 7 (*excluding 101 shot by police*)

According to official estimates more than 100 persons died during clashes between Hindus and Muslims in Uttar Pradesh and also in Delhi between 18th and 26th May. But the British and Indian press cited that unofficially the death toll might have been nearer 300 and attributed much of the violence to the security forces.

Many Muslim deaths in and around Meerut were blamed on the (mainly Hindu) Provincial Armed constabulary (PAC). According to the "Far Eastern Economic Review" of June 11, a PAC contingent had on May 22 entered Hashimpura (the Muslim area of Meerut), where they arrested around 170 to 200 Muslims who were driven to an area outside the city where the majority were killed and thrown into a canal.

The following day a Provincial Armed Constabulary's contingent entered the village of Malyana near Meerut and, according to the Far Eastern Economic Review report, killed at least 110 Muslims.

- *Places affected:* Hashimpura (Meerut), Delhi's old sector, i.e., the north of New Delhi and Malyana near Meerut

Communal Riots in Meerut, Uttar Pradesh[152]

Immediate Cause: Trouble broke out on 18th May in Meerut after 9 p.m. There is a lot of confusion about how the violence began. The exact sequence of events was difficult to establish as there were many versions even by those who were present on scene of events in the Hashimpura locality and nearby *Imliyan* mosque. It is alleged a *khoka* (stall) belonging to a Muslim was set on fire by some miscreants. Thereafter electricity suddenly went off. It is difficult to say whether it was a deliberate act or the usual tripping. This was followed by a loud bang. Some thought it was the transformer which exploded. In the meanwhile a crowd collected. Hindus as well as Muslims collected in large numbers. Then they began stoning on the crowd from Surajkund side and the crowd went berserk.

Real Cause: The situation had become highly explosive after the Babri Masjid rally. A large number of Muslims had participated in it from Meerut. The militancy among the Muslims was growing on this question. The Hindus too were getting very aggressive. Provocative slogans against each other's community were painted on the walls of Meerut.

Also, the power struggle within the Congress had sharpened. The high percentage of Muslim population made it difficult for the Hindu Congress candidates to get ticket for the assembly and parliamentary seats from here. This, and the Ram Janambhoomi controversy had brought about a sharp polarisation within the Congress. It was vertically divided between Hindus and Muslims and the riots further sharpened this communal division. It is really difficult to estimate how many died in the riots. It was rumoured that more than 20,000 died. But it is ridiculously high figure. The Government admits only little over 100 deaths, which again seems far below the actual number.

- *Number of persons dead*: 91 (officially), 182 (unofficially)
- *Number of persons injured:* 131
- *Number of persons arrested:* 2,530
- *Loss of properties:* 250 houses were burnt in Shashtri Nagar
- *Places affected:* Hashimpura, Imliyan mosque, Shastrinagar and Moradnagar

Note: The PAC came to the village, some 6 kms away from Meerut, situated on its outer periphery, on the pretext that Muslims of Malyana were hiding some who had fled from Meerut evading arrest. The Harijans joined the PAC in the loot and burning. Almost all the houses were looted. Many got burnt alive inside the houses. In all, according to the list prepared by the village Muslims, 78 died in firing and burning operations. Many persons were burnt alive in Shastrinagar. In two houses alone in which many had taken refuge, some 33 persons were burnt alive. On the night of May 22 more than 300 persons were arrested by the PAC on that fateful night from Hashimpura, the main trouble spot and were carried away in trucks. Most of them were young and middle aged. Some were taken to jail but around hundred, who were not shown on record, were taken in several trucks to Moradnagar near Ganga canal. They were lined up near the canal and shot one by one. The horrid story was narrated by three boys who miraculously survived by feigning death. Many alleged that not less than 100 persons were shot by the PAC near the canal; and many were reported missing during the investigations.

Communal Riots in Old Delhi[153]

Immediate Cause: Trouble broke out on 22nd May in Delhi during Ramzaan. It all started after the Muslims came out of the Jama Masjid after offering their afternoon prayer. It was alleged that the Shahi Imam delivered a provocative sermon and the provoked Muslims came out of the Mosque and began to stone the areas dominated by Hindus. The Muslims allege that when they came out of the Mosque at about 2.30 p.m. they were surrounded by a Hindu mob from two sides near Hauz Kazi and stoned. Many were injured in this incident.

- *Number of persons dead:* 15 (12 in police firing and 3 died due to stabbing) (Out of 12 persons who died in police firing, there were 3 Hindus)
- *Number of persons arrested:* 250 (Muslims)
- *Loss of properties:* Extensive damage was done to Sima Lodge in Churiwalan where mostly those coming from Pakistan reside. More than 13 shops were burnt, among them were the shops of foodgrains, pan-cigerattes, gram roaster and milk vendor. In Kutcha Pandit a few shops were looted and damaged. Shamshad Ali, a fruit vendor sustained a loss of around Rs. 10,000. One Hindu shop was also set ablaze in this area.
- *Places affected:* Sita Ram Bazar, Zeenat Mahal, Lalkuan, which is a Harijan colony.

Communal Riots in Fatehpur, Uttar Pradesh[154]

Immediate Cause: Trouble broke out on July in Fatehpur when the members of Bajrang Dal chose to conduct an Akhand Ramayan Paath in a small temple built in a private house next to a mosque. The mosque authorities objected to the use of loud-speaker for the recitation of the Ramayana. *The exact date of the outbreak of the riot not available.*

Other details not available

Communal Riots in Surat, Bardoli and Rajpipla[155]

Immediate Cause: Trouble broke out in three towns of South Gujarat, i.e., Surat, Bardoli and Rajpipla on 6th September, during the Ganesh immersion processions. The trouble started when the processionists were subjected to stone throwing when passing through the sensitive areas.

Other details not available

Communal Riots at Ahmednagar, Maharashtra[156]

Immediate Cause: Trouble broke out in Ahmednagar when people going for Ganesh immersion processions were stoned.

The exact date of the outbreak of the riot not available.

- *Number of persons dead:* 2
- *Number of persons injured:* 60 (40 in police firing, and 20 policemen in stone throwing)

1988

Communal Riots in Pune, Maharashtra[157]

Immediate Cause: Trouble broke out on 19th April in Pune when tensions prevailed after attempts were made by some people to burn a Shiv-Sena water booth and in which a youth was attacked with swords.

- *Number of persons injured:* 5
- *Curfew imposed areas:* Nana Peth and Ganesh Peth

Communal Riots in Aurangabad, Maharashtra[158]

Immediate Cause: Trouble broke out on 17th May just one day before the Id, a large crowd had gathered outside the court where a petition challenging the election of the Mayor had come up for hearing, Chagan Bhujbal, the Sena leader, who was sitting right outside the court threatened that the whole city of Aurangabad would be burnt if the judgement would be against them (i.e. if the mayoral election was not set aside). But something quite unexpected happened, the hearing was adjourned for a week. The unruly Sena crowd went berserk and started towards the city, burning rickshaws and shops.

- *Number of persons dead:* 11
- *Number of persons injured:* 136 (18 belonged to Muslim community)
- *Number of persons arrested:* 600
- *Loss of properties:* Many shops and houses were burnt down
- *Places affected:* Baujipura, Jinsi, Kaisar colony, Chistiya colony, Indiranagar, Sector No-7 in CIDCO, Lota Karanja, Shahganj, Mulumchi Bazar, Gandhi Chowk, Roshan Gate, Kasari Bazaar, Aurangpura, Gulmandi, Rangar Gali, Jijamata colony, Nehru Bhavan, Juna Bazaar, Khara Kunwa, Sarafa Bazaar, Pan Dariba, Nizammudin Chowk and Kokanwadi

Note: The real cause was the political strategy of the Shiv Sena which was trying to exploit Hindu sentiments for its own ends.

Communal Riots in Paithan, Bidkin, Marathwada District, Maharashtra[159]

Immediate Cause: Trouble broke out on 19th May in Paithan, 55 kms away from Aurangbad, and in a village called Bidkin. Both in Paithan and Bidkin, violence broke out in reaction to what had happened in Aurangabad and was directed against the Muslims. The violence apparently started in Paithan after a dead body was discovered near a cinema house.

- *Number of persons killed:* 9 (8 in Paithan) 1 (in Bidkin)
- *Number of persons injured:* 11 (9 were injured in Paithan). 2 (in Bidkin)
- *Loss of properties:* In Paithan, 6 houses were burnt and 13 shops belonging to the minority community were also burnt down.
- *Places affected:* Kavasan, Narala, Rangar Harlti areas and Indiranagar slums.

Communal Riots in Jalna, Marathwada District, Maharashtra[160]

Immediate Cause: Trouble broke out on 20th May in Jalna May when the Shiv Sena tried to hoist its flag near the Jama Masjid which led to tensions.

- *Number of persons killed:* 2
- *Number of persons injured:* 45
- *Other details not available*

Communal Riots in Surankot, and Mendhar, Jammu and Kashmir[161]

Immediate Cause: Trouble broke out on 23rd July in the towns of Mandi and Loran in Poonch where unruly mobs looted shops belonging to two communities. Surankot and Mendhar were also affected by the riots.

Other details not available.

Communal Riots in Bidar, Karnataka[162]

Immediate Cause: Trouble broke out on 14th September in Bidar when Sikh students armed with weapons attacked a Ganesh pandal after an altercation with pandal volunteers, as reported by the "Deccan Herald".

- *Number of persons dead*: 6
- *Number of persons injured:* 60
- *Number of persons arrested:* 126
- *Loss of properties*: The loss of properties was estimated to be worth Rs. 5.2 million

Communal Riots in Aligarh, Uttar Pradesh[163]

Immediate Cause: Taking advantage of the communally surcharged atmosphere some communalists from the majority community sought to hang a banner renaming Aligarh as Harigarh. This banner was being hung on 8th October near Sabzi Mandi Chauraha in between Jama Masjid and Abdul Karim chowk. This place in fact divides the Hindu and the Muslim localities. Some Muslims on 8th October prepared a banner which read 'aqal ke andhon yeh Harigarh nahin, Aligarh Hai' ('oh! you with blind reason, it is not Harigarh but Aligarh). When some Musilms were tying this banner, a mob of about 300 Hindus emerged from one of the roads leading to Kanvarganj from Sabzimandi Chauraha and began to throw stones on those who had gathered near the banner. By then about 300 Muslims emerged to retaliate. Then, a big group of Hindus marched towards Dahi Wali Gali where there was phatak of Muslims in a narrow lane called Bisatian Ka phatak. Violence occurred near this phatak.

- *Number of persons dead:* 5 (3 Hindus and 2 Muslims)
- *Number of persons injured:* 28 (20 were Hindus and 8 Muslims)

- *Loss of properties:* 8 shops were burnt down
- *Places affected:* Bisatian ka Phatak, Subzimandi Chauraha and Abdul Karim Chauraha

Communal Riots in Muzzaffar Nagar, Uttar Pradesh[164]

Immediate Cause: Trouble broke out on 8th and 11th October, when the ministers Hukam Singh and Saiduz Zaman were present in the town. On 8th October, a call for Uttar Pradesh *bandh* was given by the Hindu communal organisations. It was in protest against the call for march given by the Babri Masjid Action committee on 14th October. On the day of the *bandh* the Shiv Sena volunteers forced the Muslims to close down their shops which the Muslims resented. On 11th October, a peace committee was formed at the residence of Saiduz Zaman. During the curfew hours, the peace committee took out a procession. The Shiv Sena activists began to beat up the Muslim peace marchers sparing the non-Muslims. This led to the massacre of innocent people.

- *Number of persons dead:* 35 (unofficially) But the exact figure is not known. Several figures varying from as high as 200 to as low as 32 were quoted. According to a fair estimate, 60 Muslims and 27 Hindus were killed
- *Number of person injured:* 1 (Muslim)
- *Number of persons arrested:* 2
- *Loss of properties*: 48 shops were set on fire, out of which 45 belonged to Muslims
- *Places affected:* Nallapura and Khalapar

Communal Riots in Khatauli, Uttar Pradesh[165]

Immediate Cause: Though the Babri Masjid/Ram Janmabhoomi controversy seems to be the apparent cause of communal riots in Khatauli, the real dynamics of communal violence was provided by the Municipal election which was due on 30th November. Then came the call for the march to retrieve Babri Masjid. This coupled with the call for *bandh* on 8th October provided the needed spark. A call was also given on 8th October for Prabhat Pheri by the Hindu orgnisations. After this, the Hindu students took over the responsibility for the bandh. Muslims resented the enforcement of the *bandh* and refused to close their shops. The students entered the Muslim localities to force them to close their shops and the Muslims retaliated.

- *Number of persons killed:* 2 (1 Hindu and the other a Muslim)
- *Number of persons injured:* 10
- *Number of persons arrested:* 7
- *Loss of property:* One sweetmeat shop in front of Jama Masjid was damaged.

Communal Riots in Muzaffarnagar, Uttar Pradesh[166]

Immediate Cause: Trouble broke when a bandh was called on 8th October, by Hindu organisations. This was also joined by a call given by Muslim organisations to retrieve Babri Masjid on 14th March.

Other details not available.

Communal Riots in Faizabad, Uttar Pradesh[167]

Immediate Cause: Trouble broke out on 21st October in Faizabad at 10 p.m. when a procession was passing through Wazirganj area in the city. Provocative slogans led to rival groups clashing with each other. The city as such was reeling under a tense atmosphere ever since the Babri Masjid-Ram Janambhoomi controversy started three years ago.

- *Number of person dead:* 1
- *Number of persons injured:* 12

Communal Riots near Srinagar, Jammu and Kashmir[168]

Immediate Cause: Trouble broke out in Srinagar when a priest of a temple was beaten to death by a policeman on 9th December as he refused to recite from a scripture of another religion, as reported by 'Tribune' newspaper.

1989

Communal Riots in Jammu city, Jammu and Kashmir[169]

Immediate Cause: Trouble broke out on 13th January in Jammu city. The violence flared up when some one objected to certain slogans being raised by some of the processionists.

- *Number of persons dead:* 6
- *Number of persons injured:* 100
- *Other details not available*

Communal Riots in Jamshedpur, Bihar[170]

Immediate Cause: Trouble broke out on 21st February in Jamshedpur due to a Bandh which was called in protest against the publication of a sketch in a Hindi daily, "Aaj" in its Sunday edition.

- *Number of persons injured:* 24 (in police firing)
- *Other details not available*

Communal Riots in Dhule, Maharashtra[171]

Immediate Cause: Trouble broke out on 22nd March. According to police the spilling of water from a tanker near a mosque led to the riots, but the local MLA denied this reason as baseless. According to him some miscreants had thrown colour on the mosque which led to riots.

- *Number of persons killed:* 1 (Nihal Ahmed – a Muslim was killed in the Macchi Bazar area)
- *Number of persons injured:* 4 (Muslims)

Communal Riots in Kalpi, Uttar Pradesh[172]

Immediate Cause: Trouble broke out on 14th April between two communities in Kalpi during a religious procession.

- *Number of person killed:* 1
- *Number of persons injured:* 4
- *Number of persons arrested:* 25

Communal Riots in Tonk, Rajasthan[173]

Immediate Cause: Trouble broke out on 10th May in Tonk, Rajasthan following the murder of a 22 year old youth, Mr Jagdish Gujjar, by some members of another community. He had been involved in many criminal cases, including one relating to attempted murder. It is stated that he was on friendly terms with his alleged killers. It is believed that he was killed after a dispute that arose while they were allegedly under the influence of liquor. His body, which was dumped near Gehlot ghat, was recovered five days later. Even as members of Jagdish community joined hands to seek justice on behalf of the family of the victim, those belonging to the other community had been organising themselves alleging undue harassment by the police. The Gujjar's took out a procession in support of their demands, including ex-gratia for the victim's family members and search of houses of members of the other community to seize arms allegedly in their procession. While the procession was passing through Kafla Bazaar, the participants reportedly hurled stones at members of the other community.

- *Number of persons injured:* 24
- *Number of persons arrested:* 58
- *Loss of properties:* 3 hutments were burnt down
- *Arms and ammunitions recovered:* A gun and over 175 weapons were seized.

Communal Riots in Amravati, Maharashtra[174]

Immediate Cause: Communal riot broke out on 12th August in Amravati over the attack made by Shiv Sainiks on some Muslims for taking oxen for slaughtering which led to clashes between the two communities.

- *Number of persons dead:* 2
- *Number of persons injured:* 30
- *Number of persons arrested:* 70

Real Cause: The Bajrang Dal activists were keeping the watch near the slaughter house and prevented the Muslim butchers from taking their animals for slaughter, often attacking them. The tensions had always prevailed in the town between Shiv Sainiks, Bajrang Dal and Muslim butchers.

Communal Riots in Mathura, Uttar Pradesh[175]

Immediate Cause: Trouble broke on 16th April in Mathura when Bajrang Dal activists gathered at the doorstep of the Jama Masjid in Chowk Bazar at around 7 p.m. to install an idol of Hanuman. Muslims who had assembled for the evening *namaz* came out of the mosque to the sound of cymbals, drums and *chants* of Jai Bajrang Bali. An altercation ensued, followed by arson and rioting.

- *Number of persons injured:* 8 (7 were police personnel.)
- *Number of persons arrested:* 26
- *Loss of properties:* 34 shops, 11 houses were looted and burnt, one small temple was also damaged. At least 4 mosques were raided and some copies of the Qoran were burnt.

- *Loss of properties:* 7 shops were damaged and 3 hutment's were set on fire.
- *Places affected:* Deshwalon ka Mohalla in the Kalipattan area was affected.
- *Ammunitions recovered:* A gun and 175 weapons.

Communal Riots in Kollegal, Karnataka[176]

The Immediate cause and comunities involved in this conflict are not available.

- *Number of persons dead* :3
- *Number of persons injured:* 8
- *Number of persons arrested:* 70

Communal Riots in Hazaribagh, Bihar[177]

Immediate Cause: Trouble broke out in Hazaribagh in May during the Ramnavmi festival. The riots reportedly started in Buchrtoli.

The exact date of the riot not available.

- *Number of persons dead:* 40 (unofficially put it at more than 200)
- *Loss of properties:* 31 shops (Muslims) were gutted in Kanti Bazar.

Communal Riots at Jawal village, Sirohi District, Rajasthan[178]

Immediate Cause: Trouble broke out on 1st June in Jawal due to an eve-teasing incident in Jawal village.

The exact and immediate cause involved in the conflict not available.

- *Number of persons killed:* 2
- *Number of persons injured:* 6

Communal Riots at Chikali, Buldhana District, Maharasthra[179]

Immediate Cause: Trouble broke out on 3rd July in Chikali during the "*Maharashtra Bandh*" called by the Shiv Sena, the Bhartiya Janata Party and the Rashtriya Swayam Sevak Sangh. 'Bandh' was called to condemn the killing of Rashtriya Swayam Sevak Sangh workers by terrorists at Moga in Punjab. Violence broke out when the, 5,000 strong procession of supporters of the ' Bandh' was stoned as it was passing through a place of worship.

- *Number of persons killed:* 4
- *Other details not available*

Communal Riots in Leh, Ladakh[180]

Immediate Cause: Trouble broke out on 7th July in Leh, Ladakh due to a quarrel between the two youths of different communities.

- *Number of persons injured:* 20
- *Other details not available*

Communal Riots in Aruppukottai, Tamil Nadu[181]

Immediate Cause: Trouble broke out on 14th July in Aruppukottai near the Muthalamman temple over the fixing of flag posts at two sites near the Muthalamman temple and the Shiva temple by the people belonging to a community living nearby.

- *Number of persons dead:* 3
- *Number of persons injured:* 11

Communal Riots in Meerut, Uttar Pradesh[182]

The Immediate cause and communities involved in the conflict were not available.

- *Number of person dead:* 1 (stabbed)
- *Number of persons injured:* 3

Communal Riots in Bhagalpur, Bihar[183]

Immediate Cause: Trouble broke out on 12th August in local Parvati Mohalla in Bhagalpur, when violence broke out between two groups of communities.

The exact cause and the communities involved in the conflict not available.

- *Number of persons injured:* Several (the exact Number of persons injured are not available)
- *Loss of properties:* 6 government vehicles were damaged
- *Place affected:* Parvati Mohalla in Bhagalpur

Communal Riots in Sasaram town, Rohtas District, Bihar[184]

Immediate Cause: Trouble broke out on 17th August in Sasaram town in Bihar.

The exact and the Immediate cause involved in the conflict not available.

- *Number of persons dead:* 5

- *Number of persons injured:* 16

Communal Riots in Ramnagram, Karnataka[185]

Immediate Cause: Trouble broke out on 2nd September in Ramnagram due to the dispute between two persons belonging to two different communities. It soon assumed a communal form and riots broke out.

- *Number of persons dead*: 7
- *Loss of properties:* 1 petrol bunk, a saw mill and 50 huts were burnt. Also 4 industrial sheds were ransacked and machinary damaged.

Communal Riots at Satbharawa village, Palamau District, Bihar[186]

Immediate Cause: Trouble broke out on 21st September in Satbharawa. Violence erupted when a group of one community allegedly damaged a burial ground of another community in the village.

- *Number of persons dead*: 5
- *Number of persons injured:* 4
- *Number of persons arrested:* 47

Communal Riots at Nagpur, Maharashtra[187]

Immediate Cause: Trouble broke out in old Nagpur city in October, due to a clash between the Vishwa Hindu Parishad activists and supporters of a tribal organisation protesting against the burning of Ravana on Dassehra day. The Gond Dharma Parishad had organised a procession from Anand talkies chowk to Patwardhan ground in West Nagpur. The tribals considered themselves descendants of Ravana and were hence opposed to burning an effigy of the demon king. The police said that feminists Seema Sakhare and Yamini Chaudary, and others, who had gone to participate in the procession, were attacked and abused by a group of people, alleged to be supporters of Vishwa Hindu Parishad supporters. Chanting "Jai Sri Ram" slogans, they scuttled the procession and stoned policemen who had gone to the rescue of the women activists. Workers of the Gond Parishad and some Dalit organisations protested against the attack and retaliated by throwing stones.

The exact date of the riot not available

- *Loss of properties:* 2 auto rickshaws, 1 police motorcycle, 1 moped and a few bicycles were set on fire.

Communal Riots at Saraula, Jhalawar District and Jahajpur, Bhilwara District, Rajasthan[188]

Immediate Cause: Trouble broke out on 10th October in Saraula, Jhalawar district and Bhilwara district in Rajasthan when an unauthorised religious procession was being conducted.

- *Number of person dead:* 1
- *Number of persons injured:* 4

Communal Riots in Aurangabad, Maharashtra[189]

Immediate Cause: Trouble broke out on 12th October in Aurangabad in Maharashtra at Balanagar village in Bidkin when members of a particular community reportedly stoned a place of worship where Dasshera processionists were playing a band. A clash immediately followed between the members of the two communities in which lethal weapons were used.

- *Number of person dead:* 1
- *Number of persons injured:* 4
- *Number of persons arrested:* 24

Communal Riots in Ahmedabad, Gujarat[190]

Immediate Cause: Trouble broke out on 11th October in Ahmedabad when a religious procession was reportedly stoned in the Ram Baug area.

- *Number of person dead:* 1
- *Number of persons injured:* 10
- *Number of persons arrested:* 54
- *Loss of properties:* 4 shops were set ablaze.

In Basankhanta

- *Number of persons injured:* 5
- *Number of persons arrested:* 40
- *Loss of properties:* 4 shops were set ablaze.

In Bulsar

- *Number of persons injured:* 9

Communal Riots in Gulbarga, Karnataka[191]

Immediate Cause: Trouble broke out on 12th October in Gulbarga immediately after the Dasshera procession when some miscreants climbed rooftops and started pelting stones. Discontent over the use of a piece of land for worship was suspected to be the cause for the trouble.

- *Number of persons injured:* 5 (in stone throwing)
- *Other details not available*

Communal Riots in Jaipur, Rajasthan[192]

Immediate Cause: Trouble broke out in Jaipur during the Dassera procession.

The exact cause and the communities involved in the conflict are not available.

- *Number of person dead:* 1
- *Number of persons injured:* 4

In Jahajpura, Bhilwara district

- *Number of persons injured:* 21. (13 policemen)
- *Loss of properties:* Several shops and a tractor were burnt down.

Communal Riots in Dhar, Madhya Pradesh[193]

Immediate Cause: Trouble broke out on 13th October in Dhar when some one threw crude bombs on an Id procession in the district town of Dhar, near Indore. (other details not given)

- *Number of persons injured:* 6

Communal Riots in Indore, Madhya Pradesh[194]

Immediate Cause: Trouble broke out on 14th October, in Indore around 11.30 am with the bursting of crackers at the rear end of the nearly 30,000 strong Barawafat procession. This triggered off a stampede and riot broke out between the two communities.

- *Number of persons dead*: 22
- *Places affected:* Bombay Bazaar, Kadaoghat and adjoining areas in the heart of Indore
- *Ammunitions recovered:* A huge quantity of illegally acquired arms including rifles, pistols, bombs, acid bottles, swords, spears and iron rods

Note: This riot which broke out in the commercial capital reflects the worst ever expression of communal divide in the state. There was hardly anything unexpected about the violence that erupted for the second time in a fortnight in the Malwa region of the state. The Ram Shila procession had set a tone for communal tension visible even as preparation for the Barawafat procession was made. Although forewarned by some citizens, the district administration took the situation lightly.

Communal Riots in Palanpur, Gujarat[195]

Immediate Cause: Trouble broke out in October in Palanpur with the expected arrival of Ram Jhanmabhoomi "Shila Poojan" processions from near by villages and towns. The trouble started when a person was beaten up by some goondas with sharp edged weapons.

The exact date of the outbreak of the riot not available.

- *Number of person dead:* 1
- *Number of persons injured:* 24
- *Number of persons arrested:* 24

Communal Riots in Sidhpur town, Mehsana District, Gujarat[196]

Immediate Cause: Trouble broke out on 15th October in Sidhpur town when a religious procession was being taken out in the town according to the police.

- *Number of person dead:* 1
- *Number of persons injured:* 4

Communal Riots in Patan Town, Mehsana District, Gujarat[197]

Immediate Cause: Trouble broke out on 17th October in Patan town after the public meeting of Bhartiya Janata Party.

- *Number of person injured*: 1 (Muslim)
- *Loss of properties:* 1 Dargah and 20 Muslim shops were set on fire

Communal Riots in Jharia, Bihar[198]

Immediate Cause: Trouble broke out on 17th October in Jharia town in Bihar after violence erupted when a Ram Shila procession was disturbed and a group of people spread rumours about riots in Dhanhad. Tension had been simmering for three days after Muslims took out a procession on the eve of Id-ul-milad-e-Nabi.

- *Number of person dead:* 1
- *Number of persons injured:* 20
- *Number of persons arrested:* 100

Communal Riots in Bhagalpur, Bihar[199]

Immediate Cause: The Ram Shila pujan procession (procession of consecrated bricks) was supposed to be taken out on 24th October. The Muslims objected to the passing of the procession from Tartarpur (a Muslim Mohalla in Bhagalpur) area saying that it was not a usual religious·procession taken out on Hindu festival, for they argued that the Ram Shila pujan procession was a political one. Despite this Arun Jha, the District Magistrate, and Superintendent of Police, Dvivedi, not only allowed the procession, but allowed it to pass through Tartarpur. Provocative anti-Muslim slogans added to the tension. The procession was being led by two alleged notorious anti-socials, Kamleshwar Yadav and Mahadev Singh. The District Magistrate and Superintendent of Police were also accompanying the procession in a jeep. Some bombs were thrown on the procession and it caused great turmoil in the procession. The District Magistrate and Superintendent of Police escaped narrowly. Soon, the procession broke and maurading mob killed people, looted and burnt shops and houses. The wild rumours were also spread. It was rumoured that hundreds of Hindu students were killed by Muslims and their bodies were thrown into nearby wells. These rumours spread very fast to the villages from where the students came and soon mobs in these villages started killing their Muslim neighbours. Many villages (Timoni, Madaninagar, Chanderi) on the outskirts of Bhagalpur were very badly affected by communal frenzy.

- *Number of persons dead:* 1,026 (876 Muslims 150 Hindus)
- *Number of persons injured:* 269
- *Number of persons arrested:* 2,000 (1,100 were Hindus and 900 Muslims)
- *Loss of properties*: houses burnt to ashes: 6,200 (6,000 of Muslims); houses looted 3,000; shops looted 891; looms other than powerlooms destroyed 3,000 (almost all of Muslims); damaged mosques 42, tombs 10, Madrasas 6, and Imambadas 6.

The number of Hindu houses gutted completely not exactly known, but in any case it was more than 300.

Communal Riots in Susaram, Rohtas District, Bihar[200]

Immediate Cause: Trouble broke out on 6th November in Sasaram over the Ram Shila Puja Procession.

- *Number of persons dead*: 6 (officially), 10 (unofficially)
- Number of persons injured: 51
- *Number of persons arrested:* 102
- *Loss of properties*: 2 shops were burnt down in Chauhatti locality of the town.
- *Places affected:* Chauhatti, Laksheraigang and Nogitala localities
- *Ammunitions recovered:* 113 bombs

Communal Riots in Fatehpur town, Uttar Pradesh[201]

Immediate Cause: Trouble broke out on November in Fathepur when an activist of a Hindu Jagran Manch was murdered in Fathepur.

The exact date of the riot not available.

- *Number of person dead:* 1 Hindu
- *Loss of properties:* Immediately after the killing, hundreds of VHP activists and Bajrang Dal workers came out on the streets and burnt banners of all the party candidates and set a Uttar Pradesh State Regional Transport Corporation bus ablaze.

1990

Communal Riots in Ahmedabad, Baroda and Palanpur, Gujarat[202]

The Immediate cause and communities involved in the conflict were not available.

- *Number of persons dead*: 53
- *Places affected:* Jamalpur, Khanpur and Gomtipur

Communal Riots in Batala, Punjab[203]

Immediate Cause: Trouble broke out on 3rd April in Batala when a bomb which the police suspected had been planted by Sikh separatists exploded near a Hindu religious procession celebrating Ram Navami in Batala.

- *Number of persons dead*: 35

Communal Riots in Ahmedabad, and other places in Gujarat[204]

Immediate Cause: Trouble broke out on 4th April in Ahmedabad when a Muslim was stabbed to death. Clashes between Muslims and Hindus ensued and spread to several other towns.

- *Number of persons dead*: 60
- *Loss of properties:* Extensive damage to properties was done.

Communal Riots in Kanpur, Uttar Pradesh[205]

Trouble broke out on 18th April in Kanpur. This broke out as a sequel to two mafia dons trying to establish their foothold in politics by communalising the incident. This was due to an outburst of the minority community's anger with the police, especially the PAC.

The exact and the Immediate cause and the communities involved in the conflict are not available.

- *Number of persons dead*: 24
- *Number of persons arrested:* 220
- *Ammunitions recovered:* During the raids conducted at residential places a huge quantity of arms and ammunition including petrol bombs, hand made country grenades, pistols and sharp-edged weapons were seized.

Communal Riots in Mathura, Uttar Pradesh[206]

Immediate Cause: Trouble broke out on 21st April in Mathura when the Virat Hindu Sammelan, organised by the Vishwa Hindu Parishad was going on. Some miscreants in a religious procession hurled stones, which triggered of violent incidents.

- *Loss of properties:* 6 shops were partially burnt down

Communal Riots in Manori village, Maharashtra[207]

Immediate Cause: Trouble broke out in Manori village when clash occurred between two large groups of people belonging to different communities. *The exact date of the out-break of the riot not available.*

The exact cause involved in the conflict not available.

- *Number of persons injured:* 60

Communal Riots in Baroda, Gujarat[208]

The exact and the Immediate cause involved in the conflict not available.

- *Number of persons dead*: 5
- Number of person injured*:* 1
- *Loss of properties:* According to fire brigade sources, a shop and a luxury bus were set on fire
- *Places affected:* Moghulwada and Badri Mohalla

Communal Riots in Nandgaonpeth, Amravati District, Maharashtra[209]

Immediate Cause and the communities involved in the conflict not available.

- *Number of person dead:* 1
- *Number of persons injured:* 26
- *Loss of properties:* 10 huts were destroyed by setting on fire by violent mob.

Communal Riots in Lohardagga, Bihar[210]

Immediate Cause: Trouble broke out on 21st July in Lohardagga district. Disturbances triggered when blood was sprayed on some school going girls near a religious place. The incident was a sequel to an alleged rape and murder of a girl at Chitra Daru village in Senaha police area a few days earlier.

- *Number of persons arrested:* 45
- *Loss of properties:* 6 shops were burnt down.

Communal Riots in Banṣawara city, Rajasthan[211]

Immediate Cause: Trouble broke out in Banswara city when police opened fire at a religious procession that turned violent.

- *Number of person dead:* 1
- *Number of persons injured:* Several (the exact number not available)

Communal Riots in Madras, Tamil Nadu[212]

Immediate Cause: Trouble broke out on 2nd September, when the 'Vinayak Chaturthi' procession was passing through the Triplicate area where a mosque is situated. Anti-Muslim slogans were shouted as soon as the procession started. The procession stopped near the mosque and some of the processionists began to beat drums at a high pitch. It was 2.30 pm and late noon prayer was going on. It was also alleged that the processionsts threw firecrackers into the mosque. Some chappals and stones were thrown on the procession from the mosque, resulting in utter confusion and people began running helter skelter. Many eyewitnesses reported that police shot and killed some innocent Muslims inside the nearby houses. The Muslims came out on the street and began to fight. However, they were outnumbered and had to flee.

- *Number of persons dead*: 3 (officially), 6 (unofficially); Police firing caused all the deaths.
- *Number of persons injured:* 12
- *Loss of properties:* The *Loss of properties* was estimated to be worth lakhs of rupees.

Communal Riots in Ramnagaram town, Karnataka[213]

Immediate Cause: Trouble broke out on 2nd September in Ramnagaram, some 50 kms away from Bangalore when two persons belonging to two different communities quarrelled which assumed communal overtone resulting in the riot.

- *Number of persons dead*: 7
- *Loss of properties*: miscreants set 1 petrol pump, 1 saw mill and 50 huts on fire. Also, 4 industrial sheds were ransacked and machineries were damaged by them in a nearby industrial estate.

Communal Riots in Baroda[214]

Immediate Cause: It was well-established fact that the BJP Health Minister of Gujarat Shri Nalin Bhatt was instrumental in provoking riot in Baroda. Trouble started when a huge Ganesh procession led by Bhatt was passing through the heart of the city. Provocative slogans were shouted against Muslims in Muslim localities and the Muslims reacted by throwing stones. Within minutes of stone throwing, there was a rumour in the procession that the Muslims had killed Hindu women and children. What followed was looting and burning of every Muslim shop on the route of the procession. For breaking shutters, gas-cutters were used. (The exact date of the riot not available)

- *Number of persons dead*: 8
- *Number of persons injured:* 24
- *Loss of properties:* According to Prof. J.S. Bandukwala, Professor of physics in the M.S. University, Baroda, the Jama Masjid was partially damaged.

Communal Riots in Anand Town, Gujarat[215]

Immediate Cause: Trouble broke out in Anand town in Gujarat when the procession accompanying Ganesh idol raised provocative slogans against Muslims while passing through a Muslim locality. *The exact date of the riot not available.*

- *Number of persons dead*: 3
- *Number of persons injured:* 12

Communal Riots in Surat, Gujarat[216]

Immediate Cause: Trouble broke out in Surat in Gujarat during Ganesh festival. *The exact date of the riot not available.*

The exact cause and communities involved in the conflict were not available

- *Number of person dead:* 1
- *Number of persons injured:* 4

Communal Riots in Uthampuram, Madurai District, Tamil Nadu[217]

Immediate Cause: Trouble broke out on 15th September in Uthampuram. A long-standing dispute over the right to worship a peepal tree led to the clashes.

- *Number of persons dead*: 6

Communal Riots in Gonda, Uttar Pradesh[218]

Immediate Cause: Uttar Pradesh also witnessed communal violence in Gonda district during the immersion of idols of goddess Durga on 30th September. The trouble broke out when processionists raised provocative slogans against Muslims and Muslims retaliated by throwing stones on the processionists. Communal violence in Colonelganj area was also quite serious.

- *Number of persons dead*: 14 (officially), 300 (unofficially)
- *Number of persons injured:* 1,000 (unofficially)
- *Number of persons arrested:* 150

- *Properties destroyed:* The loss of properties was estimated to be worth lakhs of rupees.

Communal Riots in Udaipur, Rajasthan[219]

Immediate Cause: Trouble broke out on 3rd October, in Udaipur. It was also said that some people attacked a place of worship situated in the Bhimashah area. It is said that some people attacked a place of worship. They also stoned the "RAMJYOTI" procession according to V.K. Thanavi, I.G., Police. Thereafter a mob collected near clock tower area and demanded action against the mischief makers and also wanted ban on the procession of Miladun Nabi (Prophet's birthday). The Muslims also collected near the clock tower and challenged the people of the other community. The police stopped the religious procession near Mukherji chowk but the mob attacked the police with stones, lathis and other weapons. An indefinite curfew was imposed.

- *Number of person dead:* 1
- *Number of persons injured:* 13
- *Loss of properties*: Miscreants ransacked and set ablaze several shops and damaged the welcome arches for the Ram Jyoti procession.

Communal Riots in Chennapatna, Karnataka[220]

Immediate Cause: Trouble broke out on 3rd October in Chennapatna in Karnataka. It is said that the trouble started after an incident of eve-teasing which resulted in clashes between two groups of students but latter assumed communal colour.

- *Number of persons dead*: 2
- *Number of persons injured:* 30
- *Loss of properties*: Many properties were burnt down

Communal Riots in Kollar, Karnataka[221]

Immediate Cause: Trouble broke out on 3rd October in Kollar and in its surrounding areas on Id-ul-Milad. Trouble broke out when one student was stabbed to death.

- *Number of persons dead*: 16
- *Number of persons injured:* 15
- *Loss of properties:* Many shops were burnt down.

Communal Riots in Bombay, Maharashtra[222]

Immediate Cause: According to the police, the trouble broke out when some miscreants pelted stones at people returning in about 200 trucks and five jeeps from the traditional Id-e-Milad procession in South Bombay which was led by the then Uttar Pradesh Chief Minister, Mulayam Singh Yadav. *The exact date of the riot not available.*

- *Number of person dead:* 1
- *Number of persons injured:* 24
- *Places affected:* Kalachowkie, Bandra, Mahim and R.A. Kidwai Marg police stations
- *Loss of property*: The Bandra mosque was stoned by miscreants.

Communal Riots in Morba village, Raigad District, Maharashtra[223]

Immediate Cause: — Communal riot broke out in Morba village when a group of persons pelted stones at a Ram Rath Yatra procession. *The exact date of the riot not available.*

- *Number of persons dead:* 1
- *Number of persons injured:* 13
- *Loss of properties*: As the news of the riot spread to Manegaon, a Hindu dominated village about 10 km away from Morba, the shops belonging to Muslims were stoned by miscreants.

Communal Riots in Devangere, Karnataka[224]

Immediate Cause: Trouble broke out on 6th October in Devangere when Ram Jyoti processionists went berserk.

- *Number of persons dead*: 18
- *Other details not available*

Communal Riots in Gujarat[225]

Immediate Cause: Trouble broke out on 30th October in Gujarat. The Gujarat bandh and 'rasta roko' agitations called jointly by the Vishwa Hindu Parishad and the Bhartiya Janata Party to mark the Kar Seva for construction of the Ram temple in Ayodhya turned violent forcing the police to open fire in troubled areas.

- *Number of persons dead*: 24 (officially)
- 34 (2 killed in police firing)

- *Loss of properties:* About 60 to 70 shops were set on fire in Ahmedabad and an equal number of shops were looted, the police said. Mobs set fire to the compartment of the Hapa Jammu Tawi Mail at Chanakyapuri railway crossing near Ahmedabad. A Western Railway official said that some air conditioned coaches were also damaged. Some coaches of the Baroda-Viramgam passenger train were also damaged at Chandlodia near Ahmedabad. A mob also set ablaze a government jeep at Muli in Saurashtra.
- *Places affected:* In Ahmedabad the *places affected* were Kalupur, Dariapur, Gomtipur, Juhapur, Vasna, Shahipur, Khanpur, Pald, Sattelite road in Ahmedabad, Astodia, Maninagar and Paldi. In Baroda, the *places affected* were Wadi, Panigate, Karelivbag; Godhra, Baroda, Baruch, Jamjodhpur, Padra, Halol, and Ahmedabad. The areas of Bharuch and Muli in Saurashtra were also affected.

Communal Riots in Bijnor, Uttar Pradesh[226]

Immediate Cause: Trouble broke out on 30th October in Bijnor on the day when the Kar Sevaks reached Ayodhya tensions had dramatically escalated and the atmosphere was very tense. Around 11 a.m., a police officer who had been listening to the radio rushed to the Arya Samaj Mandir with news, he claimed he had heard over the British Broadcasting Corporation, that Kar Sevaks had reached Ayodhaya, placed their flags on the mosque and started to demolish it. Within an hour, a victory procession of several hundred people marched through Bijnor shouting slogans about their determination to build a temple in Ayodhaya. The procession marched towards *'Ghanta Ghar'*, a clock tower in the centre of the town and entered the Muslim dominated area shouting provocative slogans. At some point, Muslims began to pelt stones at the processionists who responded immediately.

- *Number of persons dead*: 87 (officially) 200 (unofficially)
- *Number of persons injured:*127 (officially) 400-500 (unofficially)
- *Loss of properties:* A large number of shops were looted and burnt.

Communal Riots in Karnataka[227]

Immediate Cause: Trouble broke out in different parts of Karnataka in October as wild rumours was going around that the Babri Masjid in Ayodhya had been bombed.

- *Number of person dead:* 1

- *Number of persons injured:* 30
- *Number of persons arrested:* 27
- *Places affected:* Doddaballapur near Bangalore, Chikballapur, Kyatsandra near Tumkur, Tumkur town, Bangalore pet in Kolar district, Thyamagondala village near Bangalore, Northern Bijapur district, Sumwarpet in Coorg district
- *Loss of properties:* In Chikballapur, a house was set on fire. An autorichshaw was set ablaze in Kyatsandra near Tumkur. A place of worship was slightly damaged in Thyamgondala village near Bangalòre and another burnt in the Northern Bijapur district. At Sumwarpet in Coorg district, a mob attacked a house.
- *Ammunitions recovered*: 2 guns

On 25th October, at least 5 persons were killed in police firing and stabbing incidents in Kolar, Mysore, district in response to a 'Bandh' call by the Bhartiya Janata Party and a number of Hindu organisations against the arrest of Bhartiya Janata Party chief Lal Krishna Advani.

Communal Riots in Delhi[228]

Immediate Cause: Trouble broke out in old Delhi when a Sikh-Muslim Harmony march turned to become violent. Delhi was tense on account of news reports about the Kar Seva in Ayodhya on 30th October and the peace march turned into bloody rioting. It is alleged that some youths were leading the peace march and they raised slogans which were not very sober. The Hindus termed them as provocative. When the peace march terminated at the old Idgah it was turned into a public meeting. Muslims and Sikhs spoke. When the Sikh leader rose to speak, there was heavy brickbatting from the vicinity. The police had to fire several rounds to send the rioters packing. The trouble began when a Muslim resident of Qasabpura went to buy some provisions in a shop near Basti Harphool Singh. Some youngsters who had assembled there, warned the shopkeeper not to sell anything to the man as he belonged to another community. An altercation ensued and the man was very badly beaten up. Shortly, heavy brickbatting followed between the residents of Qasabpura and Basti Harpool Singh.

- *Number of persons dead*: 6
- *Number of persons injured:* 25
- *Number of persons arrested:* 237

Communal Riots in Hyderabad and adjoining areas of Ranga Reddy District, Andhra Pradesh[229]

Immediate Cause and the communities involved not available.

- *Number of persons dead*: 107
- *Number of persons injured:* 300
- *Number of persons arrested:* 418
- *Ammunitions recovered:* 45 weapons
- *Places affected:* Rein Bazar, Santoshnagar, Gokulnagar, Rajendranagar, Budwel village near Rajendranagar, Shamsheergunj, Saroorangar, Malakpet, Chanderghat, Lal Darwaza, Chatri naka, Kacheguda, Falaknuma and Idi Bazar

'The Telegraph' reported on 2nd November, that as many as 30 persons have died in stray stabbing incidents in the State, including Hyderabad, since early October. There had been 48 stabbing incidents, leading to three communal flare-ups. Communal clashes broke out when a noted anti-social, Sardar Mohammed, was killed in a police encounter. Fresh violence also broke out in Hyderabad in the last week of October, as the news of the arrest of the BJP President L.K. Adavani spread in the city.

Communal Riots in Hyderabad, Andhra Pradesh[230]

Immediate Cause: Trouble broke out when the Hindu agitation around the disputed shrine at Ayodhaya in early December fuelled serious communal unrest in many parts of India. Ironically, the fresh agitation which started on 6th December was based on the concept of satyagraha ("peaceful protest") so that as violence erupted in other parts of the country, Ayodhaya itself remained relatively calm.

- *Number of persons dead*: 200

Real Cause: Riot broke out in Hyderabad as a result of Lal Krishna Advani's Rath Yatra. In October the BJP President was arrested which resulted in minor rioting. But it was only on 7th December, that an incident triggered off major disturbances. An extremely poor Hindu hawker boy was fatally stabbed. Since he was a Hindu, it was assumed that the killer must have been a Muslim, though it is difficult to know who stabbed him. No sooner had this happened than 150 persons, (it is alleged that they belonged to the dissident Congress lobby) descended on Karwan, a place where the Hindu boy was killed and went on a stabbing spree.

- *Number of persons injured:* 300
- *Loss of properties:* According to Salahuddin Owaisi, President of the Majlis-e-Ittihadul Muslemin, 58 mosques were demolished and 200 religious sites were destroyed. According to Kodard Ram Reddy of Andhra Pradesh Civil Liberties committee, in Shakerpali and Dhobiper villages in Ranga Reddy district, properties worth Rs. 30 lakhs were destroyed.
- *Places affected:* Karwan, Shankarganji, Chatrinaka, Shankaranpet, Dhobipet, Nawabpet, Pahadisharif, Shamshabaugh, Sabzimandi and Shankerpali and Dhobipet villages.

Communal Riots in Uttar Pradesh and Bihar[231]

On 23rd October the Bhartiya Janata Party President, Lal Krishna Advani was ordered to be arrested by the then Prime Minister Vishwanath Pratap Singh for taking out the Rath Yatra.

On 24th October, the Bhartiya Janata Party called a nationwide strike during which 16 persons were killed and 400 persons were arrested.

Immediate Cause: Trouble broke out on 1st November in Uttar Pradesh in reaction to the Kar Seva incident. The Hindu agitation around the disputed shrine at Ayodhaya in early December fuelled serious communal unrest in many parts of India.

Real Cause in Lucknow: The clash occurred when a place of worship was damaged.

- *Number of persons dead*: 2

Agra and Aligarh too Witnessed Riots.

- *Number of persons dead*: 100

In Bihar:

- *Number of persons dead*: 2
- *Places affected:* Sadar Gali, Noon Ka Chauraha, Lodi-Ka-Katra and Fasad-Ka-Maidan

Communal Riots in Modusa town, Sabarkantha District, Gujarat[232]

Immediate Cause: Trouble broke out in Modasa in Gujarat when the rumours of violent incidents during the curfew relaxation spread and the mob got indulged in stone pelting. (The exact date of the riot not available)

- *Number of person dead:* 1

Note: In the communal violence in different parts of Gujarat in the month of December, 38 persons were killed of which, 34 persons were killed in Ahmedabad.

Communal Riots in Aligarh, Uttar Pradesh[233]

Immediate Cause: Trouble broke out on 7th December in Aligarh. It became so intense that an army was called out in the riot-torn area. The apparent cause was an attack on some jawans by some Muslims who were returning home after Friday papers. The PAC Jawans were stoned by these angry Muslims who were told that some PAC. men had raped a Muslim widow in the town. On the same day the Gomti Express was stopped by a Hindu mob a few furlongs from Aligarh station, Muslims pulled out and several of them killed.

Real Cause: Aligarh is the center for lock manufacturing. This industry provides employment for around a lakh of people in Aligarh. There are both household units as well as large scale units. The former are owned mostly by the Muslims whereas the latter are controlled by the Hindus. The large scale industrialists used to provoke communal riots to damage small-scale industries financially. Communal violence had hit the small scale units financially and caused them heavy losses

- Killed in train incident: 11
- *Number of persons dead:* 16 (official) 24 (unofficially)

Note: Violence in Aligarh took a new turn on 13th December, when the policemen stationed in the civil lines and university areas refused to assume duty after an assault on two of them by a group of students. They alleged that the Senior Superintendent of Police was pro-Muslim and had ordered them not to fire on the students, though they were being attacked every day.

Violence spread to Meerut and Varanasi from Kanpur and Aligarh on 13th December raising the number of districts affected in the state to six. Newspaper reports estimated the death toll in the state as 125.

- *Number of persons dead*: 85 (officially), 500 (unofficially)

Communal Riots in Kanpur, Uttar Pradesh[234]

Immediate Cause: Trouble broke out in Kanpur on 10th December. A few Muslim hawkers selling clothes on Babbar road were attacked and their clothes burnt. They came to their locality and complained about it with the result that Muslims came out of their house and went around their area shouting slogans and protesting and looting and burning Hindu shops. The Hindus retaliated by burning chappal shops belonging to the mosques. On 12th December the Muslim–PAC confrontation began. By 11.30, a large mob of Muslims in these localities came out of their houses and raised slogans of Allah-o-Akbar and began confronting the PAC. and the police. The authorities found the situation beyond their control and appealed to the Muslims to go back to their houses, convincing them that their demands would be fulfilled. Their demands were (1) withdrawal of PAC, (2) restoration of water, (3) electric and telephone connections

- *Number of persons dead*: 20
- *Number of persons arrested:* 600
- Loss of property*:* 1mosque was damaged
- *Places affected:* Bacongang, Chamanganj, Kanghi Mahal, Colonelganj, Anwarganj

Communal Riots in Agra, Uttar Pradesh[235]

Immediate Cause: Trouble broke out in December in Agra when the audio cassettes incited two communities to indulge in rioting. The cassettes started with "Allah-o-Akbar" and then "Jai Shri Ram" followed by "Bachao-bachao" and "Maaro maaro". These were played by Maruti Car stereos at full volume in the night. The unidentified cars then zipped off leaving behind two panic striken and suspicious communities who then began screaming and pelting stones at each other.

The exact date not given.

- *Number of persons dead*: 22

- *Places affected:* Dholi Khar, Tila Ajmeri Khan and Ghati Mamu Bhanja in the Mantola police station area

Communal Riots in Ahmedabad, Gujarat[236]

Immediate Cause: Trouble broke out in Ahmedabad when a group of boys belonging to the minority community while playing cricket hit the ball unintentionally towards a group of State Reserve Police men. An altercation followed resulting in police firing in which one of the boys was injured. This seemingly innocuous incident occurred on 9th December. Two days later, the minority community called for a *"bandh"* to protest against police firing. Meanwhile tensions escalated in the capital.

- *Number of persons dead*: 39
- Number of persons injured: 12

1991

Communal Riots at Ghaziabad, Uttar Pradesh[237]

Communal violence erupted at Ghaziabad on 26th January.

The exact and the immediate cause involved in the conflict not available.

- *Number of persons dead*: 10
- *Number of persons arrested:* 254

Communal Riots in Sullia, Karnataka[238]

Trouble broke out on 2nd February at Sullia near Madikeri.

The Immediate cause and the communities involved in the conflict not available.

- *Number of persons injured:* 5
- Loss of Property: A large number of houses and shops were badly damaged

Communal Riots at Nadia District, West Bengal[239]

Immediate Cause: Trouble broke out on 11th March at Nadia district in West Bengal over an ice-cream vendor using a loudspeaker. The objection later on took a communal turn.

- *Number of persons dead*: 7
- *Number of persons injured:* 13

Communal Riots in Bhadrak, Orissa[240]

Immediate Cause: Trouble broke out on 24th March at Bhadrak in Balasore district. Bhadrak is a town with a total population of 1,20,000, of which the 70,000 Muslims form a major chunk. In Bhadrak the economy is controlled by the Marwaris and Oriya Hindus. The Bhartiya Janata Party was trying to gain a foothold in Orissa, having its eye on the Hindu votes and had its supporters and financers in the Marwaris. They therefore decided to take out Ram Navami processions in many places in the state. As usual, abusive slogans were raised and the Muslims protested. Soon brickbatting was resorted to. The police force accompanying the procession was very small.

- *Number of persons killed:* 17 (4 Hindus)
- Number of person injured: 1
- *Loss of properties:* Muslim shops in Naya Bazaar were looted and burnt. Marwari shops in Chandan Bazaar area were also looted and burnt

Communal Riots in Soro, Orissa[241]

Immediate Cause: Soro is situated 32 KM away from North of Bhadrak. The Bhartiya Janata Party had given a call for Bandh in the State and processions were taken out. There was an altercation between Hindus and Muslims, which led to breaking out of the riot.

- *Number of persons killed:* 16 (2 Hindus)

Communal Riots at Saharanpur, Uttar Pradesh[242]

Immediate Cause: Trouble broke out on 24th March, when a Ram Navami religious procession was to pass from Jama Masjid around 6.00 p.m. before the evening prayer started. However deliberately or otherwise, the procession came near Jama Masjid when the evening prayer had started and hence was stopped. As a result there was a confrontation between the police and the processionists. The processionists withdrew, they started a campaign against the district administration, demanding the right of Hindus to complete the procession through the traditional route. The Bhartiya Janata Party and its supporting organisations like the Vishwa Hindu Parishad, RSS and Bajrang Dal were vocal in their attacks at street corner meetings. On 26th March, the

District Magistrate gave permission to complete the procession on the assurance from the BJP that no riots would take place. The procession was later taken out on 27th March. Provocative communal slogans were raised. A large section of processionists were activists of Bajrang Dal, Vishwa Hindu Parishad and the Rashtriya Swayam Sevak Sangh. The sloganeering soon degenerated into abuses and slandering of Muslims as the procession neared the Jama Masjid. But a section of the processionists soon broke off from the main procession, squatted on the steps of the Jam Masjid and began shouting vulgar slogans. All efforts to remove them failed. The small police force was ineffectual. This resulted in stone-throwing incidents. Later, the police resorted to firing.

- *Number of persons dead:* 15 (officially) (7 killed in police firing) 40 (unofficially)
- *Number of persons arrested:* 284
- *Loss of properties:* 140 shops were burnt down

Communal Riots in Mustafabad village, Uttar Pradesh[243]

Immediate Cause: Trouble broke out on 8th April at Mustafabad village near Varanasi. The trouble broke out when a buffalo entered a cane farm.

- *Number of persons dead*: 3
- Number of person injured*:* 1

Communal Riots in Calcutta, West Bengal[244]

Immediate Cause: Trouble broke out 17th April, in Calcutta. The riots broke out after a bomb explosion near a prayer meeting.

- *Number of persons injured:* 25
- *Places affected:* Canal road under the Hastings police station, Bekari road, Commissariat road and ST George's Tier

Communal Riots in Surat city[245]

Immediate Cause: Trouble broke out on 21st April in Surat.

The exact and the Immediate cause involved in the conflict not available.

- *Number of persons dead*: 2
- *Other details not available*

Communal Riots in Baroda, Gujarat[246]

Immediate Cause: The main cause of rioting on communal lines on 23rd April was aggressive electionering by Bhartiya Janata Party. The apparent cause was a minor incident in which a boy was hit by an autorickshaw.

- *Number of persons dead*: 9
- *Number of persons injured:* 9
- *Places affected:* Fatehpura, Mathikhana, Patel, Falia

Communal Riots in Gurgaon, Madhya Pradesh[247]

Immediate Cause: Trouble broke out on 16th May in Gurgaon, 17 km from Khargone near Indore. It was a consequence of a clash between two Hindus and a Muslim youth.

- *Number of persons dead*: 5
- *Number of persons injured:* 20
- *Loss of properties*: More than 115 Kiosks, shops and houses were completely or partially damaged.

Communal Riots at Kanpur[248]

Immediate Cause: Trouble broke out in April. This was a sequel to two-mafia dons trying to establish their foothold in politics by communalising the incident.(the exact date of the out-break of the riot not available)

- *Number of persons dead:* 24 (Killed in police firing)

Communal Riots in Baroda, Gujarat[249]

Immediate Cause: Trouble broke out on 23rd April in Baroda. The main cause was aggressive electioneering by the BJP, but the apparent cause was due to a minor incident in which a boy was hit by an autorickshaw. As a result the mobs clashed and the police fired 148 teargas shells and 27 rounds.

- *Number of persons dead:* 9 (7 in stabbing and 2 in police firing)
- *Loss of properties:* 4 houses, 8 roadside stalls and 6 vehicles burnt by the miscreants

Communal Riots in Rajpara, Gujarat

Immediate Cause: Trouble broke out in Rajpara in Gujarat where a State Transport bus was stopped. Similiarly a staff bus of the

Indian petrochemicalsLimited was stopped by a mob and one of the victims stabbed brutually. *The exact date of the outbreak of the riot are not available*

- *Number of person dead:* 1

Communal Riots in Surat, Gujarat

- *Number of persons dead*: 2

Commual Riot in Kanpur, Uttar Pradesh[250]

Immediate Cause: Trouble broke out on 19th May in Kanpur due to aggressive BJP storm troopers taking out an election procession in Muslim dominated Lakkarmandi area and hurling abuses at the community. A few Muslim youths retaliated with vengeance. BJP's protest meeting in Navin market, heavily populated by Muslims, on 20th May sparked off a new wave of violence. Violence continued unabated until the army was called in on 21st May to control the situation.

- *Number of persons dead*: 4

The next day, disturbances began again due to the BJP protest meeting in Navin Market, heavily populated by Muslims. The rioting spread like a wildfire and a Hindu shopkeeper was dragged out of a police jeep and lynched and a young Muslim bride was kidnapped and brutually murdered.

- *Number of persons Killed:* 5 (3 in police firing and 2 murdered and stabbed)

Note: Kanpur witnessed communal riots in April and December 1990. The last riot in December was linked to the Ayodhya issue.

Communal Riots in Sikandarabad, Uttar Pradesh[251]

Immediate Cause: Trouble broke out on 20th May in Sikandarabad in Bulandshahar district of U.P. The town fell victim to communal-cum poll violence. The violence was sparked off by a poll clash between activists of two parties.

- *Number of persons dead*: 12
- *Loss of properties*: 49 shops and 9 houses were set ablaze

- *Arms and ammunitions recovered:* 250 high power bombs, 19 "paper bombs", a large quantity of petrol bombs and country made pistols

Communal Riots in Benares, Uttar Pradesh[252]

Immediate Cause: Trouble broke out on 20th May and again during 8-12 June in Benares. It started on voting day when Muslims were allegedly prevented from voting by the Hindus, while Hindus allege that it started when Muslims in their localities prevented Hindus from voting. It was difficult to establish who provided the spark. There was a complete polarisation between Hindus and Muslims as most of the Muslims and the Scheduled castes were to vote for the Janata Dal candidate and most of the Hindus for the Bhartiya Janata Party.
In Riots on 20th May:

- *Number of persons dead:* 28 (officially) (24 Muslims, 8 Hindus) 50 (unofficially)
- *Number of persons injured:* 75 (15-20 Hindus)

In Riots during 8-12th June:

- *Number of persons dead*: 3 (Hindus)
- *Loss of properties:* Hindu shops were burnt

Communal Riots in Delhi[253]

Immediate Cause: Communal riot broke out on 3rd July, when an autorickshaw ran into a pushcart in the congested market at Bhogal. An altercation followed, during which the autorickshaw driver was beaten up by the pushcart owner and his friend. Later, the autorickshaw driver returned and stabbed both of them. Soon after, 30 people from two communities collected and fought each other.

- *Number of persons injured:* 2
- *Loss of Property:* A police vehicle was attacked by the rioters
- *Place affected:* Bhogal area.

Communal Riots in Basavakalyan, Kerala[254]

Immediate Cause: Trouble broke out on 20th July in Basavakalyan. The trouble began a few days earlier when a man teased a woman belonging to a different community. Members of the woman's community allegedly assaulted him, thus instigating the rival gangs sparking off clashes.

- *Number of persons dead*: 3
- *Number of persons injured:* 10
- *Loss of properties*: 3 huts were burnt down.

Communal Riots in Baroda, Gujarat[255]

Immediate Cause: Trouble broke out on 22nd July in Baroda on the ocassion of the Muharram procession when the Tazia procession was stoned in Mandvi area but soon the entire walled city was engulfed.

- *Number of persons dead:* 7 (5 killed in police firing 2 killed in stabbing)
- *Places affected:* Babampura, Mandvi, Fathepura
- *Curfew imposed areas:* Vadi city and Panigate police stations

Communal Riots in Broach city and Jambusar town, Broach District, Baroda[256]

Immediate Cause: Communal riot broke out on 24th July when large-scale violence occurred during a Moharrum procession.

- *Number of persons dead*: 17
- *Places affected:* Baroda, Broach, Jambusar

Communal Riots in Benares[257]

Immediate Cause: There was practically no communal riots in Benaras between 1947 and 1966, but between 1966 and 1991 there were about 12 communal riots. There were riots in 1967 (trouble started with a *tazia* procession in which 3 persons died). On 16th June 1972, Muslims were taking out a procession protesting against the Aligarh Muslim University Bill. The police had clamped section 144 and hence tried to stop the procession, which resulted in eruption of communal violence. On 23rd October 1977, trouble started on the occasion of Durga Puja, clashes occurring between Muslims and Bengalis on the question of land at Deonathpura. It was a very serious communal trouble resulting in several deaths and excesses by the PAC. On 23rd November 1985, it was again the procession of Durga being taken for immersion during which trouble broke out near Katupura. On 14th February 1986, Muslims observed black day as the lock of Barbi Masjid was opened. There was stone throwing followed by stabbing and rioting. On 24th July 1986, brickbatting took place at village Kotwa and stone throwing on *Tazia* procession in village Lohta near

Imambara. These are some of the major and minor incident, which have occurred in Benares in the last few decades.

Immediate Cause: Riots broke out on 8th November 1991, in Varanasi during the immersion of the Kali idol in the Ganga. Speaking in Parliament, the Minister of State for Home, M.M. Jacob stated that riots broke out following an accidental injury to a person of one community due to a fire cracker.[258]

- *Number of persons dead*: 17
- *Paces affected*: Madanpura and Godowlia

1992

Communal Riots in Hapur town, Uttar Pradesh[259]

Immediate Cause: Trouble broke out on 12th February in Hapur town following a dispute over the construction of a temple.

- *Number of persons dead*: 9
- *Number of persons injured:* 20

Communal Riots in Bilaspur, Rampur District, Uttar Pradesh[260]

The exact and Immediate cause involved in the conflict not available.

- *Number of persons dead*: 2
- Number of person injured*:* 1
- *Number of persons arrested:* 24
- *Other details not available*

Communal Riots in Pandu, in Hooghly District, West Bengal[261]

Immediate Cause: Trouble broke out in Pandu in Hooghly district, when people from two different communities clashed with each other.

- *Number of person dead:* 1
- *Other details not available*

Communal Riots in Ahmedabad, Gujarat[262]

Immediate Cause: Trouble broke out on 2nd July on the eve of Lord Jagannath Rath Yatra, in Dariapur area of Prem Darwaza at about 4 p.m.

- *Number of persons dead*: 27

- *Number of persons injured:* 100
- *Loss of properties:* The *Loss of properties* estimated to be worth crores of Rs. was damaged.

Real cause of the riot in Ahmedabad in July, 1992:

The Ramjanmabhoomi-Babri Masjid controversy raised communal temperature throughout the country, especially in Gujarat, wherein too the BJP was making a serious bid for power. Thus, the riot which occurred on 2nd July in Ahmedabad was a by-product of the communal politics of the BJP.

Many observers and analysts of the Gujarat political scene have also felt that the BJP had an eye over forthcoming municipal elections in many cities and towns in Gujarat like Ahmedabad, Surat, Baroda, Rajkot, etc. According to these observers, the BJP felt that engineering communal violence would benefit it in these elections.

Writing about the 2nd July riots, Ashraf Sayeed of *'The Times of India'* says, 'The main characters have not changed. Anti-social elements, particularly bootleggers, still play a major role in connivance with the police, politicians and religious bigots. There was a time when the Congress was suspected to be the main culprit. Now it is the turn of the Bhartiya Janata Party (BJP), with its blatantly Hindu card designed to instill fear in the minds of the minority community.

Communal Riots in Thiruvananthapuram, Kerala[263]

The exact and the Immediate cause involved in the conflict not available.

- *Number of persons dead*: 6
- *Other deta.'s not available*

Communal Riots in Malegaon, Maharashtra[264]

Immediate Cause: Trouble broke out on 19th July in Malegaon Trouble broke out due to the Ayodhya controversy.

- *Number of persons dead:* 3
- Number of persons injured: 116
- *Number of persons arrested:* 101

Communal Riots in Gujarat[265]

Immediate Cause: Trouble broke out in Gujarat during the Ganesh idol immersion procession.

The exact date of the out-break of the riot and the exact and the immediate cause involved in the conflict not available.

- *Number of persons dead*: 3
- Number of persons injured: 24

Communal Riots in Anand Town, Kaira District, Gujarat[266]

Immediate Cause: Trouble broke out in Anand town over the issue of diversion by the police of the route of the Ganesh idol immersion procession. *The date of the outbreak of the riot available.*

- *Number of person dead:* 1
- *Number of persons injured:* 16

Communal Riots in Sitamarhi, Bihar[267]

Immediate Cause: Trouble broke out on 6th October in and around Sitamarhi due to the tension created by Durga pooja procession.

- *Number of persons dead*: 48
- *Number of persons injured:* 100

Communal Riots in Sitamarhi, Bihar[268]

History of communal riot in Sitamarhi: Sitamarhi has a history of communal riots and a number of riots have taken place in this small town. In 1948, it witnessed communal violence in a place called Belsand, followed by a communal riot in 1959 on the question of Mahavir flag. It was a major riot and about 50 persons were killed in it. Most of those who died in the riots were Muslims. Again communal riots started due to a false rumour that the Muslims slaughtered a cow though the cow was traced out alive near Jankyoshthan. In 1959, another riot took place again on the cow slaughter issue at a place called Balminiya Akta and in this riot about 11 people were killed and 200 houses were reduced to ashes. Again those killed were mostly Muslims. Riots broke out in 1967 in Sitamarhi along with Ranchi on the controversy about Urdu. There was a coalition Government in Bihar at that time. The riot which took place at Sursan claimed about 50 lives and 400 houses. Mostly, Muslims were affected. Again in 1969 riot erupted at Revasia and Rupsi.

Communal Riots in Ajmer, Rajasthan[269]

- *Number of persons arrested:* 32
- *Places affected:* Delhi Gate, Langarkhana Gali, and Moti Katla
- *Loss of properties*: A few shops and vehicles were damaged.
- *Other details not available*

Communal Riots in Bombay, Maharasthra[270]

Immediate Cause: As soon as the news of the demolition of the Babri Masjid on 6th December 1992, spread many Muslims in many areas of Bombay came out on the streets and expressed their anger by attacking buses, taxis and other public property. Some temples were also attacked in certain areas resulting in partial damage. Some of the anti-social elements among them looted Hindu shops also. Many innocent people were killed due to indiscriminate firing by the police.

- *Number of persons dead:* According to police sources, from 6th to 12th December 1992, a total of 202 persons were killed, of which 137 were killed in police firing. However, the death toll actually seems to have crossed 400, with most of the people having died in police firing.
- *Places affected:* Behrampada, Govandi, Malad (East)-Pathanwadi and Islampura, Bandra (East)-Bharat Nagar and Nirmal Nagar, Dharavi, Mahim and Dargah Makhdum Mohiuddin, Behram Baug, Jogeshwari (West), Kurla, Halau Pul and other areas, Ghatkopar Asalfa village, Bhendi Bazaar and Null Bazaar.

Communal Riots in Surat, Gujarat[271]

Immediate Cause: After the demolition of the Babri Masjid on December 6th, Surat, like other towns in the country became tense. The rioting in Surat began a day after the demolition of the Babri Masjid i.e., on 7th Dec. 1992 and continued till 14th Dec. 1992. There was anger and resentment among Muslims. This was sought to be exploited by one Mahmood Pardewala who heads the Bhartiya Minority Suraksha Sangh (BMSS) and has underworld connections. He gave a call for *'Surat Bandh'*. BMSS is a small organisation with little following among the Muslims and Dalits. However, some men belonging to this organisation tried to stop traffic and force a *'Bandh'* on unwilling people. Shops were also stoned and damaged. The two communities indulged in brickbating near the railway station.

- *Number of persons dead*: 21 (officially), 300 (unofficially)
- *Number of persons injured:* 39
- *Loss of properties*: In all about 20 industries were looted, burnt and destroyed of which eight were large scale industries while twelve belonged to the small scale industries category. Out of the eight large-scale industries affected, one belonged to a Hindu. Also, more than 1,000 houses and shops were looted and burnt, of which more than 900 belonged to Muslims. Also, 15 mosques and 2 temples were partially or wholly damaged
- *Places affected:* Varachha Road, Udhna, Rander, Limlayat, Dindoli, Neol, Pandesara, Gulshan Nagar, Geeti Nagar, Raghu Nagar, Ambika Nagar, Swaminarayan Nagar, Apeksha Nagar, Gauri Nagar, Jyoti Nagar, Jai Javan Jai Kisan Nagar, Kailash Nagar, Pundit Nagar, Prayog Nagar, Mukti Nagar, Jeevandeep Nagar, Karamyogi Nagar I & II, Ved Road, Bhatena Nagar, Surat Railway Station, Pandol Industrial Estate, Gopipura, Limda Chowk and Rani Talao.

Communal Riots in Delhi[272]

Immediate Cause: Trouble broke out in Delhi as soon as news of the Babri-Masjid demolition took place. There was tension in the area and the Muslim families put up black flags on their houses and had black bands on their arms as a mark of protest. However this peaceful protest was not liked by the police. The policemen directed the concerned families to remove black flags and black bands. This led to the altercaton between some agitators and the police. Meanwhile some miscreants set a Delhi Transport Corporation bus on fire. Later, a policemen on duty was allegedly mishandled. It was alleged by the residents that local police organised anti-social elements and with their help let loose a reign of terror — looting, arson and killing.

- *Number of persons killed:* 12 (officially) 100 (unofficially)
- *Loss of properties:* 75 shops of wood merchants in a single row were reduced to ashes. A large number of houses and jhuggis of the minority community were also burnt. Even some of the Hindu shops were also burnt.

1993

Communal Riots in Bombay and Ahmedabad, Gujarat[273]

Immediate Cause: Trouble broke out on 5th January due to the destruction of the Babri Masjid at Ayodhya. Intense communal violence occurred in the western cities of Bombay and Ahmedabad.

- *Number of persons dead:* 215 persons, (80 in Bombay)
- *Figures for Ahmedabad not available*
- *Number of persons arrested:* 1,700 persons; and 2,000 were placed in preventive detention.

Communal Riots in Bombay, Maharashtra[274]

Immediate Cause: Trouble broke out again on 6th January in Bombay. It is very difficult to say with certainty as to how the riots in the second phase began. One possible reason might have been due to the murder of two Mathadi workers in Dongri area inside a godown. It was alleged that Muslims had murdered them out of communal vengeance. However, it is far from certain as to who the murderers really were. According to another view, the riots began in Bhendi Bazar, Null Bazar and Mohammed Ali Road area on account of rumours that the Muslim dargah in Mahim was demolished by Hindus. A few cases of stabbing were reported from this area and undoubtedly this became a flash point for the riots. However it would be utterly simplistic to say that riots started only because of these stabbing cases, with no other factors at work. Apart from other things, the *'Maha Artis'* (road side worship of Hindu deity) had done a lot of damage to communal peace.

- *Number of persons dead:* In the second phase, according to '*The Times of India*' the death toll was 557 on January 22, 1993. Official sources put the death toll at 458 only. According to police commissioner Bapat, out of the 458 persons killed, 288 were Muslims and 170 Hindus. 133 persons died in police firing (75 Muslims and 50 Hindus, 8 unknown), 259 in mob violence (186 Muslims, 73 Hindus) and 66 in arson (39 Hindus and 27 Muslims). Of the remaining 99, it is difficult to say which community they belonged to, but it is very likely that a majority of them were Muslims. In any case, the figure of 557 also seems to be an underestimate for the death toll in all probability would exceed 1,000.

- *Loss of properties*: There was a loss of property worth about Rs. 4,000 crores.
- *Places affected:* Dongri, Bombay Central, Tulsiwadi (Tardeo), Girgaum, Jacob circle, Byculla, Cotton Green, Wadala, Antop Hill, Mahim, Dharavi, Behrampada (Bandra East), Kherwadi, Nirmal Nagar, Vakola, Andheri East, Jogeshwari east, Goregaon, Malad east and west, Malvani, Borivali, Dahisar, Ghatkopar, Asalfa village, Vikhroli, Bhandup, Mulund and Pratika Nagar.

Real Cause of the Bombay Riots in the Second Phase in January 1993

The Shiv Sena was preparing for the violent outburst on a large scale. It was waiting for the flash point and the incidents in Bhendi Bazar-Mohammed Ali Road area provided one. Apart from other things, the *Maha Artis* had done a lot of damage to communal peace. Hundreds of Shiv Sainiks, BJP men and others participated in each 'Maha Arti' which invariably ended with anti-Muslim propaganda that exacerbated communal tensions and prepared the atmosphere for eruption of communal violence. The police commissioner of Bombay himself had admitted on 7th Janauary that the 'Maha Artis' were aggravating the situation. By 8th Janauary, 113 such Aartis had been already organised.

Communal Riots in Surat, Gujarat[275]

Immediate Cause: The trouble broke out after the Babri Mosque was demolished.

- *Number of persons killed:* 197 175 (Muslims) 22 (Hindus)

Communal Riots in Ahmedabad, Gujarat[276]

Immediate Cause: The trouble broke out on 6th December soon after the Babri mosque was demolished.

- *Number of persons killed:* 70

Communal Riots in Delhi[277]

Immediate Cause: Trouble broke out on 27th January afternoon in Delhi following the rumours of desecration of a religious place. The violence was triggered off by the desecration of a religious place, behind the Gokha cinema theatre. One section attributed the alleged desecration by the monkeys which abound in the area, while according to another version, the locks were broken by some anti- social elements who gained entry despite the presence of a picket nearby.

- *Number of persons dead:* 2 (1 in police firing and 1 in stabbing)
- *Number of persons injured:* 6 (3 in stabbing)
- *Loss of properties*: Some shops were burnt and 2 religious places were damaged. 2 scooters and a paint shop were burnt.
- *Places affected:* Jama Masjid, Chandni Mahal, Hauz Qazi, Kamla Market, Daryaganj, Kucha Chelan, Tehra Bahram Khan, Suiwalan, Kamra Bangash, Chitli Qbar, Matia Mahal, Sikriwalan, Bazaar Sita Ram, Haveli Azam Khan, Kala Mahal, Sadar Bazaar and Bara Hindu Rao

Communal Riots in Belgaum, Karnataka[278]

Immediate Cause: Trouble broke out on 6th April, in Belgaum between two communities due to the stabbing of a youth while returning from the cinema. An orgy of violence was let loose.

- *Number of persons dead*: 9
- *Number of persons injured:* 52
- *Number of persons arrested:* 178
- *Loss of properties:* Large number of shops were destroyed.

Communal Riots in Manipur[279]

Immediate Cause: Trouble broke out on 3rd May in the tiny border State of Manipur. The fact that Manipur so far had been relatively free from communal antipathy added a new dimensions to the tragedy.

- *Number of persons dead*: 98
- *Other details not available*

Communal Riots in Karnataka[280]

Immediate Cause: The riot broke out in Bhatkal when a lecturer in a private college at Bhatkal was shot and seriously injured. Enraged by the incident, members of one particular community went on rampage.

- *Number of persons dead*: 3
- *Number of persons injured:* 15

Communal Riots in Jawad Town, Mandrasaur District, Madhaya Pradesh[281]

Immediate Cause: Trouble broke out on 27th September in Jawad town on the occasion of Ganesh festival. The violence broke out due to stone-throwing on a procession which led to retaliatory violence and burning of small shops and hutments.

- No casualties were reported.
- *Number of persons arrested:* 58

Communal Riots in Surat, Gujarat[282]

Immediate Cause: Trouble broke out on 29th September in Surat during the Ganesh immersion procession. Also on 30th September, trouble erupted when some miscreants heavily stoned a procession from a place of worship. A Ganesh Visarjan Yatra which was passing in front of a place of worship in the Limbayatt area came under heavy stone-throwing.

- *Number of persons dead*: 3
- *Number of person injured:* 1
- *Place affected*: Limbayat area

1994

Communal Riots in Mapusa, Goa[283]

Immediate Cause: Trouble broke out in Mapusa over the Ganesh Mandir issue. According to police superintendent (north), Dilip Kumar, riots broke out after the police foiled an attempt by some groups to build an illegal temple structure. *The exact date of the riot not available.*

- *Number of persons arrested:* 22 (activists of Maharashtra Goan Party, Bhartiya Janata Party and Shiv Sena)
- Loss of Property: 4 buses of the State owned Kadamba Transport Corporation (KTC) were damaged.

Communal Riots in Kanpur, Uttar Pradesh[284]

Immediate Cause: Trouble broke out on 10th February when Hindu mobs attacked Muslim residents, blaming them for a bomb explosion on 9th February which killed local Bhartiaya Janata Party politician Kala Bachcha. Bachcha was implicated in raids on several

Muslim homes during communal rioting which followed the destruction of the Ayodhya mosque in December 1992.

- *Number of persons dead*: 4
- *Number of persons injured:* 6

Trouble broke out on 13th February in Kanpur when the two rival groups in Babupurwa area hurled bombs at each other, while members of a particular community gheraoed a pose of PAC personnel in Baquargang. The calm was broken when two rival groups hurled bombs at each other.

(Other details not given.

Communal Riots in Uttar Pradesh

Immediate Cause: Trouble broke out on 28th February in Uttar Pradesh due to the clashes which erupted when a person was arrested for obstructing a prayer meeting by playing songs over a loudspeaker in his house. A mob then gathered outside the police station and hurled stones and shot at the members of other community.

- *Number of persons injured:* Several (The exact Number of persons injured are not available)
- *Number of persons arrested:* 25

Communal Riots in Vizhinjam, Kerala[285]

Immediate Cause: Trouble broke out on 15th May in Vizhinjam following an arguement between the two fishermen over the use of a common space meant for keeping fishing equipments. The heated exchange soon took a violent turn with rival sides using country bombs and swords against each other.

- *Number of persons dead*: 2
- *Number of persons injured:* 15
- *Loss of properties*: 100 boats and fishing equipments worth several lakhs of rupees was destroyed in the violence.

Communal Riots in Nadiad, Gujarat[286]

Immediate Cause: Trouble broke out in July in Nadiad. Four villages of Nadiad taluka were disturbed by the communal tensions which erupted on Muharram day.

The exact and the Immediate cause involved in the conflict and the exact date not available.

- *Number of person dead:* 1

Communal Riots in Asangaon, Maharashtra

Immediate Cause: Trouble broke out on 8th June in Asangaon in Mumbai over the issue of children playing marbles. The fragile equilibrium and peace which held its 7 Muslim houses together with the rest of Hindus flared into a communal hate wave because of the innocuous game. As they were playing, a marble hit 10 year old Shabana who was passing by. She went home crying. Her mother, and a relative, Saira Banu Mughal came out to enquire and a squabble erupted between the boys playing the game and the women. Soon the heated exchange took communal tone as expletives started. Then three men came out of Shabana's house, all armed with revolvers. With large sticks, axes and stones, went on a rampage picking out each of the 7 Muslim houses.

- *Loss of properties:* Furniture, roof of the thatched houses

Communal Riots in Hubli, Karnataka[287]

Immediate Cause: Trouble broke out on 15th August when the police lathi charged the supporters of the Bhartiya Janata Party who wanted to hoist the national flag in the Idgah maidan, despite a ban on them.

- *Number of persons dead:* 6
- *Number of persons injured:* 34
- *Number of persons arrested:* 300
- *Ammunitions recovered:* Dozen javelins, handrods and acid bulbs were recovered.
- *Places affected:* Deshpande Nagar, Dhaji banpeth, Ganeshpeth and Durgadbyle Broadway

Communal Riots in Bhadravathi, Karnataka[288]

Immediate Cause: Trouble broke out on 21st August when the Id-e-Milad procession was hit by a soda bottle. However, the police force escorting the procession managed to avert any trouble at that moment, but the processionists, on their return, are said to have pelted stones and missiles at some Hindu owned shops and a temple. Meanwhile, as the funeral procession of a Muslim was coming from another part of the city, rumours spread among the Id-e-Milad processionists that the funeral procession was attacked. This led to the Muslim youths attacking some vehicles with stones.

- *Number of persons dead*: 2 (1 Hindu and 1 Muslim)
- Loss of Property: The loss of private property, most of it belonging to Muslims came to about Rs. 3 crore. Over 200 vehicles were burnt. Hotels and shops, numbering about 50 were razed or looted. One cinema theatre, 3 saw mills were vandalised and burnt. 250 bicycles were burnt.

Communal Riots in Bangalore, Karnataka[289]

Immediate Cause: Trouble broke out on 7th October in Bangalore when anti-Urdu telecast protesters turned violent.

The riots were apparently caused by introduction of a ten minute Urdu bulletin on Doordarshan at a prime time slot, *i.e.*, immediately after the Kannada language news cast from 7.45 to 7.55 p.m. The telecast of Urdu news began from 2nd October. This created an explosive situation. It remained a linguistic protest only for a short while. Very soon the protest against the Urdu telecast acquired communal overtones. By 6th October the involvement of the Hinudutva forces became obvious. Members of the Akhil Bhartiya Vidyarthi Parishad (ABVP), the student wing of the BJP, stoned and damaged the official cars of the chief justice of Karnataka, G.T. Nanavati, and Health Minister, Maalaka Reddy. On 7th October the situation further worsened and took a definite communal turn. The protest procession was deliberately routed through Muslim dominated areas of South Bangalore and provocative slogans were shouted before a Masjid where Muslims were offering Friday prayers. It was also not by accident that Friday was chosen for the protest procession which was led by Akhil Bhartiya Vidyarthi Parishad affiliated student organisation from the V.V. Puram college. The procession made its way to the K.R. Market circle where the biggest mosque in the city is located. Near the mosque, the processionist who had already turned unruly about a kilometer away started attacking a few autorickshaws whose Muslim drivers fled and took shelter inside the mosque. The police managed to disperse the processionist but now those inside the mosque came out and started attacking buses. The same thing happened which the processionist had desired, that is, to provoke the Muslims. The deputy commissioner of police's attempt failed to restrain the mob which was now pelting stones indiscriminately, the police then opened fire killing 3 persons on the spot. Some police men sustained injuries and the DCP himself was hit with broken bottle. The fact that the violence continued even after the announcement suspending the telecast of Urdu news bulletin, reflected that violence was communal in nature.

- *Number of persons dead*: 25
- *Number of persons injured:* 350
- *Loss of properties*: Properties worth crores of rupees was destroyed

Communal Riots in Davengare and Chitradurga, Karnataka[290]

Immediate Cause: Trouble broke out on 14th October in Davengare during the Dassera procession when the procession was attacked by another group with stones.

- *Number of persons dead*: 4 (2 persons died in police firing, and 2 persons died in stabbing incidents)
- *Number of persons injured:* 53
- *Number of persons arrested:* 50
- Loss of property: Some shops, autorickshaws, a private bus and a timber depot were burnt down.

Communal Riots in Ahmedabad, Gujarat[291]

Immediate Cause: Trouble broke out on 7th December in Ahmedabad when a group of people wanted to perform 'Maha Arti' on the second anniversary of demolition of Babri Masjid. However, the Commissioner of Police, Ahmedabad, himself rushed to the spot and defused the situation. However there was tension between the residents of Khadia and the police over the issue of alleged police lathi charge on a group of people who wanted to perform 'Maha Arti'.

Other details not available.

1995

Communal Riots in Moradabad, Uttar Pradesh[292]

Immediate Cause: Trouble broke out on 10th February in Mordabad when members of a particularly community objected to the construction of a boundary wall around a well.

- *Number of persons dead*: 5
- *Places affected*: Moradabad city and Sambahal town

Communal Riots in Aligarh, Uttar Pradesh[293]

Immediate Cause: Trouble broke out on 10th March in Aligarh due to a scuffle between a Hindu and a Muslim trader in the Malar Gate area which happens to be near Sultan-Sarai locality, predominantly a Hindu area. It was initially rumoured that the riot started as some miscreants teased a woman in the Sultan-Sarai area. There is also another version which depicts that some women came to buy wool and they were proceeding towards a Muslim shop, but a Hindu shopkeeper Pavan tried to woo the women customers leading to an argument between the 2 shopkeepers and this perhaps led to the outburst of communal violence.

- *Number of persons dead*: 8
- *Number of persons injured:* 19. (17 were Hindus and 2 Muslims)
- *Number of persons arrested:* 308 (219 were Hindus and 89 Muslims)
- *Places affected*: Malar Gate, near Sultan Sarai

Communal Riots in Balasore, Orissa[294]

Immediate Cause: Trouble broke out on 19th March in Balasore, in Orissa following a quarrel between the two groups of children during the festival of Holi. Police opened fire to disperse two clashing groups belonging to two different communities.

- *Number of persons dead*: 2
- *Loss of properties*: More than 50 houses were burnt down.

Communal Riots in Agra, Uttar Pradesh[295]

Immediate Cause: Trouble broke out in Agra in Uttar Pradesh.

The exact and the immediate cause involved in the conflict not available.

- *Number of person dead:* 1
- *Other details not available*

Communal Riots in Hubli, Karnataka[296]

Immediate Cause: Trouble broke out on 21st March outside a mosque. The lane in front of the mosque was very narrow. The riot allegedly started when some pranksters threw colour on those inside the mosque.

- *Number of persons dead*: 5
- *Number of persons injured:* 50

Communal Riots in Tamil Nadu[297]

Immediate Cause: Trouble broke out on 14th April in Madras and other places in Tamil Nadu when the bomb blast took place in Hindu Munani office and near a place of worship in Rameshwaram in which a Bhartiya Janata Party activist and a milk vendor were stabbed to death.

- *Number of persons dead*: 4
- *Places affected*: Coimbatore, Nilgiris, several areas of Madras city like Triplicane, Royapettah, Pudapet

Communal Riots at Holakere, Karnataka[298]

Immediate Cause: Trouble broke out on 29th April in Holakere in the Chitradurga district of Karnataka. Tensions between the two groups of bus agents belonging to two different communities over business competition first took a personal and later a communal turn. Violence flared up after a verbal altercation between the two groups who turned violent attacking each other with cycle chains and clubs.

- *Number of person dead:*1
- *Number of persons injured:* 2
- Number of persons arrested: 7
- *Loss of properties*: A shop, house, hotel and school were set on fire.

Communal Riots in Vizhinjam, Kerala[299]

Immediate Cause: Trouble broke out on 15th May following an argument between the two fishermen over the use of a common space meant for keeping the fishing equipments. The heated exchange soon took a violent turn with rival sides using country made bombs and swords against each other.

- *Number of persons dead:*2
- *Number of persons injured:*15
- *Loss of properties:*100 boats and fishing equipments worth several lakhs of rupees was destroyed in the violence.

Communal Violence in Madras, Tamil Nadu[300]

Immediate Cause: Trouble broke out on 16th April, in Madras when an activist from Bhartiya Janata Party due to a powerful bomb explosion near a place of worship at Rameswaram. The Bhartiya Janata Party activist and a milk vendor, was attacked and stabbed to death by unidentified persons. An explosion near a place of worship brought down a portion of a wall and the tin roof.

- *Number of persons dead:*2
- *Number of persons injured:*8
- *Number of persons arrested:*4

Communal Riot in Ramkhandi, Uttar Pradesh[301]

Immediate Cause: Trouble broke out 29th June, in Ramkhandi, when Muslims obtained conditional permission to build a mosque. Later the crowd collected, and attacked and demolished the mosque

- *Number of persons dead:*2
- *Number of person injured:*1

Highlights of the riot: (1) Muslims alleged that police were silent spectators and when the situation went out of control they started firing.

(2) There was an attempt to forcibly take-away a Muslim girl but some secular Hindus prevented it at the risk of their own lives.

Communal Riots in Palamu, Bihar[302]

Immediate Cause: Trouble broke out on the first week of July in Palamu. The Hindus and Muslims had quarreled on the issue of the boundary wall of a cemetery land. The dispute was about including a tree within the boundary. When the contractor insisted on including the tree within the boundary a mob collected to protest and violence broke-out. *The exact date of the riot not available.*

- *Number of persons dead*: 5.(4 Muslims)
- *Number of persons arrested:* 8
- *Other details not available*

Communal Riots in Qazi Bakri village of Manato Thana in Daltanganji, Bihar[303]

Immediate Cause: Trouble broke out on the second week of July in Qazi Bakri village, Bihar.. The police made an unsuccessful attempt of reconciliation, and arrested some Muslims. Then a few Muslims were murdered and the violence broke-out. *The exact date of the riot not available.*

- *Number of persons dead*: 4

Highlights of the riot: The superintendent of Police, Arvind Pandey, effectively controlled the situation, and prevented further spreading of the riot.

Communal Riots in Dlierganji, Uttar Pradesh [304]

Immediate Cause: Trouble broke out on 6th July in Dlierganji. It is said that a Member of Legislative Assembly of Uttar Pradesh assembly was behind the riot. It is his way of dealing with any one who opposes his supremacy.

- *Number of persons dead*: 4 (Muslim girls)
- Lose of properties: 24 houses in Dlierganj village, all belonging to minority community were razed to the ground.

Communal Riots in Jalgaon-Nasik, Maharashtra[305]

Immediate Cause: Trouble broke out on 26th August, in Jalgaon, situated about 24 km, away from Nasik, where members from the majority community armed with lathis, iron rods and other lethal weapons raided a settlement of minority community and assaulted the inmates of the houses after breaking down doors and windows of the houses.

- *Number of persons injured:* 14
- *Other details not available*

Communal Riots in Madras, Tamil Nadu[306]

Immediate Cause: Trouble broke out during the Ganapati procession, whereby the the processionists pelted stones at police when the police urged the processionists not to disturb prayers inside the mosque. This was followed by clashes.

- *Number of persons injured:* 100
- *Other details not available*

Communal Riots in Hyderabad[307]

Immediate Cause: Trouble broke out in Hyderabad when the processionists stopped near a mosque in the Charminar area and refused to move. *The exact date of the riot not available.*

- *Number of persons dead*: 5
- *Number of persons injured:* 21
- *Loss of properties*: A tourist bus and two scooters were burnt.

Communal Riots in Shimoga, Karnataka[308]

Immediate Cause: Trouble broke out in Shimoga, Karnataka during Ganpati festival.
The exact cause of the riot and the date not available.

- *Number of person dead:* 1
- *Other details not available*

1996

Communal Riots in Coimbatore and Madurai[309]

Immediate Cause: Trouble broke out in Coimbatore and Madurai districts in Tamil Nadu in the month of june. A lot of incidents of stone pelting, and burning of buses and show-rooms took place. A number of stabbing incidents also took place in Mettupalaym and in surrounding areas. *The exact date of the riot not available.*

- *Number of persons dead*: 2
- *Number of persons injured:* 7
- *Number of persons arrested:* 35

Communal Violence in Santrampur, Gujarat[310]

Immediate Cause: Trouble broke out on 4th February in Santrampur in the Panchmahal district of Gujarat. Use of loud speakers near a place of worship was the reason which led to a group clash and subsequent police firing.

- *Number of person dead:* 1
- *Number of persons injured:* 15
- *Other details not available*

Communal Riots in Bejraul, Meerut, U.P.[311]

Immediate Cause: Trouble broke out on 20th February, in Bejraul. The fight was between the majority and minority community.

The exact and the immediate cause involved in the conflict not available.

- *Number of persons injured:* 4
- *Number of persons arrested:* 6
- Loss of properties: 4 houses belonging to minority community were burnt down, and a place of worship was also destroyed.

Communal Violence in Bahraich, Uttar Pradesh[312]

Immediate Cause: Trouble broke out on 6th March, *i.e.*, on Holi, in Bahraich in Uttar Pradesh. An independent member of Local Nagar Panchayat, Raju Bhujwa, threw coloured water on Shahid, which resulted in an altercation between them resulting in stabbing and death of Shahid.

- *Number of person dead:* 1
- *Other details not available*

Communal Riots in Ahmedabad, Gujarat[313]

Immediate Cause: Trouble broke out on 13th March, in Ahmedabad, following India's defeat in semi-final of the Wills World Cup cricket against Sri Lanka at Calcutta. The violence started at Dabgharwad in Dariapur, when a group of people burst firecrackers and raised slogans in favour of the Pakistani cricket team, following the defeat of the Indian team which was strongly objected to by a large number of residents of the adjoining area, who had come out on the road to voice their protest. The police fired 28 rounds and lobbed more than 70 teargas shell.

- *Number of persons injured:* 2
- *Places affected*: Dariapur, Gomtipur, Astodia and Jamalpur areas of Ahmedabad

Communal Riots in Zeba Bagh, Hyderabad[314]

Immediate Cause: Trouble broke out on 18th March, in Zeba Bagh in Hyderabad after two groups of youngsters belonging to two different communities abused each other over a trivial issue. Some scooterists were stated to have abused some persons sitting near a hotel leading to confrontation. Though the groups did not clash the youngsters retreated to their respective areas and informed the elders of the locality about the incident. As people from both communities gathered in lanes and bylanes stones were hurled on houses and chaos prevailed in the locality.

- *Number of person dead:* 1
- *Other details not available*

Communal Riots in Moradabad, Uttar Pradesh[315]

Immediate Cause: Trouble broke out on 23rd May in Moradabad when some women activists from Bhartiya Janata Party tried to capture the disputed land of Heut Muslim degree college. Police tried to prevent them. Instead of dispersing, these women pelted stones on the police as a result of which police had to resort to firing.

- *Number of persons injured*: 4
- *Other details not available*

Communal Riots in Calcutta, West Bengal[316]

Immediate Cause: Trouble broke out on 29th May, in Calcutta. This started when those taking out Tazia procession did not follow the allotted route and suddenly changed it. Police refused permission for the changed route as it was surrounded by Hindu dominated locality in a Muslim Island. The authorities tried their best to persuade the processionist but in vain. The processionists attacked the Rapid Action Force and the police. A mob of six hundred attacked Ekbalpur police station with stones, bombs and pipeguns. In Alipur area bombs were thrown.

- *Number of persons dead*: 6
- *Number of persons injured*: 30
- *Places affected*: Garden Reach, Ekbalpur, Watgunj and South port

Communal Riots in Darbhanga, Bihar[317]

Immediate Cause: Trouble broke out on 30th May, in Darbhanga town on the occasion of Muharram-Tazia procession. However, the police denied that the clash was related to the Tazia procession and described it as settling the personal scores.

- *Number of persons dead*: 2
- *Number of persons arrested:* 2
- *Other details not available*

Communal Riots in Shrivardhan in Raigad District, Maharashtra[318]

Immediate Cause: Trouble broke out on 7th June, in Shrivardhan after a scuffle between some Hindu and Muslim youths. The trouble was brought under control but two police platoons were posted as a precautionary measure.

- *Number of persons injured:* 12
- *Other details not available*

Communal Riots in Dehradun, UP[319]

Immediate Cause: Trouble broke out on 17th June, in Dehradun over the question of cow slaughter. The police were attacked and a lot of large scale arsoning took place.

- *Number of persons injured:* 17 (policemen)
- *Number of persons arrested:* 43

Communal Riots in Bhensa, Adilabad District, Andhra Pradesh[320]

Immediate Cause: Trouble broke out on 23rd September in Bhensa during Ganesh Visarjan procession when some Muslim youth threw stones on the Ganesh procession which was passing through an area where a mosque was situated. The stones were thrown as processionists disturbed the prayer and did not pass through quickly. The processionists went berserk and looted nearby shops and set them on fire. The police had to open fire when the mob frenzy could not be controlled by lathi charge.

- *Number of persons dead*:2
- *Number of persons injured:* 9
- *Loss of properties*: 14 shops were looted and burnt and completely destroyed.

Communal Riots in Pen, Maharashtra[321]

Immediate Cause: Trouble broke out on 26th September in Pen in Raigadh district, when the Ganesh procession was stopped in front of a mosque and the processionists continued to throw gulal (red vermillion) on the mosque and refused to move despite all the police efforts to persuade them failed and therfore the police opened fire.

- *Number of persons dead*: 4
- *Number of persons injured:* 2
- *Loss of properties*: Some Muslim houses, a dargah and a mosque were damaged.
- *Places affected*: Pen and Antorabunder

Highlights of Riot: Pen which had only a small Muslim population of 1.000 among 50,000 Hindus had not experienced any communal trouble before. The Hindu Muslim relations in town were generally cordial. The trouble was mainly caused by the Ganesh processionist who were dead drunk.

Note: The same type of violence on Ganesh procession happened at Junnar in Raigad district, where processionists threw gulal at a mosque, as a result of which there was stone throwing in which some people were injured but no one was killed.

Communal Riots in Lucknow, Uttar Pradesh[322]

Immediate Cause: Trouble broke out on 27th September in Lucknow when a Mandir was sought to be constructed adjacent to an old mosque in the old city in a narrow lane. The police fired to control the situation.

- *Number of person injured:* 1
- *Number of persons arrested:* 563 (Muslims)

Highlights of the riot: This happened on the eve of Uttar Pradesh election. One Bhartiya Janata Party leader who wanted to get the Hindu votes in his favour is said to have instigated this violence.

Communal Riots in Hyderabad[323]

Immediate Cause: Trouble broke out on 6th December, in Hyderabad, when a procession was taken out on the occasion of the fourth anniversary of the demolition of the Babri Masjid. When the trouble started, the police opened fire without giving any warning. Ahmad Asadullah a passer-by was killed in firing. He was hit by the bullet when he was going on his motor cycle.

- *Number of person dead:* 1
- *Number of persons injured:* 25
- *Number of persons arrested:* 50
- *Loss of properties*: 30 vehicles were burnt.

Communal Riots in Mulbal near Kolar, Karnataka[324]

Immediate Cause: Trouble broke out on 14th December, 1996, in Mulbal village in Kolar in Karnataka when a piece of pork was thrown inside a mosque. It was followed by violent demonstrations and clashes. The police opened fire to disperse the mob. The trouble came under control but the curfew continued for a couple of days.

- *Number of persons dead*: 3
- *Number of persons injured:* 20

1997

Communal Riots in Coimbatore, Tamil Nadu[325]

Immediate Cause: Trouble broke out on 28th January, in Coimbatore with the murder of one Ranganathan a local organiser of Hindu Merchants Association, affiliated to the Hindu Munnani at Pudapet. The murderers were suspected to be Muslim fundamentalists. About the same time two Bhartiya Janata Party leaders were also murdered in Dindigul.

- *Number of persons dead*: 6
- *Places affected*: Coimbatore, Triruppur, Keezhakarai, Palani and Dindigul

Communal Riots in Dhady in Buldhana District, Maharashtra[326]

Immediate Cause: Trouble broke out on 26th January in Dhady in Buldhana district of Maharashtra. The clashes between Hindus and Muslims occurred on the question of eve-teasing. When people were returning from the cultural programme on Republic day, some Muslim boys began teasing a Hindu girl. This led to group clashes between the two communities. Police resorted to firing to disperse the mob.

- *Number of persons dead*: 3; 2 in stabbing incidents and 1 (Muslim) in police firing
- Number of persons injured: 14 (1 injured in police firing)

Communal Riots in Patna, Bihar[327]

Immediate Cause: Trouble broke out on 23rd January in Patna in Bihar, when a Saraswati procession was attacked on Friday afternoon by some anti-social elements which led to Hindu-Muslim clashes in which one State Telephone Department booth owner, a Muslim, was killed. Again the clashes occurred when his body was taken for burial. In fact, the Muslims maintained that this procession was attacked because the Saraswati processionists were engaged in looting the Muslim shops near Sabzi Mandi and also indulged in eve-teasing.

- *Number of person dead:* 1
- *Other details not available*

Communal Riots in Hubli, Karnataka[328]

Immediate Cause: Trouble broke out on 20th March, in Hubli during Holi festival. The exact and the immediate cause of the riot not available.

- Number of persons killed: 4
- *Number of persons injured:* Several (The exact number of persons injured are not available).

Communal Riots in Belgaum, Karnataka[329]

Immediate Cause: Trouble broke out on 24th March in Belgaum in Karnataka when a group of people after playing Holi went to a well for a bath. One of them lost his gold chain and the group assaulted four youths belonging to a particular community (*i.e.*, Muslim) suspecting them to be thieves.

- *Number of persons dead*: 4 (1 in police firing)
- *Number of persons injured:* Several (The exact number of persons injured are not available).

Communal Riots in Jammu[330]

Immediate Cause: Trouble broke out on 25th March in Jammu when an altercation broke out over the massacre issue of seven Kashmiri Pandits in the valley which had taken place seven days before the incident and the police firing on 25th March against the demonstrators in the city. This led to looting and arsoning and disruption of vehicular movement.

- *Number of persons injured:* 228
- *Number of persons arrested:* 27
- *Loss of properties*: 1 shop and 1 State road transport corporation bus was burnt.
- *Places affected*: Sherkhani and Subhashnagar

Communal Riots in Mathura, Uttar Pradesh[331]

Immediate Cause: Trouble broke out on 26th March, in Mathura due to the stabbing of a Hindu youth by a notorious Muslim criminal on 25th March. Police interfered with lathi charges and bursted tear gas shells. This happened in a slum where the scavengers—Valmiki community people lived side by side with Muslim fishing community. The riot broke-out after Jaffer, a Muslim youth in an inebriated condition quarrelled with Pappu from Valmiki community, who was also drunk. Jaffar, a petty criminal, against whom there were 16 registered cases, stabbed Pappu on the thighs who bled to death. Soon there was violence and stone throwing next day when Pappu's body was being taken for cremation. Trouble broke-out once again when some one fired and a person named Arjun died.

- *Number of persons dead*: 2
- *Number of persons injured:* 21
- *Places affected*: Macchli Mandi and Bharatpur Gate

Communal Riots in Shahid Nagar near Delhi[332]

Immediate Cause: Trouble broke out on 6th April, in Shahid Nagar near Delhi. It started with a dispute about a piece of land adjacent to a place of worship. Some people were trying to construct a wall on that, which resulted in communal clashes and the police had to resort to firing. The police tried every thing to stop the violence. The construction of wall was stopped. The local people alleged that the policemen entered their houses and broke them and molested their women but the police denied this and said they had entered some houses to arrest suspected people.

- *Number of persons injured:* 8 (1 Superintendent of police and 7 policemen)
- *Number of persons arrested:* 49

Communal Riots in Mohammadpur, Kamrahia area of Laksar in Roorkee District, Uttar Pradesh[333]

Immediate Cause: Trouble broke out on 19th May, in Muhammadpur. The trouble started after members of a particular community objected to the procession being taken out by the other community. The communities involved were Hindus and Muslims.

- *Number of person dead:* 1 (a teenager was shot)
- *Number of persons injured:* 8 persons were injured (7 with bullet injuries and one policemen was pulled out of his Jeep and stabbed when he was taking some of the injured to hospital)
- Number of persons arrested; 40

Communal Riots in Rajpalayam, Tamil Nadu[334]

Immediate Cause: Trouble broke out on 22nd June, in Rajapalayam in Tamil Nadu. The riot sparked off when the convoy of vehicles in which leaders of a community were touring the riot hit villages, were attacked by miscreants.

- *Number of persons dead*: 3
- *Number of persons injured:* 13
- Loss of Property: 5 huts and a van set ablaze in Desikapuram

Communal Riots in Bangalore, Karnataka[335]

Immediate Cause: Trouble broke out on 17th September, in Bangalore over the Idgah property which led to rioting. The disputed Idgah property lies in the middle of Jayanagar, a posh and elitist locality in Bangalore. This Idgah is surrounded by a bus stand on two sides and houses and shops on other sides, besides four urinals are attatched to the wall. One part of the Idgah is used as burial grounds and in another part *namaz* is offered in a makeshift mosque. This Idgah property was donated to Wakf Board in 1935 by the then Maharaja of the princely state. Since then there was hardly any Muslim living there in the vicinity of Jayanagar Mutavalli or custodian from Basavangudi. But later the

Muslims from Jayanagar demanded that the property be handed over to them to construct a mosque for prayers. This was resented and this later went to court. Later, the corporation demanded the portion of land from Idgah to broaden the main road. The Muslims were prepared to hand over to the corporation the piece of land. The court then gave the order that their possession cannot be disturbed except in due course of law. The problem got aggravated when Muslims not only formed the youth forum but also started digging a bore well inside the Idgah property. A stone thrown from no where triggered the controversy which sparked off the riot.

- *Number of persons dead*: 5 (police constable Satyanarayana was lynched by a mob; bus passenger Kreshappa Reddy died of shock following an attack on the vehicle; Irfan and Kaleem Pasha died in police firing)
- *Number of persons injured:* 83
- *Number of persons arrested:*100
- *Loss of properties*: 2 petrol bunks, 12 Bangalore Municipal buses, 34 private vehicles, were damaged and destroyed. Cloth shops, jewellery shops, a pawn broker shop were looted.

Communal Riots in Hyderabad, Andhra Pradesh[336]

Immediate Cause: Trouble broke out on 17th October in Hyderabad when a Hindu mob attacked a Muslim religious procession. The attack took place during an annual procession to mark the death of Muslim Saint Hussain Shah Nali. The policemen accompanying the procession could not control the fighting between two groups and fled. The attackers, according to the police threw glass bottles and stones at the procession. Some were even armed with swords. The attack was certainly unprovoked.

- *Number of persons injured:* 20
- *Other details not available*

Communal Riots in Khampurban, Sambhal, Uttar Pradesh[337]

Immediate Cause: Trouble broke out on 21st October in Khampurban, Sambhal, in Uttar Pradesh. The clashes erupted when members of a particular community objected to opening a ration shop in the village by the district administration.

- *Number of persons dead*: 24

- *Loss of properties*: Some places of worships were damaged.

Communal Riots in Nagar Deola in Pachora Taluka of Jalgaon District, Maharashtra[338]

Immediate Cause: Trouble broke out on 14th November in Nagar Deola in Jalgaon district when a procession of Lord Balaji's disciples was stoned near a mosque. The police had to fire nine rounds in the air to disperse the mob.

- *Number of persons injured:* 50
- *Loss of properties*: Five shops were burnt down

Communal Riots in Osmania University, Hyderabad[339]

Immediate Cause: Trouble broke out on 15th November in Osmania University campus in Hyderabad between two groups when a religious pankha procession passing through the campus allegedly indulged in provoking the passers-by and bursting crackers. Eye-witness said that the processionists threw crackers on girl students waiting at the bus stop. When some male students objected, the processionists chased them with lathis and rods. This was the after effect of an incident a few months earlier, in which an Akhil Bhartiya Vidya Parishad student was murdered in the campus.

- *Number of person dead:* 1
- Number of persons injured;-Several (the exact number of persons injured not available)

Communal Riots in Coimbatore, Tamil Nadu[340]

Immediate Cause: Trouble broke out on 29th November in Coimbatore when a traffic constable charged two Muslim fundamentalists belonging to Al-ulama for violating traffic rules and took them to police station. They raised hue and cry but police officers pacified them and let them go. On their way back, they were again booked by a traffic constable for traffic rule violations. They stabbed the constable and ran away. The policeman died. The Hindu Munnai and Hindu People's Party workers gathered in numbers in government hospital where the dead body was kept. They attacked Dravida Munnetra Kazham party legislator C.T. Dhandapani and set his car on fire. Dhandapani was admitted to the hospital with serious head injuries. The riots soon sparked off, with attack from both sides and on 1.30 at night police firing also took place. In the mean time, a large section of the police struck work in protest against the killing of the constable.

- *Number of persons dead*: 23 (3 persons died in police firing, and 1 Muslim was burnt alive)
- *Number of persons arrested:* 200

Serial bomb blasts in Tamil Nadu[341]

Immediate Cause: Trouble again broke out in Tamil Nadu on 6th December, the day on which Babri Masjid had been demolished. Some Muslim extremists planted bombs on three trains starting from Chennai, namely Chennai-Madurai Pandiyan Express, Chennai–Coimbatore Cheran Express and Chennai–Alleppey Express.

- *Number of persons dead*: 50
- *Number of persons injured:* 70

Communal Riots in Hyderabad, Andhra Pradesh[342]

Immediate Cause: Trouble broke out on 5th December, in Hyderabad following the call for *"Bandh"* given by several organisations protesting against the Babri Masjid demolition five years earlier. One youth was stabbed by an un-identified assailant, while a woman, standing on the terrace of her house, died when she was hurt by a stray bullet fired by police to disperse a rioting mob in Talabkatta area. When the funeral procession of the firing victim was being taken out from her residence fresh trouble broke out. While returning from the funeral, the mourners grew restive and indulged in stone pelting for more than 30 minutes. Police used tear-gas to disperse the crowds.

- *Number of persons dead*: 2
- *Number of persons injured:* A few police personnel including special branch Deputy Commissioner of Police, Umapathy, sustained minor injuries.

Communal Riots in Jaipur, Rajasthan[343]

Immediate Cause: Trouble broke out on 15th December in Shastri Nagar in Jaipur in Rajasthan between two sections of Muslims which ended with police firing. Some Muslims had constructed unauthorised stalls on a cemetery land and when Wakf board officials came to inspect, there was stone throwing which led to mob violence. Police resorted to firing. The Muslim leaders alleged that the police and anti-Muslims were waiting for an opportunity to kill Muslims. They demanded suspension of the District Collector and Superintendent of police and held them responsible for the tragedy.

- *Number of persons dead*: 6 (in police firing)
- *Number of persons injured:* Several (the exact number of persons injured is not available)

Communal Riots at Parbhani, Maharashtra[344]

Immediate Cause: Trouble broke out on 19th December at Parbhani, Maharashtra, when a clash between two different communities occurred over a land dispute in Borvan village. The report said that the case about the disputed land was in the court which had delivered its judgment recently in favour of one of the two communities. A large number of people belonging to a particular community against whom the court decision had gone, assembled at the land and proposed to construct a memorial of Ahilyabai Holkar and a temple of Ambaji which led to the clash.

- *Number of persons dead*: 2
- *Number of persons injured:* 4
- Number of persons arrested: 24

1998

Communal Riots in Daulatpur in Bulandshahar, Uttar Pradesh[345]

Immediate Cause: Trouble broke out on 4th January in Daulatpur. According to officials in Bulandshahar, the clashes took place when the village chief, Abdul Ghafoor, objected to the construction of a kuteeha bye-lane by one Satvir. When Satvir and his men refused to stop the construction work, Ghafoor's sons attacked Satvir's family members. It resulted in brick batting and firing and developed into a full scale violence.

- *Number of persons dead*: 2 (One Hindu and one Muslim)
- *Number of persons injured:* 4
- *Number of persons arrested:* 6 (which includes Abdul Ghafoor, the village Chief)

Communal Riots near Jama Masjid, Delhi[346]

Immediate Cause: Trouble broke out on 18th January in Jama Masjid area when the clash occurred between two sects of Sunni Muslims near Jama Masjid. People belonging to Deobandi Sect were attending a religious meeting inside the Masjid. When they came out they were given hand bills by a man belonging to the Barelvi Sect. The hand bill criticised the methodology of worship adopted by the Deobandi Sect. Enraged by the contents, the Deobandi sect members tore the handbill and entered into argument with the man. The Barelvi member left but returned with a few persons belonging to the sect. There was an altercation between people belonging to two sides which led to assault between the sects.

- *Number of persons dead*: 2
- *Number of persons injured:* 4
- *Number of persons arrested:* 24

Communal Riots in Kanpur, Uttar Pradesh[347]

Immediate Cause: Trouble broke out on 10th January, in Kanpur. It all started with the beating of an Imam of a Mosque. When followers of the Imam demanded the arrest of the concerned person clashes took place. Police rushed to the place to control the situation. As usual, some miscreants disconnected the light, and people thought it was the handiwork of the police and attacked them. Police had to fire in the air. According to the police the clashes were in the context of the Lok-Sabha elections, which were to take place. Muslims of Kanpur alleged that the BJP and their front organisations were terrorising them.

Other details not available

Communal Riots and Bomb Blasts, Coimbatore[348]

Immediate Cause: Trouble broke out on 14th February in Coimbatore when the bomb blast took place. The main target of attack was Shri L.K. Advani, whose flight had got delayed. The time bomb went off. It was alleged that the blast was organised by the Al-ulama and Al-Jihad organisation who were aided and abetted by the ISI of Pakistan.

- *Number of persons arrested:* 500 (including the president of Al-ulama Basha and Al-Jihad committee president, Afzal Khan)

Political angle of the riot: According to the CPI (M) Polit Bureau member R. Umanath, Bhartiya Janata Party and the All India Anna Dravida Munetra Khazam elements fanned communal hatred after the blast. He further alleged in his statement that "to wreak communal vengeance on the minority community, organised gangs of the Bhartiya Janata Party (BJP) and All India Anna Dravida Munetra Khazam (AIDMK) have indulged in mass scale shop breaking, looting and torching shops. Also to wreak political vendetta on Dravida Munetra Khazam and Communist Party of India (CPI-M) these gangsters have resorted to destruction of the offices of their parties and properties and houses of the supporters of the Dravida Munetra Khazam, Communist Party of India (Marxist) and Tamil Indira Congress (TIC).

Communal Riots in Ajmer, Rajasthan[349]

Immediate Cause: Trouble broke out on 17th February in Ajmer, Rajasthan. The cause of the rioting was not clear but it seems that it was the result of clash between the shop keepers and some customers. There are shops owned by the majority community just out side the Dargah and houses of minority community. The shops and houses were set alight by miscreants. A memorandum was presented to Prime Minister by the Khuddam (Servants) of Dargah who alleged that police entered the Dargah with their shoes on and lathi charged the people offering prayers. They alleged that rioting was incited by some communal elements among shop keepers outside the Dargah.

- *Number of persons injured:* 56 (more than 20 policemen including SP)
- *Number of persons arrested:* 16
- *Loss of properties*: Houses, Scooters, Autos, Jeeps, Cycles and Shops were looted and burnt.

Note: Ajmer is the place where famous Sufi Saint Hazrat Moinuddin Chishite is buried. Sufis always believed the doctrine of Sulh-i-Kul, *i.e.*, peace with all. This incident shows how communally sensitive situation can set even such towns a flame.

Communal Violence in Ferozabad, Uttar Pradesh[350]

Immediate Cause: Trouble broke out on 17th Februay in Ferozabad in Uttar Pradesh. It started with a dispute between a bangle seller and a buyer belonging to different communities and later the emotionally surcharged mob began setting fire to houses and shops.

- *Number of persons injured:* 10
- *Other details not available*

Communal Riots in Nagaon village of Chittorgarh District, Rajasthan[351]

Immediate Cause: Trouble broke out on 4th April in Nagaon village when some people attacked a youth of a different community with weapons, leading to his death.

- *Number of persons dead*: 3
- *Number of persons injured:* Several (the exact number of persons injured not available)

Communal Riots in Pune, Maharashtra[352]

Immediate Cause: Trouble broke out on 19th April in Pune in Maharashtra after the boisterous Shiv Jayanti celebrations. Tension had also prevailed since early morning after attempts were made by some to burn a Shiv Sena water booth. In the afternoon a youth was attacked with swords.

- *Number of persons injured:* 5

Violence also erupted at the Ad camp chowk when some miscreants threw a burning sack on the streets and phoned up the fire brigade and police as false alarm.

Communal Riots in Moradabad Uttar Pradesh[353]

Immediate Cause: Trouble broke out on 9th May in Moradabad. It began with the attack on a Moharram Taziah procession allegedly by some of the BJP supporters. It is said that trouble started when some one threw an acid bomb on the procession. The situation became so tense that the district administration had to bring in the Rapid Action Force to control the situation along with enforcement of indefinite curfew. In fact because of communal tensions the procession could not be taken out on previous day and was instead taken out on 9th May, a day after the 10th day of Muharram.

- *Number of persons dead*: 3
- *Number of persons injured:* 50
- *Number of persons arrested:* 250
- *Loss of properties*: 6 Rickshaws were burnt, 12 shops were looted and a number of houses were burnt and looted.

Communal Riots in Hyderabad, Andhra Pradesh[354]

Immediate Cause: Trouble broke out on 5th June, when the Muslim mob coming out of the mosque near the Charminar after the Friday prayers went berserk and attacked shops in the area. It started after circulation of a mysterious pamphlet lampooning the religious sentiments of Muslims. The violence continued on the second day also and areas under 13 police stations had to be put under curfew. The situation was so serious that the Army had to be alerted and the Home Ministry was urged to send the para-military forces.

- *Number of persons dead*: 8. (1police sub-inspector, who was shot dead and 1 woman stabbed to death by unruly mobs)
- *Number of persons injured:* 36. (16 in police firing and several persons suffered serious injuries either in stabbing or stone pelting incidents)
- *Loss of properties*: 15 houses, shops and vehicles were burnt, and the rioters prevented fire brigade from entering the area. A mob of about 500 persons raided Bhavaninagar police-station and ransacked it completely.

Communal Riots in Bangalore, Karnataka[355]

Immediate Cause: Trouble broke out in Bangalore when members of one community hoisted a flag on an illegal flag-post in the area. They refused to bring it down despite protests by the members of another community. In the afternoon the unruly elements belonging to both groups converged near the pole and had heated arguments. Around 3 p.m. they brought down the pole and destroyed the flag. *The exact date of the riot not available.*

- *Number of persons dead*: 6
- *Loss of properties*: 12 vehicles were burnt.
- *Other details not available*

Communal Riots in Bardoli, Gujarat[356]

Immediate Cause: Trouble broke out in July in Bardoli district in Gujarat. Vishwa Hindu Parishad and Bajrang Dal activists began to terrorise Muslims in Bardoli just because some Muslim boys had married tribal girls. They were terrorised to such an extent that the Muslims had to flee from those villages. *The exact date of the riot not available.*

Background: Bhartiya Janata Party had lost seats in tribal belts and their activists were trying to garner the tribal support for the Bhartiya Janata Party through such tactics. They held Dharma Sabhas in tribal villages and after every dharma sabha, Muslim shops and houses were looted and burnt. The police were passive. Trishuls and swords were flashed openly when Hindu organisations took out rally to protest Muslims marrying tribals. It was alleged that Muslim youths were given special training (how to attract Hindu girls) at Madrassas in Dabhel, Ahmadabad, Bharuch and other places. The Bhartiya Janata Party spokesperson claimed that " We don't have the proof yet, but a trust in Ajmer gives Rs. One lakh for enticing a married Hindu woman and Rs. 50,000 for an unmarried girl ". But it is such misinformation campaign which ultimately leads to communal violence.

Rajkot Incidents: The Christians were targeted in Rajkot. Sangh Parivar burnt some 200 copies of the Bible, distributed to school children, saying that these copies were being distributed among students with a view to convert them. One church building was attacked and a dead body of the Christian was exhumed and thrown away on the pretext that the cemetery land belonged to Hindus.

Communal Violence in Sanjeli town in Dahod District, Gujarat[357]

Immediate Cause: Trouble broke out on 18th August in Sanjeli town in Dahod district of Gujarat during Janmashtami. It started out due to a quarrel between two communities over fishing rights in a pond. Till the last month, the fishing rights were vested in a local Muslim youth, Altaf, but the contract was not renewed after it expired. The tribals went fishing in the pond to which Altaf objected and they pelted stones at each other. Then stones were thrown on Janmashtami procession and the riot broke-out. The police fired on the violent mob.

Background: In the month of July there was an alleged kidnapping of two tribal women including a married one by two Muslim youths who belonged to Sanjelli village and the women belonged to Randhikpur village. The State Minister of Home, Haren Pandya, maintained that the trouble in Sanjelli was unrelated to this incident.

- *Number of persons injured:* 2

Communal Riots in Nasik, Maharashtra[358]

Immediate Cause: Trouble broke out on 12th September in Nasik. It started with a minor quarrel regarding the parking of a Jeep. A mob ransacked shops belonging to the Muslim community. One girl was crushed to death in the stampede. She belonged to Muslim community. Muslims refused to bury the girl until the rioters were arrested. However, the police and politicians appealed to the agitators not to aggravate the situation. It was only after that the girl was buried. According to Babu Shaukh Mansuri, anti-social elements and hooligans affiliated to political parties began rioting, terrorising the people of a particular community. It was also told to the investigators that on 11th September a procession was taken out under the leadership of the president of Municipality Vijay Wagh. The participants in the procession were shouting anti-Muslim slogans and stopped the procession in a Muslim locality and stoned the Muslim houses.

- *Number of person dead:* 1
- *Loss of properties*: A hotel belonging to a Muslim and a few houses of Muslims destroyed.

Communal Riots in Nalanda and Munger, Bihar[359]

Immediate Cause: Trouble broke out on 2nd October, in Nalanda and Munger in Bihar. According to some people present on the scene, several rounds were fired from both sides and even bombs were hurled. One company of Reserved Action Force and two companies of Central Reserve Police Force had to be rushed to control situation. Hit and run tactics were employed by anti-social elements from both sides. Thus communal tensions gripped the town for several days. One Ajay Yadav was killed in firing by a Muslim miscreant Chunnu. In retaliation 15 minutes later, a Muslim was shot dead by Hindus. And on the same day in another part of the town one person named Ikram was beheaded by some Hindu miscreants. Pappu Khan, an allegedly anti-Social element who was a town president of Rashtriya Janata Dal in Bihar Sharif was provoking Muslims.

- *Number of persons dead*: 4
- *Number of persons injured:* 29
- *Other details not available*

Communal Riots in Biharsharif, Bihar[360]

Immediate Cause: Trouble broke out on 3rd October when processionists shouted slogans during procession to immerse goddess Durga's idol after the pooja.

- *Number of persons dead*: 3
- *Number of persons injured:* 3
- Other details not available

Communal Riots in Ramanathapuran, Tamil Nadu[361]

Immediate Cause: Communal riot broke out on 3rd October over a dispute relating to Ayodhya pooja.

The exact and the immediate cause and the communities involved in the conflict not available.

- *Number of persons dead*: 8
- *Loss of properties*: A number of houses set on fire
- *Other details not available*

Communal Riots in Suratkal, Mangalore[362]

Immediate Cause: Communal riot broke out in Suratkal town, Mangalore, (Karnataka) over the police inaction against miscreants belonging to a community who had indulged in eve teasing in Suratkal. *The exact date of the riot not available.*

- *Number of persons dead*: 8
- Number of persons Injured: 60

Highlight of the Riot: Many Hindus had provided protection to Muslims in Tadambailn, Dodak oppala and other places. Muslims had prevented fundamentalists from attacking Hindu families in Chokabettu and Krishnapura.

Communal Riots in Surat, Gujarat[363]

Immediate Cause: Trouble broke out on 25th December in Surat when an altercation broke out between the members of the Christian community and those taking part in Hindu Dharamajagran Manch.

- *Number of persons injured:* 43
- *Other details not available*

Communal Riots in Purnea, Bihar[364]

Immediate Cause: Trouble broke out on 15th December in Purnea due to a 20 year old dispute, when an angry mob burnt alive 6 lakh tribals. The incident occurred after a land lord, claimed to be the rightful owner of the disputed plot of land, began ploughing the field using his tractor. This infuriated the tribals, who killed him after firing an arrow. They then set fire to his tractor and dumped in the fire.

- *Number of persons dead*: 6
- *Loss of properties*: 75 houses were burnt

Communal Riots in Suratkal, Mangalore District, Karnataka[365]

Immediate Cause: Trouble broke out on 8th December in Mangalore district of Karnataka over an eve-teasing incident involving a Hindu girl and a Muslim boy. The Muslim youth was bashed up by the Hindus and as a result three of them were arrested. The Hindu Jagran Vedike organised a big crowd at the police station demanding the release of those arrested. Later, in the last week of December 1998 communal violence broke out in which Muslims suffered a great deal and it continued up to 8th January, 1999.

Attack against Christians in Gujarat

On 13th January 1999 a church in Lamancharia village of Dangs district was damaged when unidentified miscreants tried to set it ablaze. The situation became so serious that it warranted the visit by the Prime Minister, and from here the Prime minister called for a national debate on conversion. He later maintained that he did not mean debate but a dialogue on conversion.

1999

Communal Riots in Ahmedabad[366]

Immediate Cause: Trouble broke out on 16th January on the issue of kite flying. It started on 15th January with an argument between two groups of local boys over flying kites leading to uneasiness. Later, a young boy of a particular community entered the place of worship of another community while running after a falling kite. A group of people chased kite fliers and reportedly assaulted them. It took a few minutes for the situation to get out of control. By 5 p.m., it took the shape of a communal riot when people from one community started attacking the residences of the other.

- *Number of persons injured:* 25 (including 5 policemen)
- Places affected: Kalupur and Dariapur

Communal Violence in Seelampur, Delhi[367]

Immediate Cause: Trouble broke out on 19th January in Seelampur in Delhi when students of Hindi and Urdu schools fought on a wooden piece landing on the cricket ground. Heated arguments, followed by scuffling finally led to a man badly beaten-up. This was enough for both sides to get agitated as the two communities clashed with each other and people came out from each by-lane, and pelted stones and bottles at the crowd on the other side. Police had to fire 21 gun shots in air to bring the situation to an uneasy calm. The clashes here occurred mainly between Muslims and low caste Valmikis.

- *Number of persons injured:* 2

Graham Staines Case

A more shocking incident took place in Manoharpur village in Kenonjihar in Orrissa, on 22nd January 1999. An Australian born Christian Missionary Graham Staines was burnt alive along with his two children. Dara Singh, a VHP activist took a leading role in this ghastly killing. The incident shocked the entire nation. But the VHP and Bajrang Dal denied their involvement.

Communal Riots in Surendra Nagar and Songadh, Gujarat[368]

Immediate Cause: Trouble broke out in Surendra Nagar and

Songadh in Gujarat when a Muslim Dargah came under attack by the militant Hindus in Kotari village in Surendranagar district. In Songadh, a group said to be of Bajarang Dal activists was alleged to have set fire to some shops belonging to Muslims in Songadh town in retaliation to the assault reported on some of their colleagues. The Sangh Parivar, however had denied the involvement of the Bajrang Dal in the Songadh incident which occurred a day after the Congress (I) took out a rally in neighbouring Vyara town expressing solidarity with the minority communities. It is quite encouraging to note that the local Hindus in Lothari village joined hands with the administration to rebuild the Dargah demolished by the Bajarang Dal activists.(the exact date of the riot not availale)

Communal Riots in Kodala, Gujarat[369]

Trouble broke out in Kodala on 5th March during the Holi festival.

- *Number of persons injured:* 23

Communal Riots in Ranali Village in Gajapati, Orissa[370]

Immediate Cause: Trouble broke out on 16th March, in Berhampur between Christians and others. Clashes occurred after a Cross carved on a hillock, was tampered by miscreants on 15th March.

- *Number of persons injured:* 12
- Loss of Property: 157 houses burnt and a Jeep of a Block Development Officer damaged

Communal Riots in Ahmedabad, Gujarat[371]

Immediate Cause: Trouble broke out on 29th March, on the occasion of Mahavir Jayanti and Id-ul-Adha, *i.e.*, during Id festival when Muslims sacrificed animals as part of their religious ritual. The dispute arose on the question of animal slaughter. One person, whom the Bjarang Dal said was its activist, was stabbed to death at around midnight. He was reported to be accompanying the vehicle carrying the animals for sacrificial rites. Another youth was stabbed to death in Paldi area. Tension prevailed in many areas of the walled city in Ahmedabad.

- *Number of persons dead*: 2

Communal Riots in Lakhanwara, Maharashtra[372]

Immediate Cause: Trouble broke out on 26th April in Lakhanwar town of Buldana district in Maharashtra which witnessed communal flare-up. A Shiv-Jayanti procession happened to pass by the Jama Masjid during the evening (*maghrib*) prayer. Processionists raised piercing cries, threw colours on the mosque and the adjoining mausoleum. Stones were thrown by those in procession. The procession went haywire after that. They came to bus stand, looted and set fire to Muslim shops.

- *Loss of properties*: Properties worth Rs. 5 lakh destroyed

Communal Violence in Phulpur Village in Moradabad District, Uttar Pradesh[373]

Immediate Cause: Trouble broke out on 27th April (the day of Muharram) when a mosque was demolished by Hindu fundamentalist. There was large scale firing, and attack on Muslim and their properties. The steps taken by Government to restore normalcy in Phulpur was quite inadequate. Police failed to arrest even half of the 53 persons accused in the riots.

- *Number of persons dead*: 2
- *Number of persons injured:* 21
- Loss of Property: 60-70 Muslim homes attacked and a mosque demolished

Communal Riots in Shahabad Tehsil of Rampur District in Uttar Pradesh[374]

Immediate Cause: Trouble broke out on 27th April in Shahabad on the occasion of Tazia procession.

There was large scale looting and arsoning.

The exact and the immediate cause involved in the conflict are not available.

- *Number of person dead:* 1
- *Number of persons injured:* 2
- Loss of Property: 51 shops were looted and set on fire.

Highlights of the Riot: The state president of Indian Union Muslim League, Syed Shakil Miyan, alleged that it was not a Hindu Muslim riot but rather it was looting and terrorising by some goondas with the connivance of the police who had prior knowledge. He alleged that it was for this reason that the police remained mute spectators when looting and burning incidents were taking place. He said that he was told by Hindus and Muslims that despite such widespread looting the Hindus and Muslims remained attached to each other and shared each other sufferings.

Communal Riots in Madurai, Tamil Nadu[375]

Immediate Cause: Trouble broke out on 7th June in Madurai in Tamil Nadu in retaliation to burning of shops on 6th June.

- *Number of persons arrested:*16
- *Loss of properties*:15 houses looted

Communal Riots in Rampur, Uttar Pradesh[376]

Immediate Cause: Trouble broke out on 27th April in the Shahbad Tehsil of Rampur district during a Tazia procession.

- *Number of persons injured:* 3
- *Loss of properties*: 51 shops looted

Communal Riots in Lakhnwara, Uttar Pradesh[377]

Immediate Cause: Trouble broke out during the procession of Shiv-Jayanti. Hindus were permitted to take out the said procession by the district administration on 26th April. The time allowed was between 1 p.m. and 6 p.m. The procession happened to pass by the Jama Masjid during the evening prayer with the mosque being situated on the one end of the city. Revellers in the procession threw colours, raised piercing cries, threw colours on the Mosque and burst crackers.

Communal Riots in Paharganj town of Rai Bareilly, Uttar Pradesh[378]

Immediate Cause: Trouble broke out on 30th April in Paharganj town in Rai Bareilly district on the question of a disputed religious place. There were stone throwing incidents, burning and setting fire to shops.

- *Number of persons dead*: 2
- *Number of persons injured:* 20

Communal Riots in Kheoli town of Barabanki District, Uttar Pradesh[379]

Immediate Cause: Trouble broke out on 15th May in Kheoli town on the alleged provocation of cow slaughter, when a horde of over 1,000 armed men surrounded the area and set houses on fire. The hamlet has over 40 homes, and out of that 31 homes were reduced to ashes. All the Muslims of these dwellings are poor daily wage workers. The situation was prevented from going bad to worse by timely action of the police and administration.

- *Loss of properties*: 31 homes burnt to ashes

Recovery of Bombs in Tamil Nadu[380]

On 30th May bombs were recovered from, Chennai, Tiruchi and Coimbatore. There was also an explosion at a students hostel. Hand bills at the site in the name of Al-Ulama alleged torture and ill treatment of Muslim fundamentalists in Jails and condemned the police. However Chief minister of Tamil Nadu K. Karunanidhi refuted the charges and warned that the National Security Act would be used if necessary, to take action against the extremists.

- *Number of persons arrested:* 334 (as a preventive measure)

Communal Riots in Harda, Madhya Pradesh[381]

Immediate Cause: Trouble broke out on 1st July in Harda when a communal mob confronted the police in which the deputy Superintendent of Police was killed and several policemen were injured.

- *Number of person dead:* 1
- *People Injured*: Several (The exact number of persons injured not available)
- *Number of persons arrested:* 90

Communal Riots in Idar town in Sabarkantha District, Gujarat[382]

Immediate Cause: Trouble broke out on 15th July in Idar when a *Rath Yathra* procession was passing near the religious place. The slogans and counter slogans started. Many shops were subsequently looted and goods worth several lakhs were set on fire. As Idar did not have fire fighting facilities fire brigade from Ahmedabad and Himmatnagar were rushed.

- Number of persons injured: 8
- *Number of persons arrested:* 111
- *Loss of properties*: More than 35 shops and 62 three wheelers set ablaze.

Communal Riots in Ahmedabad[383]

Immediate Cause: Trouble broke out on 20th July, when a mentally unstable boy was teased. The riot spread to several parts of the city. Groups came out on the road and looted shops, burnt properties and stabbed people. From Jalampur chawl area, about 300 Muslim families were forced to flee and take refugee elsewhere.

- *Number of persons dead*: 8
- *Places affected:* Dariapur, Kalupur and Saraspur

Back ground of 20th July riot: The rath yatra of Lord Jagannath taken out on 14th July, 1999, soured the relations between the two communities. When this yatra passed through Muslim localities provocative slogans " *Maktian chor - Mian chor (Muslims are thieves)* and *"Musalman, Jao Pakistan"* (Muslims go to Pakistan) etc. were raised. They also distributed pamphlets alleging that Muslims seduced Hindu girls and hoodwinked them. However, the reports indicate the Muslims, particularly Muslim women tried to express their good will for rath yatra to prevent any untoward incident. The Muslims also prayed for communal harmony. Some Muslims on 13th July even visited Jagannath temple and presented a cheque for Rs. 50,000 towards temple repair fund. Yet riot broke out on 20th July.[384]

Communal Riots in Nagercoil, Tamil Nadu[385]

Immediate Cause: Trouble broke out during Ganesh Chathurthi festival, organisers of the celebrations, placed an extra idol of Vinayaka at the site belonging to a Hindu. Some Christians raised objection. Despite elders in the Christian community advising restraints an aggrieved sections of them declined to keep cool, leading to the theft of the idols and an attack on the youth. This led to communal violence. *The exact date of the riot not available.*

- *Number of person dead:* 1

Communal Riots in Rajasthan[386]

Immediate Cause: Trouble broke out in Rajasthan due to the alleged attack on a group of "Kavadia yatris".

- *Number of persons arrested:*4
- Loss of property: Few shops burnt down

Communal Riots in Ahmedabad

Immediate Cause: Trouble broke out in Ahmedabad on 20th July after the Bhartiya Janata Party assumed power in Gujarat. The violence started with the world cup cricket matches and the Kargil conflict. There were when Pakistan was defeated by India and Australia. The were concentrated in Muslim area as if the town had been defeated. It was a crude attempt to equate the Muslim citizens of India with Pakistan. The conflict in Kargil sent off a chain of demonstrations and the burning of the effigies of Nawaz Sharief. There was a competition between two groups of people, who could be described as Hindus and Muslims — the Hindus to denounce the betrayal by Pakistan and the Muslim fundamentalists as if to declare their allegiance to the state.

- *Number of persons dead*: 8
- *Number of persons injured:*16
- *Number of persons arrested:* 35
- Number of *places affected:* Shahpur and Karanj areas, Dariyapur, Kalupur, Gomtipur and Bapunagar
- *Number of person killed*: On 21st July1999: 1 killed in Astodia area of Ahmedabad and 18 persons including 6 police men were injured in stabbing and stone throwing incidents. On 25th July: 2 persons died and 20 persons were injured. Kalupur, Khodia, Saraspur, ReliefRoad, Gandhi road and Panchpatti. 92 cases of stabbing incidents were reported, 2 persons died, 20 scooters and autorickshaws were burnt, 25 buildings and shops were put on fire. On 27th July: *Number of persons injured:* 20
- *Number of persons killed:* 4
- Rioters set ablaze a couple of Kisoks

Communal Violence in Rampur, Uttar Pradesh[387]

Immediate Cause: Trouble broke out resulting in Communal riot in the Shahbad Tehsil of Rampur district on 27th April during a Tazia procession.

The exact and the immediate cause not available.

- *Number of persons injured:* 3
- *Loss of properties*: 51 shops were looted

Communal Riots in Surat, Gujarat[388]

Immediate Cause: Trouble broke out on 24th September in Surat during the Ganpati procession. The dispute was about the route of the procession. The police refused permission to the processionists to pass through Madina Masjid area as they anticipated trouble. The processionists went on rampage and the police had to fire to control the revelers. The revelers also set fire to the house of Ravindra Patel, the president of Ganeshutsav committee.

- *Number of persons dead*: 7
- *Number of persons injured:* 34
- *Loss of properties*: The mob torched vehicles and huts in the Sanjayanagar area.

Communal Riots in Hyderabad, Andhra Pradesh[389]

Immediate Cause: Trouble broke out on 25th September, the day of Ganesh Chaturthi, when the Ganesh procession was to be taken out from the Mecca Masjid in the Charminar area during the Friday prayer. While passing through Charminar area the processionists were stoned allegedly by some Muslim youth from the mosque. It was alleged that the MIM (Majli's Ittehadul Muslemin) provoked the incident for its own political reasons. In an effort to disperse the crowd, the police, including the Rapid Action Force commenced lathi-charge, in which Owaisi of MIM and some of his supporters were injured. As the tension escalated in the old city, mobs gathered in lanes and by lanes, pelting stones which led the authorities to lob tear gas shells and firing in the air.

- *Number of persons injured:* 35
- *Loss of properties*: Signboards of shops belonging to a particular community, police vehicle, and some scooters damaged.

Communal Riots in Aurangabad, Maharashtra[390]

Immediate Cause: Trouble broke out in Aurangabad when a procession by members of Samajwadi Party and Muslim Kirti Samiti, to mark the 7th anniversary of the Babri-Masjid demolition turned violent, forcing the police to resort to lathi charge to disperse the media-persons outside the police commissionerate. *The exact date of the riot not available.*

- *Number of persons injured:*20
- *Other details not available*

Communal Riots in Gonda District, Uttar Pradesh[391]

Immediate Cause: Trouble broke out on 27th October in Gonda district when the majority community roasted one Muslim woman and her two children. It is said that one Subhanali gave the police the names of the culprits who were involved in the theft of a boring equipment. This was the beginning of communal tension in the village. Subhanali's wife and his two children of 2 and 5 years old were then burnt alive. The matter did not rest here. On 8th November 18 houses belonging to other Muslims in the village were burnt. Those people who set fire to these houses remained on the spot until everything was burnt. Most of these Muslims were labourers.

- *Number of persons dead*: 3
- *Loss of properties*: 18 houses belonging to the Muslims in the village burnt down.

Communal Riots in Nandurbar and Raver in Jalgaon District, Maharashtra[392]

Immediate Cause: Trouble broke out Nandurbar and Raver were under communal spell on 7th, 10th and 11th November. It started when two Muslim boys bumped into a Hindu boy. Some on-lookers there beat them up. Some other Muslim boys came and began pelting stones at the Hindu boys. In another incident on 11th November a Muslim youth threw a cigarette butt on a Hindu boy and trouble flared up. A big mob of 1,000-1,500 from Muslim side started pelting stones. The police had to resort to lathi charge and then to firing. The police maintained that Rasalpura is hypersensitive as there is widespread illiteracy and poverty, especially among the Muslims. The BJP MLA Eknath Khadse alleged that the Muslims have destroyed a temple. But the Muslims categorically denied this.

- *Number of person injured:* 1 (killed in police firing)
- *Number of persons arrested:* 130 (of which 124 were Muslims)

- *Loss of properties*: 6 houses out of which 4 belonged to Muslims destroyed. The total loss was to the tune of Rs.1,33,000 but the Muslims maintained that the losses were much higher than Rs.1,33,000.

Background: Investigating teams comprising several NGO's felt that this eruption was a result of systematic efforts to build up communal tension. On 4th November some crackers were found to be having papers on which the koranic verses were written. The police had seized these crackers. Such crackers using the paper with Koranic verses were again found in Cliopda town on 8th Nov. The Muslim boys looted the shops selling these crackers when no heed was taken despite warning. In September too there was a dispute about the play-ground and heavy stone pelting had taken place. A funeral procession was also stoned. The riots had taken place particularly in the lower class Muslim localities and the Muslim women narrated the atrocities to the police committed there. The investigating team felt that the police indulged in looting and loss was much higher than Rs. 1,33,000. Muslims felt that since they voted for the Congress, they suffered. It was also alleged that loud speakers were used in some mosques for provocative speeches by Muslim leaders. Chaggan Bhujbal, the then Deputy Chief Minister and Home Minister of Maharashtra ordered that hence forth prior permission will be needed to install loudspeakers in the mosque and if it was misused the permission will be cancelled.

Communal Riots in Aurangabad, Maharashtra[393]

Immediate Cause: Trouble broke out on 6th December in Aurangabad when the procession of Muslims and Samajwadi Party on the 7th anniversary of demolition of Babri Masjid was brutally lathi charged by the police. They had also permitted Shiv Sena to organise Maha Aarti. Just before Muslims took out procession to protest against demolition of Babri Masjid, Shiv Sena had flooded the whole area with saffron flags. The Police lathi charged the journalists who were covering the event and were not a part of the procession.

- *Number of person dead:* 1
- *Number of persons injured:* Several (the exact number of persons injured not available)

Communal Riots in Phalodi town of Jodhpur District, Rajasthan[394]

Immediate Cause: Trouble broke out on 21st December, in Jodhpur when some persons tried to stop transportation of cows loaded in Railway wagons for Bihar. They unloaded over 1,500 cows but were attacked by cow traders who were sending cattle herds to Bihar after purchasing them from cattle marts. Lathis, swords and even firearms were freely used. After this, protesters went out of control and damaged and burnt several shops and vehicles and uprooted several pumps at the near by petrol pumps.

- *Number of person dead:* 1
- *Number of persons injured:* 33
- *Number of persons arrested:* 7

2000

Communal Riots in Azamgarh, Uttar Pradesh[395]

Immediate Cause: Trouble broke out on 27th January, in Azamgarh Uttar Pradesh, when students from Shibli college affiliated to Akhil Bhartiya Vidyarthi Parishad began singing 'Vande Mataram' but other students refused to sing. The controversy took a dangerous turn when many persons were injured and many shops were looted and burnt. Para-military forces were deployed to contain the situation. The Senior Superintendent of Police of Azamgarh was transferred.

- *Number of persons dead*: 2
- *Number of persons injured:* Several (the exact number of persons injured not available)
- *Number of persons arrested:* 180

Communal Riots in Ahmedabad, Gujarat[396]

Immediate Cause: Trouble broke out on 5th February in Ahmedabad when a mob of about 40-50 people attacked the newly constructed five storeyed building, owned by a Muslim, in Viswakunj Society near National Institute of Design within Paldi area. The mob was shouting 'Jai Shri Ram'. They also threatened the care-taker of the building with dire consequences. The building was owned by Wasim Kothiwala.

- Loss of Property: The loss of property was upto Rs. 20 lakhs which included building and vehicles.

Background: Since Bharatiya Janata Party captured power in Gujarat the Vishwa Hindu Parishad and Bajrang Dal have become very bold and often indulged in vandalism against minorities and the police has remained a mute witness. Many people think that people should he encouraged to live in cosmopolitan areas to increase interaction between various religious communities but the Sangh Parivar biegots are preventing minorities from settling in Hindu dominated areas.

Communal Riots in Tonk, Rajasthan[397]

Immediate Cause: Trouble broke out on 20th February in Tonk district when some khatik (low caste) students of a government college and their local supporters allegedly demolished the Qalandari mosque killing a Muslim youth, injuring many people and damaging private and public property.

- *Number of persons arrested:* 25

Fresh disturbances broke out again in Tonk district on 12th July

- *Number of persons killed:*13
- *Number of persons injured:*3
- *Number of persons arrested:* 48
- Loss of property: Some houses and shops burnt and desecrated

Curfew was extended and three companies of Reserved Action Force had to be rushed for maintaining law and order.

Communal Riots in Nanded, Maharastra[398]

Immediate Cause: Trouble broke out in Aradhapur village in Nanded when people belonging to two religious communities clashed over a piece of land. The trouble erupted when a Muslim shop owner tried to raise a permanent structure on a piece of land claimed by Dhangar Samaj who were interested in building a temple there.

- *Loss of properties*: Twelve shops were burnt down

Communal Riots in Farrukhabad, Uttar Pradesh[399]

Immediate Cause: Trouble broke out on 19th March in Farrukhabad during Holi festival, when Hindu and Muslim communities clashed over the question of throwing colour by persons who were completely drunk.

- Number of persons killed:2

Communal Riots in Calcutta, West Bengal[400]

Immediate Cause: Trouble broke out in Calcutta in West Bengal when a group of people, completely drunk, were trying to throw colour on unwilling people of another community. When the police tried to prevent it from doing so they began pelting stones on the police.

- *Number of persons dead*: 2

Another incident took place in Hoogli district.

- *Number of person dead:*1

Another incident took place in the suburbs of Calcutta when 24 year old youth was killed as he objected to being smeared with colour.

- Number of person killed: 1

Communal Riots in Ghaziabad, Uttar Pradesh[401]

Immediate Cause: Trouble broke out in Ghaziabad in Uttar Pradesh when district administration did not permit bonfire of Holi on the disputed land. The Allahabad High Court had permitted Muslims to offer Eid prayers there but had not given any instructions about Holi bonfire. The police had to make strong arrangements to guard the place in view of communal tension in the town and any untoward incident was averted.

Communal Riots in Madhupur, Behraich District[402]

Immediate Cause: Trouble broke out in Madhupur village in Behraich district between Hindu and Muslim communities who clashed with each other, when one group tried to throw colour on Muslims who protested.

- *Number of persons injured:* 12
- *Number of persons arrested:* 15

Communal Riots in Sasaram, Bihar[403]

Immediate Cause: Trouble broke out on 19th April in Sasaram, between two groups of the same community over taking out the procession of Tazia. They exchanged heated words over the issue of taking out their procession and Ajhada of Tazia which was heading towards *karbala* for *chahlam* following which violence broke out at Navratan bazaar in the heart of the town.

- *Number of persons injured:* 24

Communal Riots in Varanasi, Uttar Pradesh[404]

Immediate Cause: Trouble broke out on 19th April in Varanasi following communal clashes between the two communities. A young man was attacked by a group of unidentified people, as he was passing through a Muslim neighbourhood. Following this, two communities clashed in the area leading to the fatal stabbing of a Hindu person who was merely passing through the area on his two wheeler. Miscreants hurled bombs in the curfew bound Telabagh area under Chetagunj police station. Schools and colleges were closed for two days in curfew bound areas and the intensive police patrolling brought the situation under control.

- *Number of persons killed*: 2 (1Hindu)
- *Number of persons injured:* 4 (including a policemen)
- *Number of persons arrested:* 61
- *Places affected:* Chetganj, Luxa, Dashmasumer Ghat, Chowk and Bhelupura

Communal Riots in Madhepura Ahmedabad, Gujarat[405]

Immediate Cause: Trouble broke out on 21st May in Madhepura when a person buying vegetables near the dhobi ghat crossroads was knifed under the left ear by the member of another community. When the victim's friend intervened, he too was knifed on the leg which led to the riot. Rival groups of two hundred each gathered on both sides and started pelting stones spreading arson and looting. Shops and vehicles in the area were set on fire. Police had to resort to tear-gas in order to disperse the rioting mobs.

- *Number of persons dead*:2 (in stabbing)
- *Number of persons injured:* 3 (including a police sub-inspector)
- *Loss of properties*: 3 shops, scooter and a hand-cart were also destroyed.
- *Places affected*: Madhepura, Dudheshwar

Communal Riots in Kopergaon Ahmednagar District, Maharashtra[406]

Immediate Cause: Trouble broke out on 25th May in Kopergaon in Ahmednagar on the question of eve-teasing near a Dargah and a temple. Hindu groups demanded that the Dargah be removed from there or they will install an idol near Idgah. Meanwhile some elements belonging to Shiv Sena and Bhartiya Janata Party began setting fire to Muslim shops. The Security Reserve Police Force had to be called to contol the rioting mobs and Article 144 was invoked to diffuse the situation.

- *Number of persons arrested:* 7
- *Loss of properties*: 3 bangle shops, 2 spare parts shops, 1 pan shop, 1 repair garage and 1 truck burnt down.

Communal Riots in Yamuna pushta, Delhi[407]

Immediate Cause: Trouble broke out on 24th June in Yamuna pushta, Delhi when a man was picked up by the police in connection with the recent blasts in old Delhi. Later, rumours spread that the police had desecrated the Holy Quran, an allegation which was denied by the police.

- *Number of persons dead*: 18
- *Number of persons injured:* 14
- *Loss of properties*: A police gypsy, 2 motorcycles burnt and completely destroyed.

Communal Riots in Guntur, Andhra Pradesh[408]

Immediate Cause: Trouble broke out on 26th June in Guntur in Andhra Pradesh following a bomb explosion in the mosque. No reports of violence were received after the curfew was imposed and no arrests were made in connection with the incident.

Chief Minister Chandrababu Naidu visited the blast site and announced the reward of Rs. 25 Lakhs to anybody providing information about the persons responsible for the attacks on religious institutions in the state. He also announced that additional police protection will be provided at all religious places belonging to minorities.

However, next day violence erupted in Guntur when groups of people went on rampage burning Andhra Pradesh State Road Transport Corporation buses and bus stations. Some trains were also detained at the Rapatla railway station.

- *Number of persons injured:* 3
- *Number of persons arrested:* 30
- *Places affected*: Kothapet, Lalapet, Mangalagiri, Rapatla, Tenali

Communal Riots in Malpura Tonk District, Rajasthan[409]

Immediate Cause: Trouble broke out on 10th July in Malpura village after the alleged killing of Kailash Mali who was accused in post—Babri Masjid demolition riots in December 1992.

- *Number of persons dead*: 6

Curfew was clamped in the area and two companies of PAC (Provincial Armed Constabulary) were deployed.

Fresh disturbances again broke out in Tonk district on 12th July.

- *Number of persons dead*: 10
- *Number of persons injured:* 4

Curfew was extended and three companies of Reserved Action Force had to be rushed in for maintaining law and order.

Communal Riots in Ahmedabad, Gujarat[410]

Immediate Cause: Trouble broke out in Kalupur, Dariapur, Jamalpur areas in Gujarat. These areas are always extremely fragile. Hindus and Muslims start fighting with each other for ordinary things. On 14th July situation became very tense over the rumour of one Muslim youth teasing a Hindu girl. Large mobs of more then 500 gathered on both sides and began pelting stones at each other. Police resorted to lathi charge, tear gas and firing in the air to disperse the mobs.

- *Number of persons arrested:* 26

Communal Riots in Ahmedabad, Surat, Rajkot, Palanpur, Gujarat[411]

Immediate Cause: Trouble broke out in certain parts of Gujarat when Vishwa Hindu Parishad gave a call for *'Gujarat Bandh'* on 3rd August after killing of about one hundred innocent Amarnath piligrims in Kashmir by Muslim extremists. Fury of irate mobs was so severe that all forms of property and businesses worth crores of rupees were destroyed, most of which belonged to the minority. Many places of worship and even schools of minority community were stormed and damaged. Rioting groups shouted anti-Pakistan and Anti-Muslim slogans and attacked people and establishments of minority community.

- *Number of persons dead*:12
- *Number of persons injured*:15
- *Number of persons arrested:*150
- *Places affected*: Kalupur, Dariapur, Jamalpur, Sabarkantha, Lambadiya, Modasa
- *Loss of properties*: Several properties and businesses worth more than Rs. Ten crores were destroyed in the riots. Many of these belonged to minority community. A dargah was razed to the ground opposite the Amdapur police chowky in Naroda area. In Khed Brahma area 6 shops were ransacked, looted and burnt. A police jeep was set on fire by a mob in Katargam area.

Communal Riots in Mathura, Uttar Pradesh[412]

Immediate Cause: Trouble broke out on 15th August in Mathura Uttar Pradesh. This was sparked by a dispute over a plot of land. When Hindus started constructing a wall on a plot of land, Muslims objected to it saying that plot was being used as a cemetery under the supervision of the Wakf Board, a claim rebutted by the majority community. The groups from both communities attacked each other with crude bombs and acid bulbs.

- *Number of persons dead*: 2 (1 Hindu, 1Muslim)
- *Number of persons injured:* 15

Communal Riots in Nanded, Maharashtra[413]

Immediate Cause: Trouble broke out on 13th September, in Nanded in Maharashtra when some Muslim miscreants stoned Ganesh procession from one of the bye-lanes of Itwara area. The news spread like wild fire and large scale riots broke out. The police resorted to lathi charge and even firing to control rioting mobs.

- *Number of persons dead*: 4
- *Number of persons injured:* 4
- *Number of persons arrested:* 25
- *Places affected:* Itwara Area

Communal Riots in Biharsharif, Bihar[414]

Immediate Cause: Trouble broke out on 9th October, on the question of installing Durga idol on the disputed piece of land. When police removed the idol and started partial demolition of the construction, the frenzied mobs started vandalising private and public properties leading to imposition of curfew. When rioting groups came out defying curfew and blocked streets with burning tyres and wooden logs, the police opened fire. Army and Reserved Action Force also had to be called to control the situation.

- *Number of person dead:* 1
- *Number of persons injured:* 3
- *Number of persons arrested:* 145

Communal Riots in Nawsari, Gujarat[415]

Immediate Cause: Trouble broke out on 3rd December in Alipur area between the two communities over the question of cow protection.

- *Number of persons injured:* 14
- *Loss of properties*:15 shops and hawker stalls set ablaze. Police had to resort to firing in order to quell the disturbances.

Communal Riots in Moradabad, Uttar Pradesh[416]

Immediate Cause: Trouble broke out on 9th December in Mordabad in Uttar Pradesh, when boundary wall of a place of worship was demolished in Galshahid area at the instance of some local politicians. Police had to lathi charge at more than 12 places as the disturbances spread to different areas.

- *Number of persons arrested:* 20
- *Other details not available*

Communal Riots in Trinuveli, Tamil Nadu[417]

Immediate Cause: Trouble broke out in Trinuveli during the month of Ramzaan where one Muslim was beheaded by two unidentified assailants. Authorities do not know the motive behind this gruesome incident. Heavy police pickets averted a major clash.

- *Number of person dead:* 1
- *Other details not available*

Communal Riots in Ahmedabad, Gujarat[418]

Immediate Cause: Trouble broke out on 17th September in Ahmedabad when an attack was made on independent candidate Ajmet Tyrewala of Dariyapur while he was on his way to cast his vote at Booth no 18. There were also reports that an incident involving an imposter couple, who tried to cast their vote but was prevented from doing so sparked off violence in other parts of Dariyapur. Another version is that the stabbing of a youth around noon near Dariyapur tower, coupled with a mob trying to capture a booth at a municipal school near the sensitive Tambu chowki had vitiated the atmosphere.

- *Number of persons dead:*6
- *Number of persons injured:*18
- *Other details not available*

Communal Riots in Ahmedabad, Gujarat[419]

Immediate Cause: Trouble broke out on 11th December in Ahmedabad on the issue of a minor boy answering nature's call near a place where a marriage ceremony was being solemonised in Shahpur.

- *Number of persons injured:* 11
- *Other details not available*

Communal Riots in Fathegarh, Uttar Pradesh[420]

Immediate Cause: Trouble broke out on 3rd March, when a woman was killed by a bullet fired during a clash between two groups of a community over throwing of colours in Fathegarh in Farrukhbad district.

- *Number of persons dead:*3

- *Number of persons injured:*12
- *Other details not available*

Communal Violence in Mau, Uttar Pradesh[421]

Trouble broke out in Mau in Uttar Pradesh following clashes between two communities during the immersion of Durga idols.

- *Number of person dead:*1
- *Number of persons injured:*3
- *Other details not available*

2001

Communal Riots in Ranchi, Bihar[422]

Immediate Cause: Trouble broke out on 29th December 2000, on Eid day when the police fired in which three Muslim youths were killed. This led to unrest among the Muslims and therefore the Minority Front and other organisations gave a call for "*Bandh*" in Ranchi on 30th December.

- *Number of persons killed:* 3 (Muslims)
- *Number of persons injured: Data not available*
- *Loss of properties*: 2 police chowkies, Reserved Action Force vehicles were heavily damaged.

Communal Riots in Kishtwar, Jammu[423]

Immediate Cause: Trouble broke out on 2nd January in Jammu after Jama Masjid was gutted apparently by short circuit. The people in the town turned violent after entire Masjid complex including the library and Madrasa were reduced to ashes. The mob turned violent after police-lathi charged to disperse swelling mob. Curfew was imposed later in Jammu.

- *Number of persons killed:* Not available
- *Number of persons injured:* Not available
- Curfew imposed areas: Kishtwar

Communal Riots in Ahmednagar, Maharashtra[424]

Immediate Cause: Trouble broke out on 5th January in Ahmednagar in Maharashtra when two dead animals were thrown into a mosque. The mob collected and stoned the passing vehicles.

- *Details not available*

Communal Riots in Mapusa, Goa[425]

Immediate Cause: Trouble broke out on 6th January in Goa when the Shiv-Sena stoked up tempers in the North Goa of Mapusa in a dispute over a make-shift prayer hall set up for *Ramzaan*. Muslims accused the Sena of damaging a religious book. The Sena made counter-accusations. Sena members apparently lodged a statue of Shivaji with saffron flags in the area and later protested that the police got it back.

- *Details not available*

Communal Riots in Nasik, Maharashtra[426]

Immediate Cause: Trouble broke out on 29th January in Nasik after a part of the mosque was demolished. The violent mob, on hearing of demolition of part of the mosque indulged in stone-throwing.

Real Cause: But the real cause was something else. Noorani Masjid's ablution house and Imam's house were not the plan approved by the Muincipal corporation and hence were demolished which led to violent incidents.

- *Number of persons injured:* 50. (2 police constables, 3 fire brigade workers)
- *Number of persons arrested:* 96
- Curfew imposed areas: Kaziapura locality and Bhadrakali

Communal Riots in Mordabad, Uttar Pradesh[427]

Trouble broke out on 5th March in Mordabad in Uttar Pradesh, when a Hindu neighbour opened fire on Muslims performing ritual of animal sacrifice on the occasion of Id-ul-Zuha (Bakri-Id) in Sambhal town in Mordabad district.

- *Number of persons dead*: 2
- *Number of persons injured:* Not available
- *Number of persons arrested:* 5
- Loss of property: 18 houses were burnt down

Communal Riots in Aurangabad, Maharashtra[428]

Immediate Cause: Trouble broke out in Aurangabad in Maharashtra in reaction to the burning of Quran incident in Delhi, which led to widespread arson and communal incidents in various parts of the country. In Maharashta also, the communal violence broke out in Aurangabad due to this main reason. The police had to resort to firing in the air and lobbying tear gas shells.

- *Number of persons injured:* 13 (in stone-pelting)
- *Places affected:* Nanded, Parbhani in Marathwada district

Communal Riots in Hyderabad, Andhra Pradesh[429]

Immediate Cause: Trouble broke out on 9th March in Hyderabad due to the burning of Quran incident in Delhi. Hyderabad witnessed stone-throwing from Mecca Masjid in Charminar area at passers by.

- *Number of persons injured:* 4
- *Other details not available*

Communal Riots in Pune City, Maharashtra[430]

Immediate Cause: Trouble broke out in Pune city after a group of people who had gathered for *namaz* had turned violent. Pune city witnessed incidents of stone-throwing and arsoning. *The exact date not available.*

- *Number of persons arrested:* 78
- *Loss of properties*: 1 bakery shop, 1 medical shop looted, an autorickshaw and a moped burnt
- *Places affected:* Gani Peth, Ghodpade Peth, Swami Vivekanand society, P.C. staff colony, Ghafurtakiya

Communal Riots in Naland District, Bihar[431]

Immediate Cause: Trouble broke out on 10th March in Shambu village of Nalanda district in Bihar between the two groups over the issue of singing Holi songs.

- *Number of persons dead*: 8
- *Number of persons injured:* 6
- *Other details not available*

Communal Riots in Kanpur, Uttar Pradesh[432]

Immediate Cause: Trouble broke out in Kanpur when the SIMI took out a protest march and put up objectionable posters in the city. The Additional Constabulary fired on this procession.

- *Number of persons killed:*12 (Muslims)

- *Loss of properties*:12 shops, a religious place was burnt down. Properties worth several lakhs of rupees were destroyed.

Communal Riots in Ajmer, Rajasthan[433]

Immediate Cause: Trouble broke out on 6th April in Ajmer after the dispute over the route of Taziyah in Nasirabad.

- *Number of persons injured*:10
- Loss of property: The outer boundary of a temple broken

Communal Riots in Kopergaon, Maharashtra[434]

Immediate Cause: Trouble broke out on 8th April in Kopergaon when two groups of people Hindus and Muslims clashed with each other during Muharram procession in which the police had to open fire.

- *Number of persons injured:* 8
- *Other details not available*

Communal Riots in Ahmednagar, Maharashtra[435]

Immediate Cause: Trouble broke out on 12th April in Ahmednagar, when a Ganesh idol was found damaged. On hearing this, the Hindus damaged a religious place of Muslims. The BJP and the Shiv Sena workers collected outside the religious place and started doing Maha Arti. This led to communal riot in Ahmednagar.

- *Number of persons arrested:* 12
- *Other details not available*

Communal Riots in Beawar Town, Rajasthan[436]

Immediate Cause: Trouble broke out on 16th April in Beawar town in Rajasthan when Vishwa Hindu Parishad and Bhartiya Janata Party procession was stoned and bottles of acid were thrown on the procession.

- *Number of persons injured:* 24

Communal Riots in Banswada, Rajasthan[437]

Immediate Cause: Trouble broke out on 20th May in Banswada in Rajasthan over the report that three persons were killed in a road accident who belonged to the other community.

- *Number of persons dead*: 3 (Muslims)

Communal Riots in Lucknow, Uttar Pradesh[438]

Immediate Cause: Trouble broke out on 5th June in Lucknow when a police constable accosted a Muslim girl near Tilewali Masjid and asked her to accompany him to police-station. This led to unrest among Muslims who had gathered to witness illumination on the occasion of Shab-e-Barat festival. The Muslim youth alleged that the constable was misbehaving with the girl whereas the constable maintained that the girl was making obscene gestures. Many people came out of the Mosque and started throwing stones.

- *Number of persons dead*: 3
- *Loss of properties*: Many autorickshaws and a police chowkie burnt down. *The exact number of autorickshaws burnt not available.*

Communal Riots in Mysore, Karnataka[439]

Immediate Cause: Trouble broke out on 2nd June in Chamrajnagar in Mysore district in Karnataka when a youth belonging to minority community was murdered.

- *Number of person dead:* 1 (Muslim)
- *Number of persons arrested:* 12

Communal Riots in Jalgaon, Maharashtra[440]

Immediate Cause: Trouble broke out on 5th June in Jalgaon district in Maharashtra after an eve-teasing incident in Anand Mela district in that town. As a result of this many arsoning incidents took place. Many communities taking advantage of this came out with swords in hands and began looting and burning properties. The MLA (Member of Legislative Assembly) and the Sarpanch both belong to the BJP. The Muslims of Jamner maintained that it was not really a riot between Hindus and Muslims but an attempt by the communalists to terrify Muslims of the town.

- *Loss of properties*: 17 shops and houses looted and burnt. (14 belonged to Muslims and 3 belonged to Hindus)

Communal Riots in Sangamner, Maharashtra[441]

Immediate Cause: Trouble broke outon 9th July in Sangamner on account of the film "Gadar". This film had become quite controversial. Actually, in the theatre the film "Lagaan" was being screened and only during the trailer, the film "Gaddar" was shown. But still after coming out of the theatre the two groups clashed and indulged in stone-pelting injuring many people.

- *Number of person dead:* 1
- *Number of persons injured:* Several (The exact number of persons injured not available)

Communal Riots in Moradabad, Uttar Pradesh[442]

Immediate Cause: Trouble broke out on 23rd July in Saraswa Gor village in Mordabad district in Uttar Pradesh when a gang of miscreants attacked houses of minority community. The whole incident is shrouded in mystery. No one knows how and why the miscreants attacked houses of minority community. The police said the motive could be robbery. But a deputation of Jamiat-ul-Ulama who visited the village said the police theory that the motive could be robbery was false on the grounds that those killed were very poor and there was hardly anything in their house worth robbing. They felt that communal violence broke out to terrify Muslims.

- *Number of persons dead*: 6

Communal Riots in Muzaffarnagar, Uttar Pradesh[443]

Immediate Cause: Trouble broke out on 5th August in Muzaffarnagar in Uttar Pradesh when some highly objectionable pamphlets were thrown on a mosque which led to clashes between Hindus and Muslims.

- *Number of persons injured:* Several (The exact number of persons injured not available)

Communal Riots in Amravati, Maharashtra[444]

Immediate Cause: Trouble broke out on 12th August in Amravati when the Shiv Seniks attacked some Muslims when they were taking oxen for slaughtering leading to clashes.

- *Number of persons dead*: 2

- *Number of persons injured:* 30
- *Number of persons arrested:* 70

Real Cause: The Bajrang Dal activists were keeping watch near the slaughter house and prevented the Muslim butchers from taking their animals for slaughter, often attacking them. The tensions had always prevailed in the town between Shiv Sainiks, Bajrang Dal and Muslim butchers.

Communal Riots in Ahmedabad, Gujarat[445]

Immediate Cause: Trouble broke out on 24th and 25th August in Ahmedabad. A call was given for *"Bandh"* by a minority organisation which resulted in closure of shops and stone-throwing incidents in Mirzapur, Kalupur, Garden Chowk and Panchkui areas.

Communal violence broke out in Daryapur area of Ahmedabad on 25th August.

On 24th August

- *Number of persons injured:* 10

On 25th August

- *Number of persons dead*: 2
- *Number of persons arrested:* 4
- Riot affected areas: Mirzapur, Kalupur, Garden Chowk, Daryapur and Pachuki areas.

Communal Violence in Jalgaon, Maharashtra[446]

Immediate Cause: Trouble broke out in Bhadgaon in Jalgaon in Maharashtra when Hanuman idol was found to be polluted with excreta.

- *Loss of properties*: Shops looted, religious places desecrated and kerosene tanks upturned.

Communal Riots in Malegaon, Maharashtra[447]

Immediate Cause: Trouble broke out on 26th October in Malegaon when a Muslim youth was distributing pamphlets outside a mosque which called for boycott of waiting police van. This angered Muslims coming out of the mosque after Friday prayers. The mobs from both sides began attacking, looting and setting fire to each other's properties.

- *Number of persons dead*: 13
- *Number of persons injured:* Not available
- *Loss of properties*: The *loss of properties* estimated to be about more than Rs. 15 crores.
- *Places affected:* Kalwan, Satana and Jaikheda

Communal Riots in Kodagu, Karnataka[448]

Immediate Cause: Trouble broke out on 9th December in Kodagu in Karnataka due to vandalism perpetrated from 6th December to 8th December with many roof tiles being damaged and cowdung (or excreta) reportedly thrown in the temple precincts. As soon as the vandalism was discovered there was an immediate outcry by the Bhaktha Jana Sangha, a Hindu religious organisation which called for a meeting of Hindus at the temple on 10th December. After the meeting, a crowd of about 2,500 people, armed with knives and other weapons marched through Kottamudi, a predominantly Muslim village just outside the temple, and stoned, looted and burnt many houses and shops.

- *Loss of properties*: Houses and shops (Muslims) damaged, Mosques and Madrasas burnt In Gonikappa, Balalmuri, Balele. Hudikeli, Shanivarasanthe, Gudugalele. The total loss of property was about Rs. 26.5 lakh in Madikeri Taluk, Rs. 15.4 lakh in Virajpet Taluk, Rs. 2.29 in Somwarpeth Taluk. Total property worth Rs. 50 lakh belonging to Muslims officially declared to have been destroyed.

2002

Communal Riots in Dahanu, Maharashtra[449]

Immediate Cause: Trouble broke out on 16th January in Dahanu, in Maharashtra after a quarrel between a Muslim community and a Hindu community over the game of cricket. When this news reached the parents of these boys, communal tensions arose and led to stone-throwing incidents.

- *Number of persons dead*: No casualties reported
- *Number of persons Injured:* No casualties reported
- *Number of persons arrested:* No arrests reported

Communal Riots in Bidar, Bangalore, Karnataka[450]

Immediate Cause: Trouble broke out on 23rd February in Bidar after a verbal duel between the two boys belonging to different communities over a trivial issue. Soon members of both communities rallied behind them and attacked each other.

- *Number of persons Injured:* 11 (7 in police firing)

Communal Riots in Godhra , Gujarat[451]

Immediate Cause: Trouble brc. e out on 28th February in Gujarat after the burning of Sabarmati Express near Godhra station in Gujarat. The Sabarmati Express arrived in Godhra at 8.45 a.m. on Wednesday morning. When the Sabarmati Express arrived at Godhra station, Kar Sevaks returning from Ayodhya started shouting slogans like 'Jai Shri Ram'. Some Kar Sevaks got into a tussle with one of them. In no time, he saw a huge crowd, carrying lathi, kerosene and sharp knives, descend on the platform. They stabbed people, set fire to the S-6 coach and left the platform all within a few minutes.

- *Number of persons killed:* 55

Later, the riot spread to other areas in Gujarat like Ahmedabad, Baroda, Panchmahal, Mehsana etc. This riot is considered to be the worst riot ever occurred in India.

- *Number of persons killed:* 1,071
- *Number of persons injured:* 1,973

Communal Riots in Murbad, Maharashtra[452]

Immediate Cause: Trouble broke out on 1st March in Murbad in Thane district in Maharashtra when the Vishwa Hindu Parishad and the Bajrang Dal called for a State-wide *Bandh* to protest against the Godhra killings.

- *Number of persons killed:* No casualty
- *Number of persons injured:* No casualty
- *Number of persons arrested:* 26
- *Loss of properties*: Many shops looted and destroyed. Property worth lakhs of rupees destroyed.

Communal Riots in Hyderabad, Andhra Pradesh[453]

Immediate Cause: Trouble broke out in the old city on 1st March in Hyderabad in Andhra Pradesh immediately after Friday prayers at the Mecca Masjid.

- *Number of persons killed:* No data available
- *Loss of properties*: Bhavaninagar police station, few houses of the majority community, a religious temple in Alijha Katla and the ruling Telugu Desam party office etc was attacked.

Communal Violence in Ajmer, Rajasthan[454]

Immediate Cause: Trouble broke out on 2nd March in Ajmer when hundreds of Vishwa Hindu Parishad activists tried to forcibly close down shops on the Jaipur–Ajmer highway. There were clashes between the members of two communities.

- *Number of persons dead*: 2
- *Places affected:* Madanganj, Kishanganj

Communal Riots in Haryana, Chandigarh[455]

Immediate Cause: Trouble broke out on 11th March in Bhiwani, Haryana, over the reports (rumours) that a family had killed a cow.

- *Number of persons arrested:* 4
- *Loss of properties*: 2 places of worship, a large number of shops destroyed, and 20 houses attacked

Communal Riots in Canning, West Bengal[456]

Immediate Cause: Trouble broke out on 11th March in Canning. A Vishwa Hindu Parishad activist was killed when the police opened fire to stop VHP from performing a "Yagna" and organising a "Dharma Sabha" near a railway station in south Paraganas district of West Bengal.

- *Number of persons dead*: 2
- *Number of persons Injured:* 32

Communal Riots in Jaipur, Rajasthan[457]

Immediate Cause: Trouble broke out on 25th March in Gangapur city in Rajasthan on the occasion of Muharram over the holding of Poornahuti Yagya and Kirtans for the Ram Mandir at various temples located on the route of the Tazia processions. The violence broke out around 1.00 PM when activists of the Vishwa Hindu

Parishad, Bhartiya Janata Party and Bajrang Dal collected at an ancient Hanumanji Mandir for a Yagya and Kirtan. The police had asked them not to gather there in large numbers as the temple was on the Tazia route but they did not agree. Violence broke out after they shouted provocative slogans as the procession drew near. The police first resorted to teargas and a lathi-charge but were pelted with stones by the mob. Finally the police had to open fire.

- *Number of persons dead*: 3
- *Number of persons injured:* 15
- *Places affected:* Gangapur

Communal Riots in Akola, Maharashtra[458]

Immediate Cause: Trouble broke out on 30th March in Akola in Maharashtra due to the throwing of colour at a Mosque in the old city area by some miscreants which led to tension resulting in stabbing and arsoning incidents.

- *Number of persons dead*: 7
- *Number of persons injured:* 15
- *Number of persons arrested:* 61

Communal Riots in Bahraich, Uttar Pradesh[459]

Immediate Cause: Trouble broke out on 30th March in Bahraich in Uttar Pradesh district over descreation of a *mazar* and a religious book.

- Number of person arrested: 1

Communal Riots in Hooghly, West Bengal[460]

Trouble broke out on 8th April in Hooghly in West Bengal due to the clashes between groups from the Hindu dominated Taatipara and Muslim-dominated Sagoon.

- *Number of person dead:* 1
- Number of persons injured: 8

Communal Riots in Kalyan, Maharashtra[461]

Immediate Cause: Trouble broke out in on 9th April in Kalyan Maharashtra over an argument over a fare between Bunty Chavan, a muncipal worker and a Muslim rickshaw driver.

Real Cause: But the real cause is something different. The cinder for the communal sparks was provided by the recent political rivalry between Shiv Sena activist Ramesh Walunj and Nationalist Congress Party member Iqbal Shaikh, the corporator from Rohidaswada. Shaikh and his associate Rasool Shaikh had been Sena loyalists before joining the Nationalist Congress Party. The two ensured the victory of Ramesh Walunj's life in the 1995 muncipal elections. The ward was then reserved for women. So the Sena was jolted when Iqbal Shaikh filed his nomination as an Nationalist Congress Party candidate. His victory communalised politics in Rohidaswada and Ambedkar Road, an ancient locality of cobblers and conservancy workers, and also in the Muslim locality of Dodh Naka. About four months ago, the police arrested 4 activists of the Students Islamic Movements of India. Around the same time, Ramesh Walunj and his uncle, Ashok, began to reconstruct a local Hanuman Temple. Clashes also erupted because of a relationship between a Muslim girl and a Hindu boy. The girl who has never been sent out of town, was allegedly abused both by her own relatives and Hindu neighbours for 'polluting the community'. Some butchers who allegedly illegally slaughtered cows had also frequently invited the wrath of Hindu neighbours. Pressure started building up on the Muslim leadership to 'protect the interests of the community'.

- *Number of persons dead*: 3
- *Number of persons injured:* Data not available
- *Loss of properties*:15 houses belonging to the minority community burnt.

Communal Riots in Haveri, Karanataka[462]

Immediate Cause: Trouble broke out in Haveri in Karanataka district when some members of a particular community objected to the Holi procession which the other group ignored. *The exact date not available.*

- *No other details given*

Communal Riots in Coimbatore, Chennai[463]

Immediate Cause: Trouble broke out in Coimbatore in Chennai after the murder of Rashtriya Sevak Sangh functionary R. Murugesan. *The exact date not available.*

- *Other details not given*

Communal Riots in Nandurbar in Nasik, Maharashtra[464]

Immediate Cause: Trouble broke out on 14th May in Nandurbar in Nasik when a youth from Kali Masjid area, Fiyazuddin Shaikh was beaten up over playing cards. He filed a police complaint against Bablu Sadashiv Bhil, Bhimsingh Ratan Bhil, Suka Visawanata More and Ganesh. Next day around 9.20 a.m. a mob from Kali Masjid area went berserk in Maliwada and Bhilhati areas. A chilli trader, Subhash Chiranjeev Agarwal who was riding a Bajaj M80 motor cycle was attacked and set ablaze with his bike. The news of Subhash being burnt alive provoked violent reaction and the mobs began to indulge in arsoning and stone throwing.

- *Number of persons dead*: 2
- *Number of persons injured:* 9
- *Number of persons arrested:* 65
- Loss of property: 12 shops and 22 hutments burnt down

Communal Riots in Vadodara, Gujarat[465]

Immediate Cause: Trouble broke out in Vadodara when Vishwa Hindu Parishad officials requested to take action against some people who had reportedly sacrificed bulls on the ocassion of Id-ul-Zuha in the Tankaria village near Bharuch. *The exact date of the riot not available.*

- *Number of person dead:* 1
- *Number of persons injured:* 3
- *Other details not available*

Communal Riots in Jamner in Jalgaon District, Maharashtra[466]

Immediate Cause: Trouble broke out on 20th June in Jamner when the riot erupted as a result of hostile feelings in the minds of both communities following a dead pig found in the Shahi mosque and the eyes of a Hanuman idol being damaged. It is alleged that full scale communal violence was triggered by inept handling of the situation by the police. This incident attracted crowds and the arguments ignited communal passions. A mob then went berserk in Shriram Peth area and the nearby areas pelting stones, damaging vehicles and shops.

- *Number of persons dead*: 5 (1 in police firing, 2 in mob violence)
- *Number of persons injured:* 22

- *Number of persons arrested:* 52
- *Loss of properties*: 80 houses, 32 shops, 14 vehicles and 2 places of worship damaged
- *Places affected:* Londhri, Pahur

Communal Riots in Bhiwandi in Thane District, Maharashtra[467]

Immediate Cause: Trouble broke out on 1st July in Bhiwandi in Thane district in Maharashtra when the dead body of a murdered man was found from a river in Khadipar area following a clash between two groups. The clash occurred due to the altercation between Akil Gaffar Shaikh (30) a rickshaw driver, and Parshuram Gharat (40) a cassette shop owner. Both of them had been on bad terms with each other.

- *Number of person dead:* 1
- *Number of persons injured:* 6
- *Number of persons arrested:* 125
- *Loss of properties*: 6 powerlooms, a grocery shop, an electronics goods store, a scrapyard and several houses ransacked

Communal Riots in Pune in Maharashtra[468]

Immediate Cause: Trouble broke out on 31st July in Pune in Maharashtra when some meat was discarded outside the Ganesh Mandal in the market area near the famous Dagdu Seth Ganpati Mandal.

- *Number of persons killed:* No causalities reported
- *Number of persons injured:* No causalities reported
- *Places affected:* Ravivar Peth, Shukrwar Peth, Guruwar Peth

Communal Riots in Badlapur, Maharashtra[469]

Immediate Cause: Trouble broke out on 21st October in Badlapur following an altercation between two youths belonging to different communities. But the police said the violence followed an eve-teasing incident. But the members of both communities insisted that the communal situation in Badlapur had been simmering even before Navratri.

- *Number of persons dead*: 10
- *Number of persons injured:* 10 (9 Hindus, 1 Muslim)
- *Loss of properties*: 1 saw mill, 1 rice mill, several shops, 2 vehicles and some houses destroyed

Communal Riots in Solapur, Maharashtra[470]

Immediate Cause: Trouble broke out on 11th November due to a call given by the Muslim Vikas Parishad to Muslim establishments in the city to shut shop to protest against a remark made by the American Baptist Minister Jery Falwell about Prophet Mohammad. The riots were triggered because the Muslim Vikas Parishad activists asked the majority community members to close down shops. Violence started from Asra Nagar township in Solapur when local businessman Nagesh Takmoge refused to close his shop after being asked to do so by the Muslim Vikas Parishad. As news of violence spread in the minority dominated area of Vijapur, the decorations for the ongoing Navratri Puja were destroyed by arsonists. This led to police firing.

- *Number of persons dead*: 9
- *Number of persons Injured:* 168
- *Number of persons arrested:* 258
- Areas affected: Shivganga Nagar, Manik Chowk
- *Loss of properties*: A fruit stall, and a shop was destroyed. Several shops and godowns set on fire.

Communal Riots in Kapasan and Balsauli, Rajasthan[471]

Immediate Cause: Trouble broke out on 23rd December in Rajasthan after a quarrel between two youth of different communities. Scores of people belonging to a certain community gathered after the quarrel and started raising slogans. Communal tension also gripped two towns in Chittorgarh district Kapasan and Balsauli where some idols were found desecrated in temples.

Other details not available.

ENDNOTES

1. *Keesing's Contemporary Archives,* (1948-50), Vol. VII, pp. 10737-38.
2. *Keesing's Contemporary Archives,* (1961-62), Vol. XIII, pp. 17958-59 and 18504.
3. *Keesing's Contemporary Archives,* (1963-64), Vol. XIV, p. 20186.
4. Ibid, p. 20185.
5. Ibid, p. 20186.
6. Dr. Zainab Banu, "*Two Sides of a Coin*: A Comparative study of riots at Godhra and Udaipur", in *Communal Riots in Post Independent India,* (ed.) Dr. Asghar Ali Engineer, Hyderbad (1991), Sangam Books, p. 232.
7. Ibid.
8. *Keesing's Contemporary Archives,* (1967-68), Vol. XVI, p. 22345.
9. Ibid, pp. 22342-43.
10. Ibid, p. 22706.
11. Ibid, p. 22831.
12. Ibid, pp. 22342-43.
13. Ibid, p. 22706.
14. Ibid, p. 22831.
15. Ibid.
16. Ibid.
17. Ibid.
18. Ibid.
19. Shah Ghanshayam, "The 1969 Communal Riots in Ahemadabad: A case study", in '*Communal Riots in Post Independence India*', (ed.) Dr. Asghar Ali Engineer, Hyderabad, (1991) Sangam Books, p. 184, 191.
20. Inquiry commission report into the communal disturbances at Ahmedabad and other places in Gujarat at on and after 18th September, 1969.
21. *Keesing's Contemporary Archives,* (1969-70), Vol. XVII, pp. 23699-700.
22. *Communal riots State and Law in India* ed. Iqbal Ansari.
23. *Keesing's Contemporary Archives,* (1969-70), Vol. XVII, p. 24183 and Inquiry Commission Report into communal disturbances in Bhiwandi, Jalgaon, Thana and Kalyan.
24. *Keesing's Contemporary Archives,* (1969-70), Vol. XVII, p. 24184.
25. Dr. Asghar Ali Engineer, "*Aligarh* riot—*An unplanned outburst*", occasional paper, April 15-30, 1995.
26. *Communal riots the state and Law in India* ed. Iqbal Ansari p. 329-331.
27. *Keesing's Contemporary Archives,* (1971-72), Vol. No. XVIII, p. 25611.
28. *Keesing's Contemporary Archives,* (1974), Vol. XX, p. 26482.
29. *Data India* (May 13-19, 1974), Issue No. 10, p. 118.
30. *Data India* (April 21-27, 1975), Issue No. 17, p. 270.
31. *Data India* (October 31-November 6, 1977), Issue No. 44, p. 707.
32. *Data India* (March 27-April 2, 1978) Issue No. 13, p. 208.

33. *Data India* (August 7-13, 1978) Issue No. 32, p. 509.
34. *Data India* (September 4-10, 1978), Issue No. 36, p. 571.
35. *Data India* (September 25-October 1,1978) Issue No. 39, p. 624.
36. *Keesing's Contemporary Archives*, (1978), Vol. XXIV, p. 29352.
37. Ibid.
38. *Keesing's Contemporary Archives*, (1979), Vol. XXV, p. 29969.
39. Ibid.
40. Ibid.
41. Ibid.
42. Ibid.
43. *Data India* (November 26-December 2, 1979), Issue No. 48, p. 571.
44. *Data India* (February 25-March 2, 1980 Issue No. 9, p. 107.
45. *Data India* (July 28-August 3, 1980) Issue No. 31, p. 370.
46. *Data India* (August 18-24, 1980) Issue No. 34, p. 408.
47. *Data India* (August 11-17, 1980) Issue No. 33, p. 396 and *Data India* (August 25-31, 1980) Issue No. 35, p. 420.
48. Ibid.
49. Ibid.
50. *Data India* (August 25-31, 1980) Issue No. 35, p. 420.
51. Ibid.
52. *Data India* (August 11-17, 1980) Issue No. 33, p. 396.
53. *Data India* (August 18-24, 1980) issue No. 34, p. 408.
54. *Data India* (September 8-14, 1980) Issue No. 37, p. 442.
55. *Data India* (August 18-24, 1980) Issue No. 34, p. 406 and *Data India* (September 15-21, 1980) Issue No. 38 p. 452.
56. *Data India* (September 29-October 5, 1980) Issue No. 40 p. 478.
57. *Data India* (October 27-November 2, 1980) Issue No. 44 p. 528.
58. *Data India* (November 3-9, 1980) Issue No. 45 p. 540.
59. Ibid.
60. Dr. Asghar Ali Engineer, "Case studies of 5 major riots from Biharsharif to Pune", in *Communal Riots in Post-Independence India* (ed.) Engineer, Asghar Ali, Hyderabad (1991) Sangam Books, pp. 253-256.
61. *Data India* (December 15-21, 1980), Vol. 51, p. 612.
62. Dr. Asghar Ali Engineer, "*Case studies of five major riots from Biharsharif to Pune*", in '*Communal riots In Post Independence India*', (ed.), Engineer, Asghar Ali, Hyderabad, (Sangam Books, 1991), pp. 256-259.
63. Ibid, pp. 238-46.
64. *Keesing's Contemporary Archives*, (1981), Vol., XXVII, p. 31257.
65. *Data India* (June 1-7, 1981) Issue No. 23, p. 276.
66. *The Times of India*, 13th May, 1981.
67. *Data India* (June 15-21, 1981) Issue No. 25, p. 296.
68. *Data India* (July 6-12, 1981) Issue No. 28, p. 334.
69. Ibid.
70. *Keesing's Contemporary Archives, (1981)*, Vol. XXVII, p. 31257.

71. Dr. Asghar Ali Engineer, "*Case studies of five major riots from Biharsharif to Pune*", in '*Communal riots In Post Independence India*', (ed.), Engineer, Asghar Ali, Hyderabad, (Sangam Books, 1991).
72. *Data India* (Aug 31-Sep 6, 1981) Issue No. 36, p. 431.
73. *Data India* (Aug 24-30, 1981) Issue No. 35, p. 418.
74. *Data India* (Sep 28-Oct 4, 1981) Issue No. 40, p. 478.
75. *Data India* (Octover 19-25, 1981) Issue No. 43, p. 515.
76. Ibid.
77. Dr. Asghar Ali Engineer, "*Case studies of five major riots: from Biharsharif to Pune*", in *Communal Riots In Post-Independence India* (ed) Engineer, Asghar Ali, (1991), Sangam Books, pp. 261-63.
78. Ibid, pp. 268-69.
79. Ibid, pp. 266-67.
80. *Data India* (April 26-May 2, 1982) Issue No. 18. p. 214.
81. Dr. Asghar Ali Engineer, "*Case studies of five major riots: from Biharsharif to Pune*", in *Communal Riots In Post-Independence India* (ed) Engineer, Asghar Ali, (1991), Sangam Books, pp. 271-80.
82. *Data India* (April 26-May 2, 1982) Issue No. 18. p. 281-87.
83. Ibid.
84. *Data India* (June 21-27, 1982) Issue No. 26, p. 312.
85. *Data India* (August 23-29, 1982) Issue No. 35, pp. 419-20.
86. Ibid.
87. *Data India* (September 6-12, 1982) Issue No. 37, p. 441.
88. *Data India* (November 1-7, 1982) Issue No. 45, pp. 537-38.
89. *Data India* (June 21-27, 1982) Issue No. 26, p. 312.
90. *Data India* (September 20-26, 1982) Issue No. 39, p. 467.
91. *Data India* (September 27-October 3, 1982) Issue No. 40, p. 480.
92. *Data India* (March 14-20, 1983), Issue No.11, p. 130.
93. *Data India* (May 23-29, 1983), Issue No. 21, p. 250.
94. *Data India* (June 6-12, 1983), Issue No. 23, p. 273.
95. *Data India* (July 4-10, 1983) Issue No. 27, p. 323.
96. Engineer, Asghar Ali, "*Hyderabad Riots—An Analytical Report*", in *Communal Riots in Post-Independence India*, (ed) Engineer, Asghar Ali, Sangam Books, Hyderabad (1991), pp. 288-93.
97. *Data India* (September 19-25, 1983), Issue No. 38, p. 452 and *Data India* (October 10-16, 1983), Issue No. 41, p. 488.
98. *Data India* (September 19-25, 1983), Issue No. 38, p. 452.
99. *Data India* (November 14-20, 1983), Issue No. 46, p. 549
100. Ibid, p. 552.
101. *Data India* (October 17-23, 1983), Issue No. 42, p. 501.
102. *Keesing's Contemporary Archives*, (Vol. XXX, 1984), pp. 33221-222.
103. Ibid, p. 33222.
104. Ibid.
105. *Keesing's Contemporary Archives*, (Vol. XXX, 1984), pp. 33222.
106. Ibid, pp. 33226-227.

107. *Data India* (May 14-20, 1984), Issue No. 20, p. 240 and *Data India* (June 11-17, 1984), Issue No. 24, pp. 285-86.
108. *Keesing's Contemporary Archives*, (Vol. XXX, 1984), p. 33227.
109. Ibid.
110. *Data India* (July 9-15, 1984), Issue No. 28, p. 336.
111. *Keesing's Contemporary Archives*, (Vol. XXX, 1984), p..33226.
112. *Data India* (September 10-16, 1984), Issue No. 37, p. 442.
113. *Data India* (December 17-23, 1984), Issue No. 51, p. 609.
114. *Data India* (November 19-25, 1984), Issue No. 47, p. 563.
115. *Data India* (December 10-16, 1984), Issue No. 50, p. 598.
116. *Data India* (November 26-December 2, 1984), Issue No. 48, p. 569. and BBC (*Asia Today* 13 January).
117. *Keesing's Contemporary Archives*, (Vol. XXXII, 1986), pp. 34173-174.
118. *Data India* (July 7-13, 1986), Issue No. 28, p. 333.
119. *Data India* (July 7-13, 1986), Issue No. 28, p. 34484.
120 . *Data India* (March 24-30, 1986), Issue No. 13, pp. 154, 155.
121. *Data India* (March 3-9, 1986), Issue No.10, p. 118.
122. *Keesing's Contemporary Archives*, (Vol XXXII, 1986), p. 34564.
123. *Data India* (May 5-11, 1986), Issue No.19, p. 227.
124. *Keesing's Contemporary Archives*, (Vol XXXII,1986), p. 34564.
125. *Data India* (June 2-8, 1986) issue No. 23, p. 275.
126. Ibid.
127. Ibid.
128. *Data India* (June 16-22, 1986) issue No.25, p. 300
129. Ibid.
130. *Data India* (July 7-13, 1986) issue No. 28, p. 333.
131. Ibid.
132. *Data India* (August 18-24, 1986) Issue No.34, pp. 404-05.
133. *Data India* (August 4-10, 1986) Issue No.32, p. 382.
134. *Data India* (July 28-Aug 3, 1986), Issue No. 31, p. 372.
135. *Keesing's Contemporary Archives*, (Vol XXXIII,1987), p. 35204.
136. *Data India* (August 18-24, 1986) Issue No. 34, p. 406.
137. Ibid, p. 35250.
138. *Data India* (November 17-27, 1986) Issue No. 47, p. 564.
139. *Ethnic Conflict in South Asia*, Dr. Asghar Ali, Engineer, 1987.
140. *Data India* (December 15-21, 1986) Issue No. 51, p. 611.
141. *Keesing's Contemporary Archives*, (Vol XXXIII,1987), p. 35250.
142. *Data India* (December 8-14, 1986) Issue No.50, p. 598.
143. *Data India* (March 10-16, 1986), Issue No.11, p. 130.
144. *Data India* (March 23-29, 1987), Issue No.13, p. 153.
145. *Data India* (February 16-22, 1987), Issue No. 8, p. 93.
146. *Data India* (March 23-29, 1987) Issue No.13, p. 153.
147. *Data India* (May 11-17, 1987) Issue No. 20, p. 238.
148. Ibid.
149. Ibid.

150. Ibid, p. 237.
151. *Keesing's Contemporary Archives,* (Vol. XXXIII, 1987), p. 35204.
152. Engineer, Asghar Ali, *'Meerut Shame of the Nation'* Occasional paper No. 6, Vol. 3, *Institute of Islamic Studies, Bombay.* (1987).
153. Engineer, Asghar Ali, *'Old Delhi in the grip of Communal Frenzy'* Occasional paper No. 7 Vol. 3 Institute of Islamic Studies, Bombay (1987).
154. *Data India* (July 20-26, 1987) Issue No. 30, p. 360.
155. *Data India* (September 21-27, 1987) Issue No. 39, p. 465.
156. *Data India* (September 14-20, 1987) Issue No. 38, p. 455.
157. Engineer, Asghar Ali, *"Aurangabad riots: An analytical view"*, in *Communal Riots in Post-Independence India* (ed) Engineer, Asghar Ali, Hyderabad, (1991), Sangam Books, pp. 335-37.
158. Ibid.
159. Ibid, p. 337.
160. Ibid, p. 338.
161. *Data India* (August 1-7, 1988), Issue No. 32, p. 383.
162. *Data India* (December 7-13,1988), Issue No. 48, p. 575.
163. Engineer, Asghar Ali, and K.S. Durrani *'Communal Riots in Muzaffar Nagar, Khataoli and Aligarh'*, Occasional paper No. 1, Vol. 5th January, 1989, Institute of Islamic Studies, Bombay.
164. Ibid.
165. Ibid.
166. *Data India* (January 1-8, 1989), Issue No. 1, p. 11.
167. Ibid.
168. *Data India* (December 12-18, 1988), Issue No. 51, p. 611.
169. *Data India* (January 9-15,1989), Issue No. 2, p. 19.
170. *Occasional paper,* Institute of Islamic Studies (March, 1989).
171. *The Times of India,* 23rd March, 1989.
172. *The Times of India,* 19th April, 1989.
173. *The Times of India,* 11th May, 1989.
174. *The Times of India,* 13th August, 1989.
175. *India Week,* 28 April, 4th May, 1989.
176. *India Week,* 14th May, 1989.
177. *Patriot,* 20th May, 1989.
178. *Data India* (July 3-9,1989), Issue No. 27, p. 323.
179. *Data India* (July 3-9,1989), Issue No. 27, p. 321.
180. *The Times of India,* 9th July, 1989.
181. *Data India* (July 17-23,1989), Issue No. 29, p. 347.
182. *Data India* (August, 21-27, 1989) Issue No. 34, p. 408.
183. *Data India* (August, 14-20, 1989) Issue No. 33, p. 395.
184. *Data India* (September 11-17, 1989) Issue No. 37, p. 440.
185. *The Times of India,* 15th September, 1989.
186. *Data India,* p. 440.
187. *The Times of India,* 15th October, 1989.

188. *Data India* (October, 16-22, 1989) Issue No. 42, p. 500.
189. *The Times of India*, 13th October, 1989.
190. Ibid.
191. *The Indian Express*, 13th October, 1989.
192. *The Times of India*, 13th October, 1989.
193. *Indian Post*, 15th October, 1989.
194. *Data India* (October 23-29, 1989) Issue No. 43, p. 514
195. *The Times of India*, 8th October, 1989.
196. *The Times of India*, 16th October, 1989.
197. Memorandum of Muslim citizens of Patan town.
198. *Data India* (October 30-November 5, 1989) Issue No. 44, p. 524.
199. Engineer, Asghar Ali, *'Lifting The Veil: Communal violence and Communal Harmony in contemporary India'*, Hyderabad (1995), Sangam Books, pp. 176-83.
200. *The Indian Post*, 9th November, 1989 and *The Times of India*, 8th November 1989.
201. *The Times of India*, 19th November, 1989.
202. *Data India* (April 2-8, 1990) Issue No. 14, p. 165.
203. *Keesing's Contemporary Archives*, (Vol. 36, No. 4, 1990) p. 37377.
204. Ibid, p. 37378.
205. *Data India* (April 30-May 6, 1990) Issue No. 18, p. 213.
206. Ibid.
207. *The Independent*, 25th May, 1990 Communal Riot in Madras and Madurai.
208. UNI, 28th May, 1990.
209. *The Times of India*, 31th May, 1990.
210. *Data India* (August, 27-September 2, 1990) Issue No. 35, p. 417.
211. *The Independent*, 3th September, 1990.
212. Engineer, Asghar Ali, *"Major communal riots during the Ganpati festival of 1990"*, op. cit.
213. Ibid.
214. Ibid and *Data India* (October 1-7, 1990), Issue No. 40, p. 479.
215. Engineer, Asghar Ali, *Major communal riots during the Ganpati festival of 1990*, op. cit.
216. Ibid.
217. *Data India* (September 10-16, 1990) Issue No. 37, p. 444.
218. Engineer, Asghar Ali, *Major communal riots during the Ganpati festival of 1990*, op. cit.
219. Engineer Asghar Ali, *Major communal riots during Ganpati festival of 1990*, (occasional paper) Vol. 11, No. 9, 1990.
220. Ibid.
221. Ibid.
222. *Indian Express*, 5th October, 1990 and *the Independent* 4th October, 1990.
223. *The Independent*, 6th October, 1990.
224. *The Times of India*, 5th October, 1990.

225. *Telegraph,* 31st December, 1990
226. Basu, Amrita, "when local riots are not merely local: bringing the state back in Bijnor, 1988-1992" in *Economic and Political Weekly,* Vol. XXIX, No. 40. October 1, 1994. pp. 2605-21 and *Data India* (October 29-November 4, 1990) Issue No. 44, p. 526.
227. *The Telegraph,* 31st October, 1990 and *Data India* (October 22-28, 1990) Issue No. 43, p. 514.
228. *The Independent,* 15th November, 1990.
229. *The Indian Express,* 13th December, 1990 and *Data India* (October 29-November 4, 1990) issue No. 44, pp. 523-24, *Keesing's Contemporary Archives,* (Vol. 36, No. 12, 1990) p. 37915.
230. Engineer, Asghar Ali, *"Lifting the Veil"* (Communal Harmony and Communal Violence in contemporary India), Hyderabad (1995) Sargam Books pp. 187-96.
231. *Keesing's Contemporary Archives,* (Vol. 36, No. 12, 1990) p. 37915 and *Keesing's Contemporary Archives,* (Vol. 36, No. 10, 1990) p. 37774.
232. *The Times of India,* 22nd December, 1990.
233. *Data India* (December 3-9, 1990) Issue No. 49, p. 586 and *Data India* (December 10-16, 1990) Issue No. 50, p. 599.
234. Engineer, Asghar Ali, *"Lifting the Veil"* (Communal Harmony and Communal Violence in contemporary India,) op. cit, pp. 108-09.
235. Ibid.
236. *Data India* (December 17-23, 1990) Issue No. 51, p. 606.
237. *Data India* (January 28-February 3, 1991) Issue No. 5, p. 103.
238. *Data India* (February 4-10, 1991) Issue No. 6, p. 122.
239. *Data India* (March 11-17, 1991) Issue No. 11, p. 227.
240. *Data India* (March 25-31, 1991) Issue No. 13, p. 265 and Engineer, Asghar Ali, *"Lifting the Veil"* (communal harmony and communal violence in India) Hyderabad (1995) Sargam Books, p. 136.
241. Ibid.
242. op. cit, p. 136.
243. *Data India* (April 8-14, 1991) Issue No. 15, p. 307.
244. *Data India* (April 15-21, 1991) Issue No. 16, p. 327.
245. Ibid.
246. Ibid, p. 145.
247. Ibid, p. 146.
248. *Data India* (April 15-21, 1991), Issue No. 16, p. 140.
249. *The Times of India,* dated 24th April, 1991.
250. Engineer, Asghar Ali, *"Lifting the Veil"* (communal harmony and communal violence in India) op. cit, p. 144.
251. *Data India* (April 15-21, 1991), Issue No. 16, p. 141.
252. Engineer, Asghar Ali, *"Lifting the Veil"* (communal harmony and communal violence in India) op. cit, p. 144.
253. *Data India* (July 1-7, 1991) Issue No. 27, p. 549.
254. *Data India* (July 15-21, 1991) Issue No. 29, p. 585.

255. *Data India* (July 22-28, 1991),Issue No. 30, p. 603.
256. Ibid.
257. Engineer Asghar Ali, *"Lifting the Veil"* (communal harmony and communal violence in India) op. cit, p. 199-200.
258. *Data India* (November 18-24, 1991) Issue No. 47, p. 946.
259. *Data India* (February 10-16, 1992), Issue No. 7, p. 115.
260. *Data India* (June 22-28, 1992), Issue No. 26, p. 438.
261. *Data India* (July 6-12, 1992) Issue No. 28, p. 474.
262. Asghar Ali Engineer, 'Ahmedabad in the grip of communal riots once again', Progressive Perspective No. 3, Vol. 1, September, 1992, Published by Institute of Islamic Studies.
263. *Data India* (July 20-26,1992), Issue No. 30, p. 506.
264. *Data India* (July 20-26,1992), Issue No. 30, p. 506.
265. *Data India* (September 7-13, 1992), Issue No. 37, pp. 616-17.
266. Ibid, p. 617.
267. *'Sitamarhi on Fire'* by Asghar Ali Engineer, in 'Progressive Perspective', No. 7, Vol. No. 1, December, 1992.
268. Ibid.
269. *Data India* (October 26-November 1,1992) Issue No. 44; p. 736.
270. Asghar Ali Engineer (ed.), *Lifting The Veil (Communal Violence and Communal Harmony)*, Hyderabad (1995) Sargam Books, p. 227 and 244.
271. Ibid., pp. 49-74
272. *Communal riots—The State and Law in India* edited by Iqbal Ansari, p. 217.
273. *Keesing's Contemporary Archives*, (Vol. 39, No. 1, 1993), p. 39270.
274. Engineer, Asghar Ali Lifting the Veil-(Communal Violence and Communal Harmony in Contemporary India) Hyderabad, (1995), Sargam Books, p. 245 and pp. 255-56.
275. Etheric society and ciric life, *"Hindus and Muslims in India"* by Ashutosh Vashney, Oxford Publications, p. 239.
276. Ibid.
277. *The Times of India*, 28st January, 1993.
278. *The Times of India*, 7th April, 1993.
279. *The Indian Express*, 13th May, 1993.
280. *The Times of India*, 5th May, 1993.
281. *The Times of India*, 29th September, 1993.
282. *The Times of India*, 1st October, 1993.
283. *The Indian Express*, 3rd January, 1994.
284. *Keesing's Contemporary Archives*, (Vol. 40, No. 2, 1994), pp. 39866-67.
285. *The Times of India*, 15th May, 1994.
286. Asghar Ali Engineer, *Communalism and Communal Violence-1994*. Published by CSSS.
287. Vaishali Kulkarni and S. Hariharan, *'Hubli Disturbances—An Investigative Report'*.
288. Secular Democracy, Vol. XIII No. 6 September, 1994., pp. 23-25.

289. Asghar Ali Engineer, *'Bangalore disturbances-linguistic or communal'*, Published by CSSS, No. 94
290. Ibid.
291. Ibid.
292. Engineer, Irfan, *"Moradabad riots: An investigative Report"*, Bombay (1995).
293. Aligarh riots: Occasional paper on Aligarh Riot — An Unplanned Outburst by A.A. Engineer of Centre for Study of Society and Secularism.
294. *The Times of India*, 21st March, 1995.
295. *The Times of India*, 25th March, 1995.
296. Ibid.
297. Asghar Ali Engineer, Communalism and Communal violence in 1995.
298. *The Times of India*, (Mumbai) May 1, 1995.
299. *The Times of India*, (Mumbai) May 15, 1995, *The Hindu* (May 15, 1995) *The Hindu* (24th July, 1995).
300. *The Hindu*, 24th July, 1995.
301. *The Times of India*, 8th July, 1995.
302. *The Times of India*, 6th July, 1995.
303. *The Times of India*, 10th July, 1995.
304. *Sunday* (Calcutta 13-19 August, 1995).
305. *The Times of India*, 27th August, 1995.
306. *The Times of India*, 25th August, 1995.
307. *The Times of India*, 15th August, 1995.
308. *The Times of India*, 15th September, 1995.
309. *The Hindu* (9th June, 1996).
310. *The Times of India*, (5th February, 1996).
311. *The Times of India*, (24th February, 1996).
312. *The Hindu*, (7th March, 1996).
313. *The Times of India*, (14th March, 1996).
314. *The Hindu*, (19th March, 1996)
315. *Secular Perspective*, Jan 1-15, 1997 (Communalism and communal violence 96).
316. *The Times of India*, (31st May, 1996).
317. *The Hindu*, (31st May, 1996).
318. *Secular Perspective*, (January 1-15, 1997).
319. *The Hindu*, (18th June, 1996).
320. *Secular Perspective*, (January 1-15, 1997).
321. *The Indian Express*, (6th October, 1996).
322. *Secular Perspective*, (January 1-15, 1997).
323. *Pioneer*, 8th December, 1996.
324. *The Hindu*, 16th December, 1996.
325. *The Indian Express*, February 3, 1997.
326. *The Indian Express*, 28th January, 1997.
327. *The Times of India News Service* (By Dipak Meshra & Soroor Ahmed).

328. *The Indian Express*, 27th March, 1997.
329. *The Times of India*, 24th March, 1997.
330. *The Indian Express*, 27th March, 1997.
331. *The Asian Age* 28th March, 1997.
332. *The Times of India*, 7th April, 1997.
333. *The Times of India*, 20th May, 1997.
334. *The Indian Express*, 23rd June, 1997.
335. *The Indian Express*, 18th September, 1997, *The Times of India*, 19th September, 1997.
336. *The Asian Age*, 18th October, 1997.
337. *The Times of India News Service* 22nd, October, 1997.
338. *The Indian Express*, 16th November, 1997.
339. *Sunday Mid-day*, 16th November, 1997.
340. *Asian Age*, 11th December, 1997 & 4th December, 1997.
341. *Asianet News Service*, (31st January, 2000 at 9.30 p.m.).
342. *The Indian Express*, 8th December, 1997.
343. *The Times of India*, 18th December, 1997.
344. *Sunday Times*, 21st December, 1997.
345. *The Times of India*, 5th January, 1998.
346. *The Times of India*, 20th January, 1998.
347. *The Times of India*, 11th January, 1998.
348. *The Times of India*, 18th February, 1998.
349. *The Times of India*, 21st February, 1998.
350. *The Times of India*, 19th February, 1998.
351. *The Indian Express*, 5th April, 1998.
352. *The Times of India*, 20th April, 1998.
353. *The Hindu*, 18th May, 1998
354. *The Indian Express*, 10th June, 1998
355. *The Indian Express*, 15th June, 1998
356. *The Indian Express*, 2nd July, 1998
357. *The Hindu*, 20th August, 1998
358. *The Mumbai Age*, 14th September, 1998
359. *The Asian Age*, 9th October, 1998
360. *The Asian Age*, 9th October, 1998
361. *The Indian Express*, 6th October, 1998
362. *The Asian Age*, 4th January, 1999 and *The Times of India*, 13th January, 1999.
363. *The Times of India*, 26th December, 1998.
364. *The Times of India*, 16th December, 1998.
365. *The Times of India*, 13th January, 1999.
366. *The Asian Age* 18th January, 1999.
367. *The Asian Age* 20th January, 1999.
368. *The Times of India*, 16th March, 1999.
369. *The Times of India*, 6th March, 1999.
370. *The Indian Express*, 18th March, 1999.

371. *The Times of India,* 30th March, 1999.
372. *Dawat Sahroza,* New Delhi, 13th May, 1999.
373. *Dawat Sahroza,* New Delhi, 19th May, 1999.
374. *Quami Awaz* New Delhi, 9th May, 1999.
375. *The Times of India,* 8th June, 1999.
376. *The Times of India,* 29th April, 1999.
377. Ibid.
378. *Daily Dawn,* New Delhi, 9th May, 1999.
379. *Dawat Sahroza,* New Delhi, 25th May, 1999.
380. *The Hindu,* 31st May, 1999.
381. *The Times of India,* 2nd July, 1999.
382. *The Times of India,* 16th June, 1999.
383. *The Times of India,* 28th June, 1999.
384. *The Times of India,* 30th July, 1999.
385. *The Times of India,* 25th September, 1999.
386. *The Times of India,* 15th October, 1999.
387. *The Times of India,* 28th April, 1999.
388. *The Indian Express,* 25th September, 1999.
389. *The Asian Age,* 26th September, 1999.
390. *The Times of India,* 7th December, 1999.
391. *The Times of India,* 28th October, 1999.
392. *The Indian Express,* 24th December, 1999.
393. *The Indian Express,* 8th December, 1999.
394. *The Asian Age,* 23rd December, 1999.
395. *Secular Perspective,* Vol. 4, No. 1, 15-30 January, 2000.
396. Ibid.
397. Ibid.
398. Ibid.
399. Ibid.
400. Ibid.
401. Ibid.
402. Ibid.
403. Ibid.
404. Ibid.
405. Ibid.
406. Ibid.
407. Ibid.
408. Ibid.
409. Ibid.
410. Ibid.
411. Ibid.
412. Ibid.
413. Ibid.
414. Ibid.
415. Ibid.

416. Ibid.
417. Ibid.
418. Ibid.
419. Ibid.
420. Ibid.
421. Ibid.
422. *Secular Perspective,* 15-30th December, 2001.
423. Ibid.
424. Ibid.
425. Ibid.
426. Ibid.
427. Ibid.
428. Ibid.
429. Ibid.
430. Ibid.
431. Ibid.
432. Ibid.
433. Ibid.
434. Ibid.
435. Ibid.
436. Ibid.
437. Ibid.
438. Ibid.
439. Ibid.
440. Ibid.
441. Ibid.
442. Ibid.
443. Ibid.
444. Ibid.
445. Ibid.
446. Ibid.
447. Ibid.
448. Ibid.
449. *The Times of India,* 17th January, 2002.
450. *The Times of India,* 24th February 2002.
451. *Muslim in India,* May, 2002, Vol. No. 233.
452. *The Times of India,* 2nd March, 2002.
453. Ibid.
454. Ibid.
455. *The Times of India,* 3rd March, 2002.
456. *The Times of India,* 12th March, 2002.
457. *The Times of India,* 26th March, 2002.
458. *The Times of India,* 1st April, 2002.
459. Ibid.
460. *The Times of India,* 9th April, 2002.

461. *The Times of India,* 10th April, 2002.
462. Ibid.
463. *The Times of India,* 13th May, 2002.
464. *The Times of India,* 15th May, 2002.
465. *The Times of India,* 21st June, 2002.
466. Ibid.
467. *The Times of India,* 2nd July, 2002.
468. *The Times of India,* 1st August, 2002.
469. *The Times of India,* 22nd October, 2002.
470. *The Times of India,* 12th November, 2002.
471. *The Times of India,* 24th December, 2002.

Communal Riots
Statistics at a Glance

Table 1
Number of Deaths in Mumbai Riots (December-1992)

	Nirmal Nagar	*Kherwadi*
Muslims	10	12
Hindus	7	-
Total	**17**	**12**

As per the police records, 6 Hindus and 1 Muslim died in rioting.

(a) Deaths due to Police Firing (December)

Date of Firing	*Nirmal Nagar*	*Kherwadi*
Dec 7	5	2
Dec 8	3	10
Dec 9	2	-
Total	**10**	**12**

Out of 22 persons who died in police firing, 1 was a Hindu.

(b) Breakdown of Muslim and Hindu Casualties

	Muslim	*Hindu*
Total number of deaths	22	12
Total number of injured	58	26

(c) Area Wise Deaths at Nirmal Nagar Police Station

	Muslims	*Hindus*	*Unknown*
Bandra East	6	-	1
Khar East	5	8	-
Santacruz East	6	3	-

(d) Property Loss at Kherwadi Police Station

Muslim	Rs. 11,58,750
Hindu	Rs. 71,650

(e) Nirmal Nagar Police Station

Shops	45
Timber	5
Depots	4
Bakeries	4

(f) Police Records, January Riots

Nature of death	*Nirmal Nagar Police Station*			*Kherwadi Police Station*		
	M	*H*	*C*	*M*	*H*	*C*
Stabbing	5	2	-	5	1	1
Police Firing	8	3	-	-	-	-
Public Firing	-	3	-	-	-	-
Riots	4	4	-	-	-	-
Total	**17**	**12**	-	-	-	-

(g) Number of Persons Injured

Nature of death	*Nirmal Nagar Police Station*			*Kherwadi Police Station*		
	M	*H*	*C*	*M*	*H*	*C*
Stabbing	10	4	1	13	3	1
Police Firing	25	12	2	-	-	-
Public Firing	1	-	-	-	-	-
Riots	10	6	-	--	-	-
Total	**46**	**22**	**3**	**13**	**3**	**1**

Source: Economic and Political weekly, February 1993.

Table 2
Statistics of the Number of Persons Killed, Injured, Arrested and Loss of Properties in December–January, 1991-1992 Mumbai Riots

Area	*Number of Persons Killed*	*Number of Persons Injured*	*Number of Persons Arrested*	*Loss of Properties*
Bhendi Bazaar	8			10 Muslim shops were looted
Null bazaar				512 shops were looted (90 Hindus and he rest belong to Muslims)
Govandi	58 (in police firing) 10 in lotus colony, 48 in Chikalwadi, Indira Nagar, Umerkhadi, Bandra plot in Govandi area	660 (450 were injured in lathi charges)		35 vehicles were burnt and damaged,45 pan-bidi shops were looted and destroyed. 1Masjid was also burnt.
Behrampada and Nirmal Nagar	6	15		
Mahim	5 (in police firing)			680 (huts were gutted)
Jogeshwari	9 (7 killed in police-firing and 2 in stabbed)			

Area	Number of Persons Killed	Number of Persons Injured	Number of Persons Arrested	Loss of Properties
Kurla Halau Pul and other areas	2 (1 stabbed,1 in police firing	3		
Dharavi	42 (40 in police firing, 2 in mob violence) 30 Muslims,10 Hindus. Out of the two who died in mob violence 1was a Christian and 1 Dalit. But according to the police sources the number of persons killed was 32 (17 Muslims and 5 (Hindus)	300		489 houses were burnt and 91 shops were looted and burnt. 35 garment factories and 60 business houses were looted.
Gh-.kopar Asalfa village	202 (137 died in police firing)			500 shops were burnt down.

Note: Dharavi: But according to the police sources:

- Number of persons killed: 22 (17 Muslims and 5 Hindus)
- Number of persons injured: 200
- Loss of properties: 489 houses were burnt and 91 shops were looted and burnt. 35 garment factories and 60 business houses were looted. The death toll in rioting in second phase was quite high. The Times of India sources placed it at 557 (unofficially) on 22nd January 1993.
- Number of persons killed: 458 (officially)
- According to the police commissioner Shri Bapat out of 458 killed, 288 (Muslims) 170 (Hindus) 133 killed in police firing (75 Muslims and 50 Hindus,8 unknown) 259 killed in mob violence (186 Muslims,73 Hindus) 66 killed in arson (39 Hindus and 27 Muslims) The death toll will exceed 600.
- Total loss of properties: Nearly 10,000 houses were demolished or burnt.

Tata services drew up a tentative estimate of the loss during January riots

According to this estimate the loss of gross value of output of goods and services comes to Rs. 1,250 Crores.

- The loss of trading business: Rs. 1,000 crores.
- The loss of exports: Rs. 2,000 crores.
- The loss of tax revenue: Rs. 150 crore
- Loss of properties worth Rs. 4,000 crores.

Thus according to the estimate the total losses came nearly to Rs. 9,000 crore.

Source: *Bombay's Shame: A Report on Bombay Riots*: Ekta Samiti, Bombay

(a) Maharashtra

Number of communal riots from March 1995 to September 1999

- Number of riots: 25
- Number of persons killed: 17
- Loss of property: 68.60%(Hindus) 30.09% (Muslims)
- Damage to Government property: 5.52 lakhs
- Number of communal riots: 44
- Number of person's dead: 41(17 died in police firing)
- Number of persons injured: 1065
- Value of the loss of property: 31.5%(13.23% Hindus) (17.22% Muslims)
- Police registered cases: 622
- Number of persons registered FIR: 4,144
- Number of persons arrested under preventive detention: 4,000
- Damage to governmental property: 1 crore

Source: *The Times of India,* October 1, 2002.

According to the State Minorities commission from October 18, 2002, 50 riots have taken place.

(b) Bhivandi, Jalgaon and Mahad (1970)

- Number of persons killed: 43 (1 Hindu) (42 Muslims)
- 2 died of stab wounds
- 39 died of suffocation and burns
- Number of persons Injured: 47; Out of 47 patients,10 had bullet injuries. Out of which 9 were Hindus
- Total loss of Hindu properties: 6
- Total loss of Muslim owned properties: 380
- Total loss of properties: 386
- Total loss of Hindu owned properties: Rs. 83,725
- Total loss of Muslim owned properties: Rs. 33,90,997
- Total loss of property: Rs. 34,74,722

(c) Bhivandi

- Number of persons dead: 78
- Total number of Hindu deaths: 17
- Total number of Muslim deaths: 59
- Total number of deaths of persons whose community could not be ascertained: 2
- Number of persons injured: 335
- Hindus: 109
- Muslims: 192
- Police personnel: 28
- Identification of communities not ascertained: 6

Table 3
Comparative Table of Loss According to the Collectorate and the District Police

Loss Suffered	*Collectorate*	*District Police*
Hindus arson	Rs. 57,15,029	Rs.60,01,192
Muslims arson	Rs.52,66,705	Rs.71,64,835
Hindus looting	Rs.16,41,177	Rs.10,38,368
Muslims looting	Rs.13,97,949	Rs.11,15,768
Total loss suffered by Hindus	Rs. 73,56,206	Rs. 70,39,560
Total loss suffered by Muslims	Rs. 66,54,654	Rs. 82,80,603
Total loss	Rs. 1,40,10,860	Rs.1,53,20,163

Source: Report of the Commission of Enquiry into Communal Disturbances at Bhivandi, Jalgaon and Mahad in May 1970, p. 138.

(a) Ranchi/Hatia (1967)

- Number of persons Killed: 184. 19 (Hindus), 164 (Muslims)
- Number of persons arrested: 611; 409 (Hindus), 102 (Muslims)
- 78 houses affected by arson
- 65 shops and business premises affected by arson
- 195 houses affected by loot or damaged
- 128 shops and business houses affected by loot or damaged
- 3 places of worship and 1 school were damaged

Source: Report of the Commission of Inquiry on Communal Disturbances Ranchi-Hatia August 22-29 1967, 1968 p. 53.

(b) Bhagalpur Bihar (1990)

On 26th October:

- Number of persons killed: 18

On 27th October:

- Number of persons killed: 108
- Villages affected: 206
- Houses burnt to ashes: 3,932
- Shops looted and burnt: 891
- Power looms looted and burnt: 3,000
- Muslims killed: 876
- Hindus killed: 150
- Missing persons: 106
- Hindus arrested: 1,100
- Muslims arrested: 900
- Persons who lost their means of livelihood: 50,000-60,000
- 37 Mosques, 7 Madrasas, 8 tombs and 5 Shiva Imam balas were destroyed. The number of Hindu houses gutted is more than 300. 100 shops were looted, burnt and damaged. Mosques were destroyed at Naya Bazar, Mundichak, Shujgunj, Maruf chak, Golghat, Burhanath.

Source: Report of the Commission of Inquiry on Communal Disturbances Bhagalpur (1990).

(c) Ahmedabad Riots (1969)

- Number of persons killed: 512 (officially)
- The breakup of number of persons Killed: 24 Hindus, 430 Muslims, 58 others
- 437 (unofficially)
- Number of persons injured: 461 (officially)
- The breakup of number of persons injured are: 232 Hindus and 329 Musims
- 1,084 (unofficially)
- (428 Hindus 592 Muslims 10 Others)
- Loss of properties: Total loss of properties: 6,742
- The loss of properties of Hindus: 573
- The loss of properties of Muslims was 4,226
- According to the government the loss of Governmental properties were: 1,943
- The loss of Hindu properties: 98
- The loss of Muslim properties: 1,845
- The damage to the properties both movable and immovable are estimated to be of Rs. 4,23,24,069.54 paise out of which the damage to Hindu properties is Rs. 75,85,845.00 and of Muslim properties is Rs. 3,47,38,224.54 paise
- *Religious places destroyed*:

  The number of religious places destroyed or damaged was 37 Mosques, 50 Darghas, 6 Kabrasthans and 3 temples.

Source: Inquiry Commission Report into the Communal Disturbances at Ahmedabad and other Places in Gujarat on and after 18th September 1969.

(d) Sabarkhanta District

- Number of Incident: 1
- Number of persons arrested: 10
- Loss of properties: 1 house,1 cabin and 1 shop belonging to Muslim was burnt.
- Village affected: Tajpur and Talod.

(e) Junagadh District

- Number of incidents: 40.
- Number of persons arrested: 6.
- Loss of property: Shops of Muslims were set on fire. 1 Mosque was also burnt down.
- Village affected: Mandvi

(f) Rajkot District

- Number of incidents: 3
- Loss of properties: Shops were looted, attacked, damaged and burnt some Muslim shops, houses and
- motor cars.
- Villages affected: Gon Dal district

(g) Mehsana District

Place	*Number of Instances*	*Place*	*Number of Instances*
Kadi	90	Unjha	11
Mehsana	64	Visnagar	31
Kalol	7	Vijapur	35

(h) Vadodara

- Number of persons killed: 7 (4 Muslims,3 Hindus)
- *Number of persons injured:* 44
- The total loss of properties: 113.
- Out of 87 Muslim shops 46 were looted and burnt.
- 2 were Hindu shops
- In the city police station: Out of 494 Muslim shops 199 were burnt or looted. 39 (Hindu shops were looted and burnt.)
- Out of 41 Mosques 12 were damaged.
- Out of 145 Darghas 35 were damaged and destroyed.
- The loss suffered by Muslims is Rs. 33,26,006.
- The loss suffered by Hindus is Rs. 4,58,210.

Source: Inquiry Commission Report into the communal disturbances at Ahmedabad and other places in Gujarat on and after 18th September 1969 Baroda p. 288.

(i) Jamshedpur, Bihar (1979)

- Number of persons Killed: 108
  79 (Muslims)
  25 (Hindus)
  1 (Christian)
  3 (unknown identity)

Source: *Inquiry Commission Report into the Communal Disturbances at Jamshedpur, Bihar*

(j) Surat, Gujarat, (1992)

- Number of persons killed: 300 (95% Muslims) 200 (official)
- Loss of properties: 20 Industries were looted, burnt and destroyed, of which 8 were of large scale
- Category, 1 large scale industry belonged to Hindu while 12 belonged to the small scale category.
- 1,000 houses and shops were looted and burnt, 900 belonged to Muslims. 15 Mosques and 2 temples were partially or wholly damaged.

(k) Kota, Rajasthan, (1989)

- Number of persons killed: 21 (officially, out of which 7 were killed by gun shot injuries and 4 were killed by sharp edged weapons.)
- 26 (unofficially out of which 22 were Muslims and 4 Hindus)
- *Number of persons injured:* 67: (26 Muslims); (41 Hindus)

Table 4
List of Life and Property Confirmed:
Gujarat Carnage February 2002

Major affected	*State*	*Ahmedabad*	*Panchmahal*	*Sabarkanth*	*Dahod*	*Mehsana*	*Anand*	*Kheda*
Districts	19	↓	↓	↓	↓	↓	↓	↓
Affected Places	198	69	14	26	10	06	10	14
Total Killed, including	1071	447	142	129	91	56	54	34
{Police firing}	200	110	08	08	06	03	06	11
{Burning}	458	2,04	42	82	44	32	15	14
Total injured	1973	-	-	-	-	-	-	-
Total religious places damaged	527	77	51	57	66	26	94	58
No. of residential properties damaged or destroyed (LRP)	10,554	1,119	115	1,924	NA	131	143	204
No. of commercial properties (LCP)	17,811	1,495	NA	1,946	NA	100	17	612
Estimated Valued	687 cr.	NA	NA	NA	NA	NA	NA	NA

Source: Muslim India 235, July 2002.

Table 5

Financial Assistance for Loss of Residential Property/Earning Assets

	Total No. of Housing Units	*Total Assistance (in lakhs)*	*Average Amount per unit*	*Maximum*	*Minimum*	*Max. Damage*
Urban Areas (Total)	1,567	110.02 Max ceiling 50,000	7,021	4,800 in Narmada	3,094 for 64 units in Kheda	4,584*for 1212 units in Ahmedabad
Rural Areas (Total)	2,902	589.88	20,327	37,172 for 110 units in Anand	6,452 for 405 units in Kheda	18,319 for758 in Panchmahal
Urban Areas (Partial)	7,716	448.56	5,813	12,412 for 68 units in Dahod	4,782 for 4280 units in Ahmedabad	4,782 for 4280 units in Ahmedabad
Rural Areas (Partial)	7,032	898.64	12,751	22,333 for 9 units in Bhavnagar	1,909 for 11 units in Valsad	16,677 for 1388 units in Panchmahal
Earning Assets (Rural)	3,926	230.46	5,870	9,000 for 35 units in Rajkot	3,000 for 1 unit in Valsad	6,268 for 500 units in Kheda
Earning Assets (Urban)	5,077	359.37	7,078	8,898 for 422 units in Panchmahal	1000 for unit in Navsari	6,570 for 1144 units in Sabarkantha

*Difference for total or partial damage is only Rs. 304

Source: Muslim India 235, July 2002.

Table 6
Gujarat Massacre: Physical and Economic Toll (30 March, 2002)

Districts	*Towns/ Villages*	*Life Lost*			*Properties Lost*	
		Torched	*Police Firing*	*Total Deaths*	*Residential*	*Commer-cial*
Ahmedabad	54	144	46	351	642	1175
Amrely	1	1	0	1	0	0
Banaskantha	6	9	6	19	220	3
Baruch	4	0	0	5	57	30
Bhavnagar	2	7	5	12	40	0
Ghandinagar	7	1	1	13	12	30*
Junagarh	2	2	2	5	0	27
Kheda	11	1	10	31	57	88
Mehsana	3	32	3	55	33	100
Panchmahal	14	40	1	106	115	0
Rajkot	1	0	0	4	70	0
Sabarkantha	22	75	8	122	822	509
Surat	7	4	4	13	0	155
Surendranagar	1	0	0	0	0	35
Vadodara	10	5	6	36	361	210
Anand	9	15	6	51	139	17
Patan	2	2	4	6	30	0
Dahod	10	19	6	53	0	0
Narmada	1	0	2	2	0	0
Total	167	357	110	885	2598	2379

Source: *Muslim India* 233, May, 2002

Table 7
Relief and Rehabilitation of Riot Victims
Goverment of Gujarat's Report (As on 6 June, 2002)

Item	*No. Cases Reported*	*No. Cases Paid*	*Amoun (Rs. in crore)*
Ex-gratia payment to next-of-kin of those killed	952	708	10.00
Cash compensation for injuries (Individuals)	1,864	1,439	0.69
Cash doles to individuals	-	40,256	0.66
Compensation for loss of household kits (Families)	NA	27,787	3.70

Table 8
Ration Distribution

No. of Relief Camps	*Inmates*	*Cash Assistance (Rs. In Lakhs)*	*Ration (in qntls)*
32	37,214	433.58	52,495.61

Source: *Muslim India* 235, July 2002.

Table 9
Cash Assistance for Loss of Earning Assets

No. of Cases Surveyed	*Estimated Damage (Rs. in lacs)*	*No. of Cases paid.*	*Amount Paid (Rs. in crore)*	*Average*
15856	8355.66	9374	6.09	6,492

Source: *Muslim India* 235, July 2002.

Table 10
Housing Assistance

Item	*No. of Cases Surveyed*	*Estimated Damage (Rs. in Crore)*	*No. of Cases Paid*	*Amount Paid (Rs. in Crore)*	*Average*
Partially Damaged Houses	19,291	39.10	15,661	13.94	8,904
Fully Damaged Houses	5,616	25.89	4,593	7.15	15,573
Total	24,907	64.99	20,254	21.10	10,416

Source: *Muslim India* 235, July 2002.

Table 11
Foodgrain to BPL Families

No. of Families Identified	*No. of Families Assisted*	*Foodgrain Distributed (in Qntls)*
19,02,745	17,73,969	1,81,775,54

Source: *Muslim India* 235, July 2002.

Table 12
Assistance to Industries/Shops/Hotels

Item	*Industries*	*Units/Shops/Show Rooms/ Go down*	*Hotels*
Application Received	630	5528	183
Cases Surveyed	528	2760	164
Damage assessed (Rs. in crores)	27.31	47.87	11.38
Units Assisted	NIL	NIL	NIL

Source: *Muslim India* 235, July 2002.

Table 13
Rehabilitation of Small Business

No. of Affected Units	*Applications Sponsored*	*Sanctioned*	*Amount Sanctioned*
4000	772	28	117.52

Source: *Muslim India* 235, July 2002.

Table 14
Bank Loan

No. of Units Surveyed	*No. of Units Recommend to Banks*	*Cases Sanctioned Cases*	*(Amt. in Crore)*	*Disbursed cases Cases*	*Amt. (in Crore)*
3452	2110	132	3.51	34	1.90

Source: *Muslim India* 235, July 2002.

Table 15
Rehabilitation of Orphans and Widows

Orphans Identified	*Widows Identified*	*No. of Pensions Granted*
38	955	555

Source: *Muslim India* 235, July 2002.

Table 16
Gujarat Massacre: Physical and Economic Toll
(as on 30 March, 2002)

Districts	*Towns/ Villages*	*Life Lost*			*Properties Lost*	
		Torched	*Police Firing*	*Total Deaths*	*Residential*	*Commercial*
Ahmedabad	54	144	46	351	642	1175
Amrely	1	1	0	1	0	0
Banaskantha	6	9	6	19	220	3
Baruch	4	0	0	5	57	30
Bhavnagar	2	7	5	12	40	0
Ghandinagar	7	1	1	13	12	30*
Junagarh	2	2	2	5	0	27
Kheda	11	1	10	31	57	88
Mehsana	3	32	3	55	33	100
Panchmahal	14	40	1	106	115	0
Rajkot	1	0	0	4	70	0
Sabarkantha	22	75	8	122	822	509
Surat	7	4	4	13	0	155
Surendranagar	1	0	0	0	0	35
Vadodara	10	5	6	36	361	210
Anand	9	15	6	51	139	17
Patan	2	2	4	6	30	0
Dahod	10	19	6	53	0	0
Narmada	1	0	2	2	0	0
Total	167	357	110	885	2,598	2,379

*This includes Wakf Board and MDFC offices Based on Gujarat relief commissioner's note.
Source: Muslim India 233, May, 2002

Table 17
Frequency and Casualities of Communal Incidents (1950–2002)

Year	*Incidents*	*Killed*	*Injured*
1950	56	50	256
1954	84	34	512
1955	75	24	457
1956	82	35	575
1957	58	12	316
1958	40	7	369
1959	42	41	1344
1960	26	14	262
1961	92	108	593
1962	60	43	348
1963	61	26	489
1964	1070	1919	2053

Year	*Incidents*	*Killed*	*Injured*
1965	173	34	758
1966	144	45	467
1967	198	301	880
1968	346	133	1309
1969	519	674	2702
1970	521	298	1607
1971	321	103	1330
1972	210	70	1056
1973	242	72	1318
1974	248	87	1123
1975	205	33	890
1976	169	39	794
1977	188	36	1122
1978	230	108	1853
1979	304	261	2379
1980	421	375	2691
1981	319	196	2613
1982	470	238	3025
1983	500	1143	3652
1984	476	445	4836
1985	525	332	3751
1986	768	418	5389
1987	711	383	3860
1988	710	259	3103
1989	922	802	3871
1990	1421	1241	3913
1991	29	877	6370
1992	37	1972	13571
1993	33	960	4496
1994	8	39	450
1995	17	54	235
1996	20	24	28
1997	70	137	495
1998	600	207	2065
1999	52	43	248
2000	24	91	165
2001	27	56	158
2002	28	1173s	2272
Total	**13952**	**14686**	**68182**

Sources: 1. *P.R. Raj Gopal* op cit pp. 16-12.
2. PhD. Thesis by Haresh Chandra Sharma at Jamia Millia Islamia, New Delhi.

Note: From 1995-2002 the data is not from the Home Ministry records. It is the data collected from the newspaper readings.

Table 18
Number of Deaths in Communal Riots in Various States/Union Territories

Name of State or Union Territories	*Number of Deaths in Communal Riots*	*Value of Loss of Properties*
Andhra Pradesh	20	Not available
Assam	94	Rs. 49 lakhs
Bihar	10	Not available
Delhi	15	Not available
Gujarat	208	Rs. 7.25 lakhs
Haryana	1	Not available
Karnataka	78	Rs. 5.97 crores
Kerala	21	Rs. 1.5 crores
Maharashtra	259	Rs. 3.9 crores
Madhya Pradesh	133	Rs. 1.5 crores
Orissa	2	Rs. 6 lakhs
Punjab	Not available	Rs. 6 lakhs
Rajasthan	49	Rs. 7.37 lakhs
Tamil Nadu	2	Rs. 68.58 lakhs
Uttar Pradesh	170	Not available
West Bengal	27	Not available.

Source: Rights of the Minorities communities in a secular state on 10th November 1995 at the Calcutta cenetary hall

Table 19
Break-up of Number of Persons Killed in Various Riots

Name of Place	*Number of Persons Killed*			*Total*
	Hindus	*Muslims*	*Others and Unidentified*	
Aligarh (1961)	1	12	-	13
Ranchi/Hatia (1967)	20	156	1	177
Ahmedabad (1969)	24	430	58	512
Jalgaon (1970)	1	42	-	43
Bhiwandi (1970)	17	59	2	78
Ferozabad (1972)	3	16	2	21
Aligarh (1978)	6	19	3	28
Jamshedpur (1979)	12	107/117	8	127/137
Mordabad (1980)	18	142	0	166

Name of Place	*Number of Persons Killed*			*Total*
	Hindus	*Muslims*	*Others and Unidentified*	
Meerut (1982)	6	21	2	29
Total	**108**	**1004/1014**	**76**	**1188/1198**
Godhra (1981)	2	2	-	4
Meerut (1982)	10	90	-	100
Meenakshipuram (1982)	150	876	-	1026
Aurangabad (1988)	5	5	1	11
Aligarh	3	2	-	5
Bhagalpur (1990)	150	876	-	1026
Sullia (1991)	-	2	3	5
Soro (1991)	2	14	-	16
Bhadravati (1994)	1	1	-	2
Palamu (1995)	1	4	-	5
Daulatpur (1998)	1	1	-	2
Varanasi (2000)	1	1	-	2
Biharsharief (2000)	-	1		1
Ranchi (2001)	-	3	-	3
Mordabad (2001)	-	2	-	2
Banswada (2001)	-	3	-	3
Mysore (2001)	-	1	-	1

Note: The data from the year 1995 is the data based on newspapers findings. So certain errors and biases may be there while recording this data.

Source: Rights of the minorities communities in a secular state on 10th November 1995 at the Calcutta cenetary hall.

Table 20
Statistics of Baroda at a Glance (1981-82)

Phases	Sr. No.	Dates of Incidents	Deaths by Firing	Deaths by Stabbing	Injured by Firing	Injured by Stabbing	Injured by Other Weapons	Destruction of Properties Worth Rs.
1	1	13-09-1981	1	3	-	41	74	1,71,492
2	2	16-12-1981	-	-	-	-	8	500
	3	17-12-1981	-	-	-	-	-	-
	4	17-03-1982	-	2	-	-	19	77,435
	5	26-04-1982	1	-	-	-	-	150
	6	04-05-1982	-	-	-	-	1	-
	7	13-05-1982	-	-	-	-	11	400
	8	19-05-1982	2	1	4	-	16	15,300
	9	04-06-1982	-	-	-	1	1	150
	10	12-06-1982	-	-	-	1	4	4,100
	11	18-06-1982	-	-	-	-	4	-
	12	19-06-1982	-	-	-	2	-	-
	13	25-08-1982	-	2	-	-	-	700
3	14	02-10-1982	-	-	-	-	-	4,900
	15	23-10-1982	-	-	22	-	12	-
	16	27-10-1982	7	1	7	20	33	3,20,198
	17	07-12-1982	-	1	-	3	-	7,700
	18	13-12-1982	4	8	3	16	29	61,00,000
Total			**15**	**18**	**36**	**84**	**212**	**67,06,621**

Source: Communalism in India Edited by Dr Asghar Ali Engineer and Moin Shakir, pp. 142, 143

Table 21
State-Base Riots Data (Death)

Year	*U.P.*	*Gujarat*	*Bihar*	*Maharashtra*	*A.P.*
1960	10	-	-	-	-
1961	30	-	-	-	-
1962	10	-	-	5	-
1963	-	-	-	15	-
1964	-	-	75	-	10
1965	5	-	-	-	-
1966	-	-	10	25	-
1967	-	-	36	-	-
1968	25	-	-	50	-
1969	-	640	-	-	-
1970	-	10	29	200	-
1971	25	-	-	-	-
1972	30	-	-	-	-
1973	10	-	15	10	-
1974	-	-	25	5	-
1975	-	-	5	10	-
1976	-	-	5	-	-
1977	10	10	-	-	-
1978	60	-	-	-	20
1979	10	-	170	-	-
1980	165	10	-	-	16
1981	-	-	75	-	35
1982	45	-	5	-	-
1983	5	-	-	20	60
1984	2	-	-	280	52
1985	-	150	-	-	2
1986	45	120	-	25	-
1987	150	20	-	5	-
1988	30	-	27	20	-
1989	25	10	435	-	-
1990	200	155	20	-	126
1991	86	15	-	5	-
1992	40	325	115	403	30
1993	-	50	-	575	-
1994	1	2	-	-	-
1995	6	-	2	1	1
1996	2	1	2	4	2
1997	27	-	-	25	3
1998	8	-	4	3	8
1999	11	17	-	1	-
2000	9	20	1	4	-
2001	22	2	11	3	-
2002	-	1071	-	45	-

Note: This data is not from the Home Ministry records.

Table 22
State-Wise Death (1960-2002)

State	*Death*
Haryana	20
Kerala	46
Tamil Nadu	216
Jammu & Kashmir	50
Rajasthan	133
Orissa	100
Delhi	2148
Assam	140
West Bengal	175
Karnataka	313
Andhra Pradesh	379
Madhya Pradesh	391
Bihar	917
Uttar Pradesh	1298
Maharashtra	1492
Gujarat	1569

Note: This data is not based on Home Ministry records.

Table 23
Most Riot-Prone Urban Areas 1960-2002

Town Name	*Total Death*
Ahmedabad	1103
Bombay (Mumbai)	906
Hyderabad	331
Meerut	263
Bhiwandi	194
Jamshedpur	194
Moradabad	166
Aligarh	146
Vadodara	126
Delhi	2148
Kanpur	86
Thane	69
Kolkatta	64
Jalgaon	52
Indore	45
Varanasi	44
Allahabad	43
Aurangabad	30
Ranchi	32

Town Name	*Total Death*
Srinagar	29
Bangalore	28
Ferozabad	25
Malegaon	35
Godhra	73
Coimbatore	110

Note: This data is not collected from the Home Ministry records.

Table 24
Year-Wise, State-Wise Break-Up of Data on Major Riots (1950-2002)

Year	*State*	*No. of Riots*	*No. of People Killed*	*No. of People Injured*	*No. of People Arrested*
1	2	3	4	5	6
1950	West Bengal & Assam	---	50	256	1719
1961	Madhya Pradesh	---	55	158	1003
1962	West Bengal	---	14	64	----
1964	West Bengal	---	285	105	----
	Bihar, Orissa &	---			
	Madhya Pradesh		346	458	----
1965	Rajasthan	—	2	12	----
	Gujarat	4			
1966	Rajasthan	---	1	----	----
1967	a) West Bengal	---	11	100	---
	b) Bihar	---	184	100	611
	c) Kashmir	---	3	162	----
	d) Maharashtra	---	4	----	----
1968	a) Assam		2	7	
	b) Uttar Pradesh	2	7	83	233
	c) Maharashtra	2	20	----	----
		2	32	----	----
1969	Gujarat	---	1000	----	1
1970	Maharashtra	---	145	382	----
1971	Uttar Pradesh	1	---	----	----
1972	Uttar Pradesh	2	16	----	----
1973	Uttar Pradesh	1	9	40	600
1974	Delhi	1	10	131	----
1975	Andhra Pradesh	1	10	8	----

1	2	3	4	5	6
1976	----	----	----	----	-----
1977	Uttar Pradesh	1	8	65	----
1978	a) Uttar Pradesh	3	43		
	b) Jammu & Kashmir	1	3		
	c) Andhra Pradesh	2	3		
	d) Madhya Pradesh	1	1		
1979	a) Bihar	3	165	483	1215
	b) Uttar Pradesh	1	7	48	----
	c) West Bengal	1	28	----	----
	d) Andhra Pradesh	1	---	100	1425
1980	a) Bihar	1	---	2	----
	b) Maharashtra	1	4	58	----
	c) Delhi	2	2	12	----
	d) Uttar Pradesh	8	142	207	883
	e) Madhya Pradesh	1	3	34	----
	f) Jammu & Kashmir	1	----	---	2000
	g) Karnataka	1	1	3	----
	h) Tamil Nadu	1	---	14	----
	i) Gujarat	1	6	30	2
	j) Orissa	1	---	---	----
1981	a) Gujarat	6	11	49	174
	b) Bihar	1	54	1000	782
	c) Uttar Pradesh	2	---	42	25
	d) Andhra Pradesh	2	28	256	1325
	e) Rajasthan	1	---	3	28
	f) Punjab	1	---	---	----
1982	a) Gujarat	3	15	62	622
	b) Uttar Pradesh	2	111	24	----
	c) Maharashtra	2	----	8	----
	d) Punjab	1	----	32	----
	e) Tamil Nadu	5	1044	5	2050
	f) Karnataka	1	1	---	----
1983	a) Jammu Kashmir	1	---	14	----
	b) Karnataka	1	5	50	----
	c) Bihar	2	4	2	115
	d) Maharashtra	2	10	3	500
	e) Andhra Pradesh	3	47	164	345
1984	a) Punjab	4	35	---	----
	b) Haryana	1	9	---	----
	c) Maharashtra	2	234	150	----
	d) Delhi	2	2000	---	8

1	2	3	4	5	6
	e) Andhra Pradesh	1	19	---	----
	f) Madhya Pradesh	2	7	---	----
	g) Assam	1	2	9	----
	h) Karnataka	1	---	---	----
1985	Gujarat	2	51	12	----
1986	a) Punjab	4	51	----	----
	b) Jammu Kashmir	2	---	200	----
	c) Delhi	2	6	76	144
	d) Madhya Pradesh	2	7	---	100
	e) West Bengal	1	---	8	20
	f) Maharashtra	3	12	105	145
	g) Uttar Pradesh	1	6	27	88
	h) Gujarat	1	40	250	6
	i) Karnataka	2	21	115	----
	j) Bihar	1	3	---	----
1987	a) Gujarat	6	20	128	50
	b) Madhya Pradesh	1	---	---	130
	c) Uttar Pradesh	1	400	131	2530
	d) Delhi	2	17	---	250
	e) Maharashtra	1	60	60	---
1988	a) Jammu Kashmir	2	---	---	----
	b) Karnataka	1	6	60	126
	c) Uttar Pradesh	5	6	51	9
	d) Maharashtra	3	21	192	600
1989	a) Jammu Kashmir	2	6	120	----
	b) Maharashtra	3	5	4	----
	c) Uttar Pradesh	5	26	215	51
	d) Rajasthan	4	19	34	58
	e) Karnataka	2	5	12	70
	f) Bihar	7	1083	91	2249
	g) Tamil Nadu	1	3	11	----
	h) Gujarat	4	3	31	24
	i) Madhya Pradesh	2	22	6	----
1990	a) Rajasthan	3	54	13	----
	b) Karnataka	5	44	75	27
	c) Maharashtra	4	3	123	----
	d) Gujarat	6	133	48	----
	e) Uttar Pradesh	5	244	127	220
	f) Bihar	1	----	----	45
	g) Tamil Nadu	2	9	12	----
	h) Delhi	1	6	25	237
	i) Andhra Pradesh	1	200	300	418
	j) Punjab	1	35	---	----

1	2	3	4	5	6
1991	a) Uttar Pradesh	7	92	1	538
	b) West Bengal	2	7	38	----
	c) Orissa	2	24	2	----
	d) Gujarat	3	28	9	----
	e) Madhya Pradesh	1	5	20	----
	f) Delhi	1	----	2	----
	g) Kerala	1	3	10	----
	h) Karnataka	1	----	5	----
1992	a) Uttar Pradesh	2	11	21	24
	b) West Bengal	1	1	---	----
	c) Gujarat	4	331	179	----
	d) Kerala	1	6	---	----
	e) Maharashtra	2	205	116	101
	f) Bihar	1	48	100	----
	g) Rajasthan	1	----	---	32
1993	a) Gujarat	2	4	1	----
	b) Maharashtra	1	458	----	1700
	c) Delhi	1	2	6	-----
	d) Madhya Pradesh	1	----	---	58
	e) Manipur	1	98	---	----
1994	a) Goa	1	---	---	22
	b) Gujarat	2	2	---	90
	c) Karnataka	4	37	430	300
	d) Uttar Pradesh	1	---	---	----
1995	a) Uttar Pradesh	6	22	21	308
	b) Kerala	6	6	15	----
	c) Karnataka	3	1	65	7
	d) Tamil Nadu	2	4	100	7
	e) Orissa	1	2	---	----
	f) Bihar	2	9	---	8
	g) Andhra Pradesh	1	5	21	----
	h) Maharashtra	1	----	14	----
1996	a) Andhra Pradesh	3	3	9	----
	b) Tamil Nadu	1	2	7	35
	c) Bihar	1	2	---	2
	d) Gujarat	2	1	17	2
	e) Rajasthan	1	1	11	----
	f) Uttar Pradesh	5	1	26	662
	g) West Bengal	1	6	30	----
	h) Maharashtra	2	4	14	----
	i) Karnataka	1	3	20	----
1997	a) Tamil Nadu	3	88	83	----
	b) Maharashtra	7	8	105	24
	c) Karnataka	2	8	28	---

1	2	3	4	5	6
	d) Jammu & Kashmir	1	----	228	27
	e) Uttar Pradesh	5	51	31	42
	f) Delhi	1	---	8	49
	g) Andhra Pradesh	3	3	55	----
	h) Rajasthan	1	6	10	----
1998	a) Uttar Pradesh	3	6	64	256
	b) Maharashtra	2	3	4	24
	c) Tamil Nadu	2	75	---	500
	d) Rajasthan	2	3	66	16
	e) Andhra Pradesh	1	8	36	----
	f) Gujarat	3	---	2	3
	g) Bihar	1	4	29	----
	h) Karnataka	1	8	60	----
1999	a) Gujarat	6	17	44	53
	b) Uttar Pradesh	7	11	61	----
	c) Tamil Nadu	3	2	---	350
	d) Delhi	1	---	---	----
	e) Maharashtra	3	1	16	130
	f) Andhra Pradesh	1	---	35	----
	g) Madhya Pradesh	1	1	15	90
	h) Orissa	1	---	12	----
2000	a) Uttar Pradesh	7	9	34	241
	b) Gujarat	7	18	47	26
	c) Rajasthan	3	16	3	25
	d) Maharashtra	3	4	4	32
	e) West Bengal	1	4	---	----
	f) Bihar	2	1	24	----
	g) Delhi	2	19	17	----
	h) Andhra Pradesh	1	---	---	----
2001	a) Bihar	2	11	6	----
	b) Jammu and Kashmir	1	---	---	----
	c) Maharashtra	11	16	126	178
	d) Goa	61	---	---	----
	e) Uttar Pradesh	5	23	9	5
	f) Andhra Pradesh	1	---	4	----
	g) Rajasthan	3	3	34	----
	h) Gujarat	1	2	10	4
	i) Karnataka	1	1	---	----
2002	a) Maharashtra	9	29	220	786
	b) Andhra Pradesh	1	---	---	----
	c) Rajasthan	2	5	15	----
	d) West Bengal	1	1	8	----

1	2	3	4	5	6
	e) Karnataka	1	---	---	----
	f) Uttar Pradesh	1	---	---	1
	g) Chennai	1	---	---	----
	h) Gujarat		1071	1973	

Note: All the data which we have collected in this table are based upon the Riots which we have recorded in narrative part. This is not based upon the Home Ministry Records. This is the data which we have collected from various newspapers. There might be errors and biases while collecting this data.

Source: Communal riots: Hindus and Muslims in India: The Minorities commission in 1986 reported that in 1985-1986, reported that in 1985-1986 Andhra Pradesh had 102 incidents in which 10 people were killed and 108 injured while Gujarat listed only 60 incidents in which 230 people were killed and 959 injured,p. 89.

Table 25

Violence in India's Riot-Prone Cities as a Proportionate of All Reported Hindu-Muslim Violence 1950-95

RP1: Minimum of 15 deaths in 3 riots over 2 five-year periods.	*RP2: Minimum of 20 deaths in 4 riots over 3 five-year periods.*	*RP3: Minimum of 25 deaths in 5 riots over 4 five-year periods.*	*RP4: Minimum of 50 deaths in 10 riots over 5 five-year periods.*	*Deaths. 1950-1995.*
1	2	3	4	5
Bombay	Bombay	Bombay	Bombay	1137
Ahmedabad	Ahmedabad	Ahmedabad	Ahmedabad	1119
Hyderabad	Hyderabad	Hyderabad	Hyderabad	312
Meerut	Meerut	Meerut	Meerut	265
Jamshedpur	Jamshedpur	Jamshedpur		198
Bhivandi	Bhiwandi			194
Surat				194
Aligarh	Aligarh	Aligarh	Aligarh	160
Moradabad	Moradabad			149
Baroda	Baroda	Baroda	Baroda	109
Bhopal	Bhopal	Bhopal		108
Delhi	Delhi	Delhi	Delhi	93
Kanpur	Kanpur	Kanpur		81
Calcutta	Calcutta	Calcutta	Calcutta	63
Jabalpur				59
Bangalore	Bangalore	Bangalore		56
Jalgaon	Jalgaon	Jalgaon		49

1	2	3	4	5
Sitamarhi				47
Indore	Indore	Indore		45
Allahabad	Allahabad	Allahabd		37
Nagpur	Nagpur	Nagpur		37
Jaipur	Jaipur			32
Aurangabad	Aurangabad	Aurangabad		30
Srinagar	Srinagar	Srinagar		30
Ranchi				29
Malegaon	Malegaon			23
Godhra				18
Deaths in Riot-prone cities	4706	4359	3887	3263
All India Deaths 1950-1995.	7173	7173	7173	7173
Riot prone cities as a percentage of all India deaths	66	61	54	45.5
Riot-prone cities as a percentage of all urban deaths	69	64	58	49
Deaths in rural India as a percentage of all deaths.			3.57	

Source: Ethenic Conflict and Civic Life, Ashutosh Varshney, Oxford Publications, pp. 104-05.

Table 26
India's Most Riot-Prone Cities 1950-95

Cities	*Deaths 1950-95*	*Cities*	*Deaths 1950-95*
Mumbai	1137	Aligarh	160
Ahmedabad	1119	Baroda	109
Hyderabad	312	Delhi	93
Meerut	265	Calcutta	63

Note: These cities experienced a minimum of 50 deaths in 10 riots over 5 five-year periods.

Table 27
(a) Communal Tensions and Violence in Aligarh, 1950-94

Year	*Reported cause*
1950	Hindu passengers stop train, kill several Muslim passengers and assault Muslim citizens following interruption of national anthem at Aligarh Muslim university.
1954	Dispute between fruitseller and customer.
1956	Aligarh Muslim University students reported insulting remarks about the Prophet Muhammad in a popular book.
1961	Clash between students in Aligarh Muslim University
1966	Government's attempt to increase powers over Aligarh Muslim University.
1969	Hindu applause for visiting cricket team at Aligarh Muslim at Aligarh Muslim University.

Year	*Month*	*Reported*
1971	March	Arrest of a Hindu nationalist student leader at the time of elections.
1972	June	Hindu seven year old knocked down by a Muslim scooter driven by accident.
1977	October	Cause insufficiently reported.
1978	October	Clash between Hindu and Muslim wrestlers.
	November	Retribution for previous violence.
	December	Retribution for previous leaders.
1979	May	Clash between Hindu nationalists and Aligarh Muslim University students going on a train to protest in Delhi.
1980	August September	Police fires at a Muslim protest, rioting three times in two weeks.
	October	Arrest of two local journalists.
	November	Random stabbing.
		Muslims attack the Provincial Armed Constabulary.
1982	July	Cause insufficiently reported.
1983	March	Stone throwing by Hindu religious processionists.
1987	June	Police arrest of a Muslim.
1988	October	A market shutdown called by Hindu nationalists for Ayodhya march.
1990	November	Tension due to the Hindu Nationalists for Ayodhya.
	December	False rumours of Hindu patient killed in Aligarh Muslim University Medical college hospital.
1992	December	Desecration of Mosque in Ayodhya.
1994	March	Random stabbing.

(b) Communal Tension and Violence in Hyderabad, 1978-95

Year	*Month*	*Reported*
1978	March-April	Police atrocity toward Muslim.
1979	July	Hindu temple near a Mosque desecrated.
1979	November	Muslim call for shopkeepers strike after the forcible occupation of Mecca in Saudi Arabia by terrorism.
1980	January	Around parliamentary elections, stabbing of Hindu boy followed by an emotional funeral procession with the body of the deceased draped in Janata party flag.
1980	March	Petty quarrel
1980	September	Arrest of a wrestler.
1981	July	Muincipal elections due, playing of music before a mosque during the procession of Bonalu, a Hindu religious festival electi̇ons postponed.
1982	June	Marriage procession playing music in front of a Mosque.
1983	January	Election violence between MIM and BJP supporters.
1983	May	Marriage procession playing music in front of a mosque.
1983	September	Simultaneous occurence of Ganesh Procession andId.
1984	May	By-election clash between MIM and TDP workers.
1984	July	Attack on Bonalu procession.
1984	September	Violence during Hindu (Ganesh and Bonalu) procession and Muslim festivals.
1985	March	Assembly elections.
1986		Small skirmishes the year round, no major violence.
1990	July	Land dispute between two spectators.
1990	October	Small skirmishes.
1990	December	Murder of a wrestler.
1992-93	Dec-Jan	Destruction of a Babri Mosque.
1995	June	Tension in the old city.

Source: *Ethenic Conflict and Civic Life*, Ashutosh Varshney pp. 158-59.

(c) Break-up Killed

Year	*Number of Incidents*	*Hindus Killed*	*Muslims Killed*	*Other/Police Killed*	*Total*
1968	346	24	99	10	133
1969	519	66	558	49	674
1970	521	68	176	54	298
1971	321	38	65	-	103
1972	210	21	45	3	70
1973	242	26	45	1	72

Year	*Number of Incidents*	*Hindus Killed*	*Muslims Killed*	*Other/Police Killed*	*Total*
1974	248	26	61	-	87
1975	205	11	22	-	33
1976	169	20	19	-	39
1977	188	12	24	-	36
1978	219	51	56	1	108
1979	304	80	150	31	261
1980	427	87	278	10	375

Table 28
(a) Bhivandi Riot

Community of the Persons Fired Upon	*Number of Occasions*	*Number of Rounds Fired*	*Number of Rounds Per Occasion*	*Casualties.*
Muslim	26	353	13.6	9 Muslims died and 5 Muslims injured.
Hindu	4	11	2.8	Nil
Could not be ascertained	6	9	1.5	Nil
In the air	1	6	6.0	Nil

Name of the place	*Hindus*	*Muslims*
Ferozabad (1972)	Nil	6
Aligarh Sept-Oct 1978	Nil	7
Meerut 1982	Nil	6

During the calendar year 1980, 89 Hindus and 275 Muslims died during communal clashes. The total number of arrests was 5457 Hindus and 5743 Muslims. This shows that for each Hindu who was killed in the riots 5743/5789, 64 Muslims were arrested, whereas for each Muslim casualty 5457/5275, 20 Hindus were arrested.

The pattern of arrests and casualties during Bhivandi clashes between 7th to 12th May 1970 were as follows.

(b) Bhivandi (7-12 May, 1970)

Arrests for cognizable	*Hindus*	*Muslims*
Offences	21	901
Casualties	17	59

The number of arrested Hindus for each casualty of Muslims works out to 0.36 whereas the number of arrested Muslims for each Hindu casualty comes to 53.0.

The pattern of arrests in Meerut riots 1982 upto 15th September was as follows:

Table 29
Meerut Riots, (1982)

Item	*Hindus*	*Muslims*
Casualty	2	8
Arrested in substantive offences	124	231
Arrested in preventive offences	112	86

The pattern of arrest in such cases where Muslims were aggressively.

Hindus Arrested	*Muslims Arrested*	*Hindus Killed*	*Muslims Killed*
23	231	2	-

The pattern of arrest in such cases were Hindus were allegedly aggressive.

Hindus Arrested	*Muslims Arrested*	*Hindus Killed*	*Muslims Killed*
-	-	-	7

Table 30
Number of Persons Arrested in Bhagalpur Communal Riot from 26.10.89 to 11.12.89

Date	*Muslim*	*Hindu*	*Total*	*Date*	*Muslim*	*Hindu*	*Total*
26.10.89	223	22	245	17.11.89	46	7	53
27.10.89	119	-	119	18.11.89	6	17	23
28.10.89	16	-	16	19.11.89	-	2	2
29.10.89	81	16	97	20.11.89	-	29	29
30.10.89	41	30	71	21.11.89	2	4	6
31.10.89	125	34	159	22.11.89	8	47	55
1.11.89	-	3	3	23.11.89	1	9	10
2.11.89	1	56	57	25.11.89	96	-	96
3.11.89	-	42	42	26.11.89	5	11	16
4.11.89	-	12	12	27.11.89	9	11	20
8.11.89	2	7	9	31.11.89	-	2	2
9.11.89	3	19	22	1.12.89.	-	4	4

Date	Muslim	Hindu	Total	Date	Muslim	Hindu	Total
10.11.89	5	33	38	4.12.89	4	-	4
11.11.89	-	6	6	5.12.89	86	4	90
12.11.89	58	-	58	6.12.89	2	-	2
13.11.89	1	-	1	7.12.89	1	3	4
14.11.89	50	4	54	8.12.89	-	4	4
15.11.89	7	47	54	9.12.89	56	-	56
16.11.89	8	-	8	11.12.89	3	2	5
Total	740	331	1071	Total	325	156	481

- Total number of Muslims arrested: 1,065.
- Total number of Hindus arrested: 487.

Source: Communal riots the State and Law in India edited by Iqbal Ansari: pp. 109-13.

The pattern of casualties and arrests upto 15th September was as follows:

Table 31
Number of Casualties and Arrests upto 15th September

Item	*Hinduo*	*Muolimo*
Casualties	2	8
Arrested in substantive offences	124	231
Arrested in preventive offences	112	86
Number of people arrested under substantive sections per casualty of the other community	15	115

Table 32
Statistics of the Number of Persons Killed--Yearwise

Year	*Number of incidents*	*Number of persons killed*	*Number of persons killed in*			
			PF	*S*	*OM*	*T*
1	2	3	4	5	6	7
1950	1	51	--	-	-	-
1961	1	55	-	-	14	14
1962	1	14	-	-	14	14
1964	2	638	56	-	-	56
1967	4	176	3	-	-	3
1968	7	62	3	3	-	6
1969	3	431	26	-	-	26
1970	5	145	1	-	19	20
1972	2	23	5	-	-	5

1	2	3	4	5	6	7
1973	1	9	-	-	-	-
1974	1	10	-	-	-	-
1978	5	43	10	3	3	16
1979	5	-	192	-	-	-
1980	11	172	7	-	19	26
1981	2	75	-	-	-	-
1982	20	1	1	-	-	1
1984	26		32	-	127	
1985	1	43	6	-	8	14
1986	8	121	-	-	13	13
1987	4	372	-	-	-	-
1989	1	100	-	-	-	-
1990	6	1301	-	-	-	-
1991	-	-	-	-	-	-
1992	13	1215	-	-	-	-
1993	3	315	-	-	-	-
1994	1	-	-	-	-	-
1994	7	40	10	18	-	28

*PF - stands for Police firing, *S - stands for stabbing *OM - stands for other methods *T - stands for total

Table 33
Statistics of the Number of Persons (Community) Injured

Year	*Number of incidents*	*Number of persons injured*					*Number of persons injured in*			
		H	*M*	*P*	*O*	*T*	*PF*	*S*	*OM*	*T*
1	2	3	4	5	6	7	8	9	10	11
1950	1	110	146	-	-	256	-	-	-	-
1961	1	-	-	-	-	158	-	-	-	-
1962	1	-	-	-	-	64	-	-	-	-
1964	4	-	53	5	4	463	11	-	-	11
1967	4	20	-	142	-	422	-	-	-	-
1968	7	-	-	-	-	92	-	-	-	-
1969	3	11	-	-	-	11	-	-	-	-
1970	5	-	-	-	-	7	7	-	-	7
1972	2	-	-	-	-	-	-	-	-	-
1973	1	-	-	-	-	40	-	-	-	-
1974	1	-	-	-	-	300	-	--	-	-
1978	5	-	-	-	-	-	-	-	-	-
1979	5	-	-	-	-	531	-	-	-	-
1980	11					7				

1	2	3	4	5	6	7	8	9	10	11
1981	2					100				
1982	20									
1984	26					11				11
1985										
1986	8			97		200			97	
1987	4									
1989	1									
1990	6					4000				
1991	-									
1992	13					5000				
1993	3									
1994	1									
1994	7		25	23	430		55	2	-	57

*PF - Stands for Police Firing.*S - Stands for stabbing *OM - Stands for other methods *T - Stands for total. *H - Stands for Hindu. *M - Stands for Muslims *O Stands for others * P - Stands for police.

Source: Communalism in India: A historical and empirical study: Dr. Asghar Ali Engineer, pp. 308-09.

Table 34
Issue-wise Analysis of Some Communal Incidents in the State of Gujarat During the Period 1950- 2002

Sl. No.	*Issue*	*No of Incidents*
1.	Shrine	8
2.	Festivals*	19
3.	Coincidence of Festivals	1
4.	Objections to Religious Riots	3
5.	Tajia-Related	1
6.	Political	6
7.	Miscellaneous	28

*Celebration of Festivals, Immersion of Idols.

Note: Due to lack of information regarding the exact cause, we are constrained to exclude some of the riots.

Table 35
Issue-wise Analysis of Some Communal Incidents in the State of Bihar During the Period 1950-2002

Sl. No.	*Issue*	*No of Incidents*
1.	Shrine	4
2.	Festivals*	5
3.	Graveyard	3
4.	Political	1
5.	Resettlement of Refugees	1
6.	Miscellaneous	3

*Celebration of festivals, Immersion of Idols

Note: Due to lack of information regarding the exact cause we are constrained to exclude some of the riots.

Table 36
Issue-wise Analysis of Some Communal Incident in the State of Maharashtra During the Period 1950- 2002

Sl. No.	*Issue*	*No of Incident*
1.	Shrine	4
2.	Festival*	9
3.	Cow-related	1
4.	Objection to Religious Riots	2
5.	Political	11
6.	Repercussion Riot	5
7.	Miscellaneous	8

*Celebration of festivals, Immersion of Idols.

Table 37
Issue-wise Analysis of Communal Incident in Certain Sensitive Centre of U.P (Aligarh, Allahabad, Bijnor, Ferozabad, Meerut, Moradabad, Muzaffar Nagar, Mathura, Saharanpur, Varanasi) During the Year 1950-2002

Sr. No	*Issue*	*No of Incidents*
1.	Shrine	15
2.	Festivals*	9
3.	Coincidence of festivals	1
4.	Objections to Religious Riots	3
5.	Aligarh Muslim University (AMU)	3
6.	Political	5
7.	Rumour	1
8.	Repercussion of Riots	4
9.	Miscellaneous	16

*Celebration of festivals and immersion of idols, (includes moradabad riots of August 1980).

Note: Certain data in the table are based according to my findings. These data are not the Home Ministry records. They are based on the incidents reported in the newspapers. So certain biases and errors would be there in these data where sources have not been written.

Figure 1
Death in India due to Riots from 1954-2002

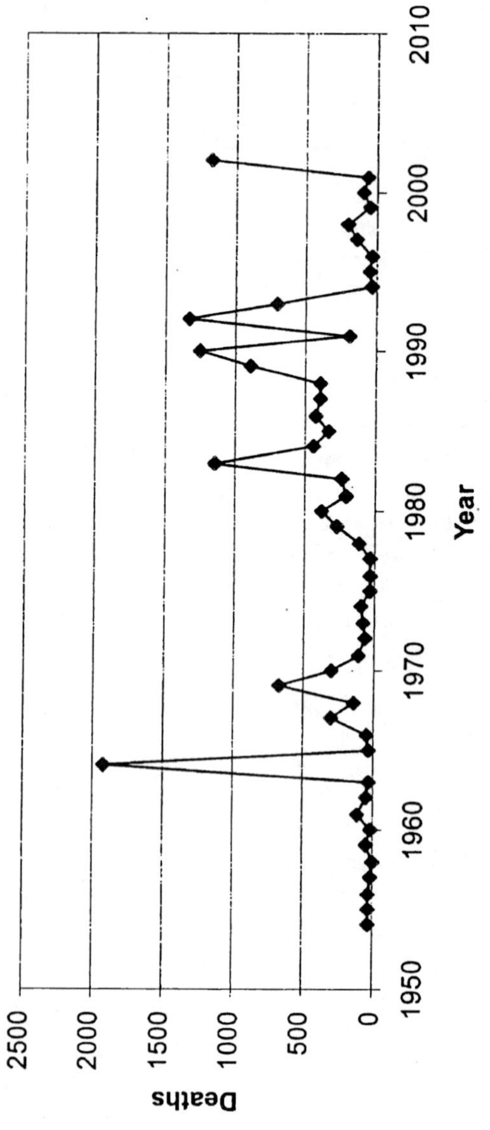

Figure 2
State-Wise Deaths

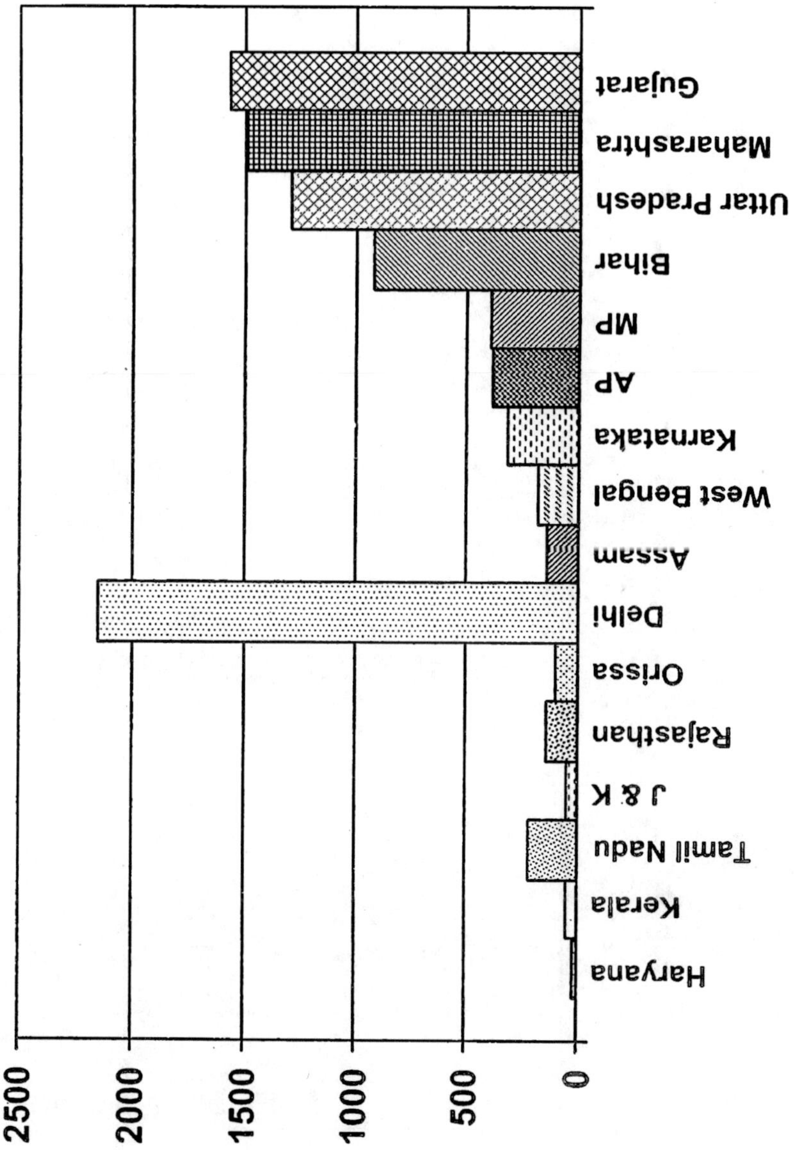

Figure 3
Most Riot-Prone Urban Areas

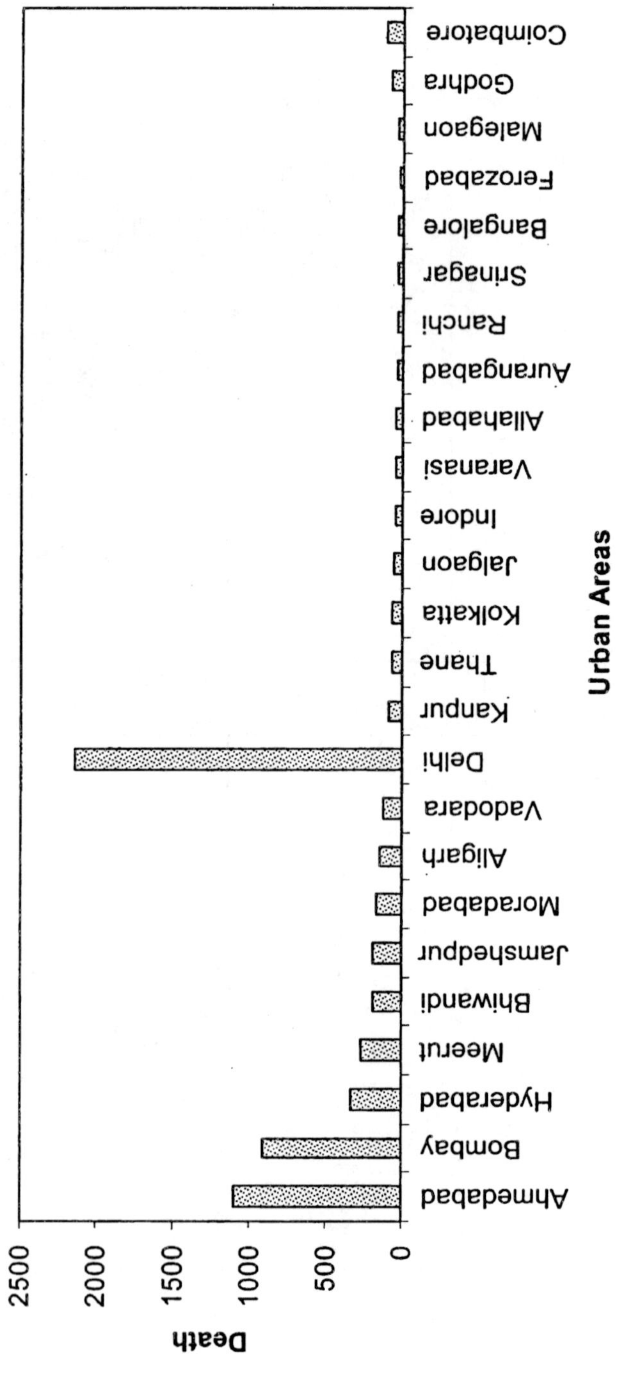

Index